THE LATER GHAZNAVIDS: SPLENDOUR AND DECAY

1040–1186

Persian Studies Series
Edited by Ehsan Yarshater
No. 7

The Persian Studies Series is devoted to works of scholarship which explore and elucidate various aspects of Iranian culture and history.

The Editor wishes to acknowledge with thanks the support received from the Iranian Minister of Culture and Arts for the publication of the present Series.

PERSIAN STUDIES SERIES
CENTER FOR IRANIAN STUDIES, COLUMBIA UNIVERSITY

Editor
Ehsan Yarshater (Columbia University)

Advisory Council
R. N. Frye (Harvard University)
I. Gershevitch (Cambridge University)
G. Lazard (University of Paris)
G. Morgenstierne (University of Oslo)
B. Spuler (University of Hamburg)

Editorial Secretary
P. Morewedge (Baruch College, CUNY)

VOLUMES PUBLISHED IN THE PERSIAN STUDIES SERIES

R. LEVY, *An Introduction to Persian Literature*
ALI DASHTI, *In Search of Omar Khayyam*, trans. L. P. Elwell-Sutton
J. PEARSON, *A Bibliography of Pre-Islamic Persia*
M. H. TABATABA'I, *Shi'ite Islam*, trans. S. H. Nasr
C. BURGEL, *Drei Hafis-Studien*
E. YARSHATER and D. BISHOP, eds., *Biruni Symposium*

In Press

C. J. BRUNNER, *A Syntax of Western Middle Iranian*
A. SCHIMMEL, *Rumi: A Study of His Works*
J. YOHANNAN, *Persian Literature in England and America*
M. MacDERMOTT, *The Theology of al-Shaikh al-Mofid*

Clifford Edmund Bosworth

The Later Ghaznavids: Splendour and Decay

THE DYNASTY IN AFGHANISTAN

AND NORTHERN INDIA

1040–1186

Columbia University Press

NEW YORK

1977

Published in 1977 in Great Britain by Edinburgh University Press
and in the United States of America by Columbia University Press

Printed in Great Britain

Library of Congress Cataloging in Publication Data
Bosworth, Clifford Edmund.
The later Ghaznavids.
Continues the author's The Ghaznavids.
1. Ghaznevids. 2. Afghanistan—History.
3. India—History—1000–1526. I. Title.
DS358.B63 955'.02 77-7879
ISBN 0-231-04428-3

1/81

Contents

Acknowledgements

It is obviously fitting that Edinburgh University Press, who published my first book on the Ghaznavids, should publish its successor volume, and I am accordingly grateful to the Press for undertaking the task in these difficult times. I must also acknowledge valuable help in elucidating difficult Persian poetry from Mr Hasan Etessami, Imperial Iranian Vice-Consul in Manchester.

C.E.B.

*

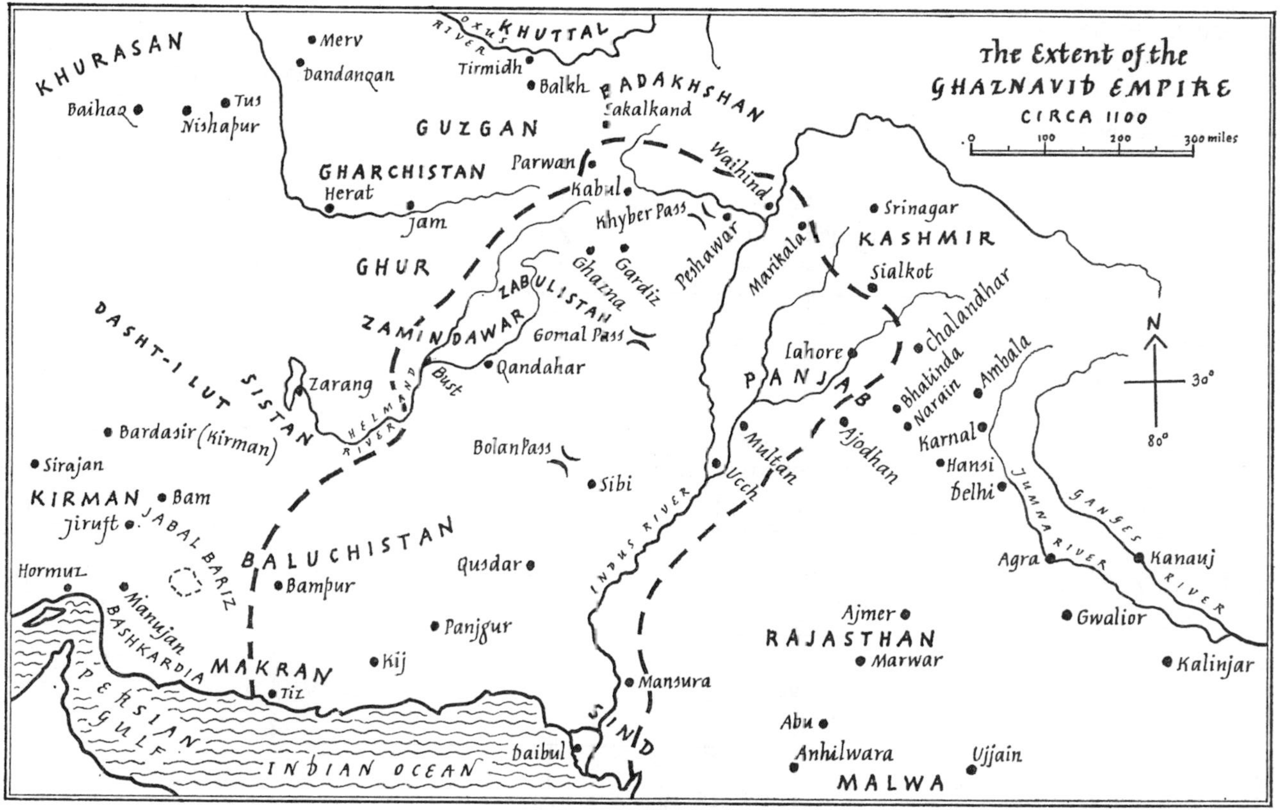
The Extent of the
GHAZNAVID EMPIRE
CIRCA 1100
0
100
200
300 miles
N
30°
80°
KHURASAN
Baihaq
Nishapur
Tus
Merv
Dandanqan
OXUS RIVER
KHUTTAL
Tirmidh
Balkh
BADAKHSHAN
Sakalkand
GUZGAN
GHARCHISTAN
Herat
Jam
Parwan
Kabul
Waihind
Khyber Pass
Peshawar
Marikala
Srinagar
KASHMIR
Sialkot
GHUR
Ghazna
Gardiz
ZABULISTAN
Gomal Pass
ZAMINDAWAR
Qandahar
Bust
HELMAND RIVER
DASHT-I LUT
SISTAN
Zarang
Bardasir (Kirman)
Sirajan
KIRMAN
Bam
Jiruft
JABAL BARIZ
Hormuz
Manujan
BASHKARDIA
BALUCHISTAN
Bampur
Qusdar
Panjgur
Kij
MAKRAN
Tiz
PERSIAN GULF
INDIAN OCEAN
Daibul
SIND
Mansura
INDUS RIVER
Bolan Pass
Sibi
Ucch
Multan
Lahore
PANJAB
Chalandhar
Bhatinda
Narain
Ajodhan
Ambala
Karnal
Hansi
Delhi
JUMNA RIVER
GANGES RIVER
Agra
Kanauj
Gwalior
Kalinjar
Ajmer
RAJASTHAN
Marwar
Abu
Anhilwara
Ujjain
MALWA

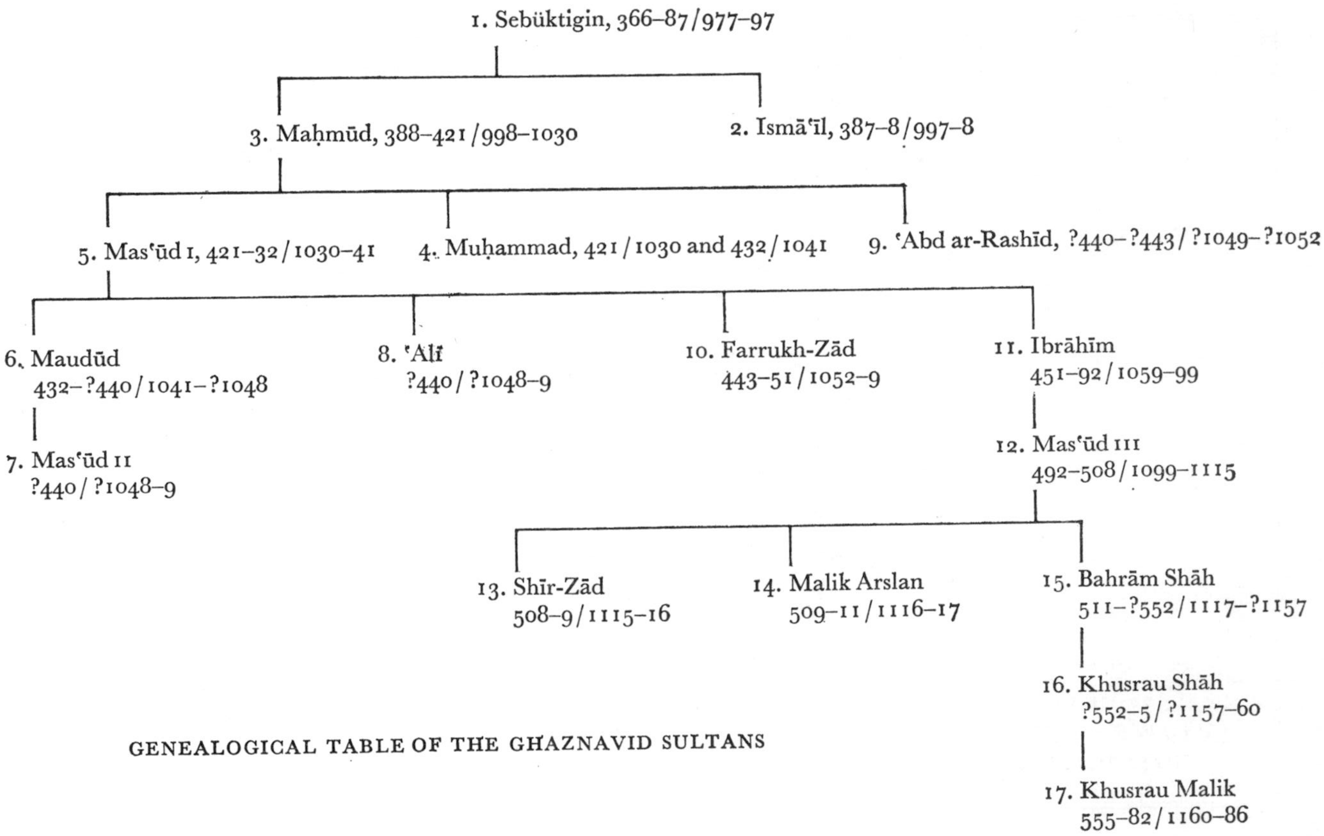
1. Sebüktigin, 366–87/977–97
3. Maḥmūd, 388–421/998–1030
2. Ismāʿīl, 387–8/997–8
5. Masʿūd I, 421–32/1030–41
4. Muḥammad, 421/1030 and 432/1041
9. ʿAbd ar-Rashīd, ?440–?443/?1049–?1052
6. Maudūd
432–?440/1041–?1048
8. ʿAlī
?440/?1048–9
10. Farrukh-Zād
443–51/1052–9
11. Ibrāhīm
451–92/1059–99
7. Masʿūd II
?440/?1048–9
12. Masʿūd III
492–508/1099–1115
13. Shīr-Zād
508–9/1115–16
14. Malik Arslan
509–11/1116–17
15. Bahrām Shāh
511–?552/1117–?1157
16. Khusrau Shāh
?552–5/?1157–60
17. Khusrau Malik
555–82/1160–86

GENEALOGICAL TABLE OF THE GHAZNAVID SULTANS

Introduction

After my previous book, *The Ghaznavids, their empire in Afghanistan and eastern Iran 994–1040*, was published by the Edinburgh University Press in 1963, various people who had found the book useful asked me when I was going to write its sequel, carrying the history of this Turco-Iranian dynasty up to its demise in the last years of the 6th/12th century. Over a decade elapsed before I was able to turn to this project, but the present book now represents the fulfilment of this expressed wish.

A cursory glance shows that the present work, covering some 150 years of history, is perceptibly shorter than the previous one, covering less than half a century. The answer is, of course, that the sources for the middle and later Ghaznavids are infinitely sparser than those for the earlier period, an exposition of which filled pp. 7–24 of my earlier book. The triumvirate of authors, ʿUtbī, Gardīzī and Baihaqī, provides for the earlier period a remarkably rich conspectus not only of military and high political affairs, the *res gestae* of the sultans and their commanders, but also of the day-to-day running of the machinery of state and more intimate, private lives of the monarchs; Baihaqī's *Mujalladāt*, in particular, are only rivalled by the *Tajārib al-umam* of his older contemporary Miskawaih as a detailed chronicle of the work of Muslim bureaucrats. Baihaqī carried his history-cum-journal of affairs up to the end of sultan Farrukh-Zād b. Masʿūd's reign in 451/1059, and it is a matter of profound regret that the richness of detail and the sapient observation, which the latter volumes of the *Mujalladāt* must have contained, are apparently lost to us, for the extant part of his work breaks off with sultan Masʿūd's ill-starred departure for India in Rabīʿ I 432/November 1040. To make matters worse, the final part of Gardīzī's more laconic but still valuable history, the *Zain al-akhbār*, which went up to ʿAbd ar-Rashīd's reign, sc. till some time just after 440/1049, has also disappeared; his narrative breaks off at the victory of Maudūd over Muḥammad and the murderers of his father in Rajab or Shaʿbān/March or April 1041.

Fortunately, something of the lost part of Baihaqī and perhaps of other lost sources seems to have been preserved in the final, historical chapter of the Persian author Ibn Bābā al-Qāshānī's *adab* work in Arabic, the *Kitāb Ra's māl an-nadīm*. The closing section of this chapter deals with the Ghaznavids, carries the account of events up to the author's own time and the accession of sultan Masʿūd III b. Ibrāhīm at the end of the 5th/11th century, and is especially detailed on the dark period of the 440s/1050s, the 'time of troubles', when the Ghaznavid state was racked by succession crises and by the usurpation of the slave commander Toghrïl. The whole text of the *Ra's māl an-nadīm* has now been critically edited by my former student Dr M.S.Badawī, but is so far unpublished; it has accordingly seemed to me worthwhile to give a translation with commentary of this section on the Ghaznavids. This forms Appendix A of the present book, pp. 132–55 below.

From the accession of sultan Ibrāhīm b. Masʿūd in 451/1059 onwards, the sources become yet scantier than for the preceding two decades. Jūzjānī's *Ṭabaqāt-i Nāṣirī* continues to be of some value, although his notices of the successive reigns are fairly brief. Ibn al-Athīr's *Kāmil* likewise provides useful information, especially for Ghaznavid-Seljuq relations, of particular significance in the reigns of Ibrāhīm and his grandson Bahrām Shāh; here too such Seljuq sources as Ḥusainī's *Akhbār ad-daula as-saljūqiyya* give supplementary material. Ibn al-Athīr was further aware that the later Ghaznavid sultans continued to fulfil the dynasty's historic mission by raiding the shrines and palaces of infidel India; but he had great difficulty, writing as he did in distant Iraq, in getting specific information and, in particular, details of places and dates. Hence his notice of Ibrāhīm's Indian campaigns, discussed below in Ch. 2, pp. 61–3, is inserted in the events of the year 472/1079–80, but it is quite uncertain in which years of this sultan's forty-year reign the campaigns actually fell, and the geographical location of the events is equally vague. Later Persian and Indo-Muslim historians, like Mīrkhwānd in his *Rauḍat aṣ-ṣafā'* and Firishta in his *Gulshan-i Ibrāhīmī*, largely utilised such sources as Jūzjānī and Ibn al-Athīr for their sections on the later Ghaznavids empire, although, as noted below in Ch. 1, p. 33, Firishta has occasional items of information that do not apparently appear in the earlier sources and whose origin is unknown.

Where the historical chronicles fail, we can only fall back on ancillary disciplines like archaeology and numismatics and on literary sources such as the *adab* literature collections of anecdotes and poetry. Apart from the valuable work of the Italian Archaeological Mission in Afghanistan in excavating and describing the palace of Masʿūd III at Ghazna, the archaeological evidence on the later Ghaznavids, whether in Afghanistan or in northern India, is virtually non-existent. Nor do we have extant such a rich series of coins for the middle and later Ghaznavid sultans as for the earlier ones. From Maudūd's reign onwards, minting in the shrunken Ghaznavid empire was concentrated on Ghazna for Afghanistan and Lahore for India, whereas under the earlier rulers there had been a rich variety of provincial mints operating in Afghanistan and Khurasan. Moreover, certain of the comparatively ephemeral sultans, such as Masʿūd II b. Maudūd, ʿAlī b. Masʿūd and Shīr-Zād b. Masʿūd III, either did not reign long enough to mint their own coins or else coins issued by them have not come down to us.

The literary sources are more illuminating. The anecdote collections, such as Fakhr-i Mudabbir Mubārak Shāh's *Ādāb al-harb wa-sh-shajāʿa* and ʿAufī's *Jawāmiʿ al-ḥikāyāt*, present stereotypes of sultans like Ibrāhīm and Bahrām Shāh, in their justice and beneficence. The poetry, however, is of first-rate importance as corroborative material for the more strictly historical sources. Much of this verse has clearly been lost, for the names of many poets, together with exiguous specimens of their verses, are known only to us from the Persian and Indo-Muslim *tadhkirat ash-shuʿarā'* literature and the literary anthologies. But we have reasonably complete *dīwāns* of such great poets as ʿUthmān Mukhtārī, Abū l-Faraj Rūnī, Sanā'ī and Sayyid Ḥasan; these writers were attached to the court circles of the sultans, and sometimes accompanied them on their Indian raids, so that their verses provide details about certain episodes and campaigns otherwise little known or wholly unknown. The value of this poetry for the historian has been demonstrated by the Indian scholar Gulam Mustafa Khan in respect of one particular poet, Sayyid Ḥasan Ghaznavī, in his monograph *A history of Bahrām Shāh of Ghaznīn*, and I have endeavoured to follow his path with reference to the other poets and their verses. Much of this poetry is nevertheless difficult, and more often allusive than specific in its historical references; I feel certain that a native Iranian scholar, thoroughly saturated in the lore and literature of his own culture, will be able to extract further items of information.

It remains to attempt a brief estimate of the historical significance of the period and dynasty under review in this book. We are dealing with the middle age and decay of the Ghaznavids. The great days of the dynasty, when it rose to its peak of power under Maḥmūd and Masʿūd, had passed by the middle years of the 5th/11th century, and the ascendant, dominating power in the Iranian east was now that of another Turkish dynasty, the rulers of the Seljuq family and their Türkmen followers. The Ghaznavids had to abandon Khurasan and the western half of modern Afghanistan to the Seljuqs, and apart from occasional outbreaks of irredentist aggression when the Seljuqs appeared temporarily to be in difficulties, the sultans coming after Maudūd generally acquiesced in what came to be the *status quo*, a state of rough equilibrium between the two empires. India, however, was left as the special war-ground of the Ghaznavids. The raids of the middle and later sultans are singularly ill-documented from the Islamic side, and the allusiveness and chronological vagueness of the native Indian sources here provide no complementary dimension of source material; but it is clear that pressure was substantially maintained on the Indian princes, who nevertheless resisted fiercely and were never really overwhelmed by Ghaznavid arms. Hence, although the temple treasures of India continued to be brought back to Ghazna for the beautification of palaces and gardens there, and although the flow of bullion continued to keep the economy of the Ghaznavid empire buoyant and its currency of high quality, there were no major gains of territory beyond the eastern fringes of the Panjab and that region of the Ganges-Jumna Dōāb which is contained today in the western half of Uttar Pradesh. The lasting successes of Muslim arms in northern India were to be the work of the Ghūrids and their slave commanders in the late 6th/12th and the 7th/13th centuries.

With the death of Masʿūd III in 508/1115, a perceptible weakening in the fabric of the empire is discernible. Because of the succession divisions after that sultan's departure, the eastern branch of the Seljuqs, under the forceful and long-lived sultan Sanjar, was able to extend its suzerainty over Ghazna, as the protector and helper of the ultimately successful candidate for the throne, Bahrām Shāh. Contemporary chroniclers felt this as a significant event in history, that the ancient and once-mighty Ghaznavid empire, which in its heyday had absorbed or brought into vassal status so many of the local dynasties in the eastern Islamic world, should now be subject in its turn to a newer power. Ghazna was, however, very much on the far periphery of the Seljuq empire, and Seljuq interference was minimal, provided that the requisite amount of tribute was paid by Bahrām Shāh. The real menace to the later Ghaznavid sultans, and the one which finally engulfed them, came from a local family within Afghanistan, sc. the Shansabānī line of chieftains in Ghūr, one of the most obscure and inaccessible regions of that country. Bahrām Shāh endeavoured to exert the control that his forefathers had exercised over the petty mountain lords in Ghūr at a time when Ghaznavid resources were shrinking and when the dynamism of the Shansabānīs was increasing. The resultant clash proved in the end disastrous for the older dynasty. The last two Ghaznavids, Khusrau Shāh and Khusrau Malik, were forced to abandon Ghazna altogether, and ruled only in the Panjab; then, once the Ghūrid leader Muʿizz ad-Dīn Muḥammad was ready for the next phase of expansionism down to the plains of India, the Ghaznavid sultanate was finally extinguished completely.

Culturally, the court life of the later Ghaznavids and the literary work of their scholars and poets continued as an extension in the east of the common Perso-Islamic culture; such poets as ʿUthmān Mukhtārī and ʿAbd al-Wāsiʿ Jabalī moved unhindered around the courts of eastern Iran, Transoxania and Afghanistan, addressing their eulogies to Seljuq, Ghaznavid, Ṣaffārid, Qarakhanid and other patrons. Ghaznavid India constituted a further focus for Islamic civilisation and literary activity, and ʿAufī already mentions such a Persian poet of Lahore as Abū ʿAbdallāh Rūzbih Nakatī, panegyrist of sultan Masʿūd I. Aziz Ahmad, in his *An intellectual history of Islam in India*, has surmised that the distinctive Indian style of Persian poetry, later called the *Sabk-i Hindī* and conventionally traced back to the 10th/16th century, began much earlier in Ghaznavid India, so that a poet like Masʿūd-i Saʿd-i Salmān exhibits two styles, a straightforward 'Khurasanian' one, and a more intellectualised 'Indian' one. Be this as it may, the place of India as an immensely fertile nurturing-ground for Persian literature clearly begins in the middle Ghaznavid period.

ONE

Defeat in the West and its Aftermath: The 'Time of Troubles'

I.

The shrunken Ghaznavid empire

The victory of the Seljuq family and their Türkmen followers in Ramaḍān 431/May 1040 at Dandānqān, in the almost waterless desert between Sarakhs and Merv, severed at a blow the Persian provinces of the Ghaznavid empire from the capital Ghazna and the heartlands, and speedily made the position in Khwārazm of sultan Mas'ūd's ally, the Oghuz ruler Shāh Malik b. 'Alī of Jand, untenable. The damage to the fabric of the empire was indeed severe, but not irreparable. It is true that Mas'ūd's nerve now failed, and his deposition and murder brought about a further temporary crisis for the remaining parts of the empire; yet this was soon surmounted, thanks to the vigour and incisiveness of Mas'ūd's son Maudūd. Maudūd speedily took command of the situation; he established a defensive bulwark against Chaghrï Beg Dā'ūd and the eastern wing of the newly-constituted Seljuq empire in Persia, and even made plans to resume the offensive and recover the lost western territories. Hence, whilst the Seljuqs inherited the Ghaznavid position in Khwārazm, western Khurasan and Jibāl, as far east as a line bisecting what is now modern Afghanistan and running through Ṭukhāristān southwards to Sīstān, the lands of northern and eastern Afghanistan, plus the Indian conquests, remained intact for over a century until the rise of the Ghūrids.

At the northern end of this Ghaznavid-Seljuq frontier zone, the Transoxanian principalities of Chaghāniyān and Khuttal eventually passed to the Seljuqs, but the main city of Ṭukhāristān, sc. Balkh, remained in Ghaznavid hands under Maudūd, as did the important Oxus crossing-point of Tirmidh (see below); it was only towards the end of Maudūd's sultanate, or conceivably perhaps during the troubled decade of the 1050s, that Tirmidh fell to the Seljuqs, and the cession of Balkh was only formally recognised in the treaty which sultan Ibrāhīm b. Masʿūd made with the Seljuqs on his accession in 451/1059 (see below, Ch. 2, p. 52). In central Afghanistan, Ghūr seems to have remained as a buffer region between the two empires, under its local chieftains. Masʿūd and other fugitive princes and commanders from the field of Dandānqān had been kindly received in Gharchistān and Ghūr during the latter half of Ramaḍān 431/first half of June 1040, and it had been at Ribāṭ-i Karvān (modern Rabāṭ-Kirmān in the region between the headwaters of the Heri Rud and the Helmand River[1]) that Masʿūd had halted to compose a message, minimising the extent of his defeat, to the Qarakhanid Arslan Khan Sulaimān b. Qadïr Khan Yūsuf.[2] We then hear little of Ghūr for the rest of the 5th/11th century, apart from one episode of intervention by sultan Ibrāhīm (see below, Ch. 2, p. 69); it remained in a state of loose vassalage to Ghazna, one which gave full play to the internecine squabbles and rivalries of its petty chiefs.

The appearance of bands of Seljuq raiders in Sīstān shortly before Masʿūd's death eventually allowed representatives of the ancient local line of Ṣaffārids to throw off the control imposed by Maḥmūd of Ghazna in 392–3/1002–3 and to recover a reasonable degree of self-government as amīrs there under Seljuq suzerainty. For the next century or so, the fortunes of the Ṣaffārids were largely bound up with those of the Seljuq royal house, to whom they supplied contingents of the famed Sagzī infantry and at whose side they not infrequently fought in person. The town of Bust at the confluence of the Helmand River and the Arghandāb, though threatened briefly at the end of Masʿūd's reign, nevertheless remained firmly under Ghaznavid control. The situation prevailing in what is now Baluchistan is obscure. The districts of Quṣdār, Makrān, Wālishtān or Sībī and Kīkānān were formally included in Masʿūd's territories as detailed in the investiture patent sent from Baghdad by the new Abbasid caliph al-Qā'im in 422/1031, and in this same year, Masʿūd had provided military help for a local claimant to power in Makrān, who thereafter became a Ghaznavid vassal.[3] From subsequent odd mentions in the sources of places under Ghaznavid control in the more westerly parts of Baluchistan and in the coastal region of Makrān as far west as Tīz (modern Chābahār), the province seems to have stayed within the Ghaznavid orbit, separated from the Seljuq amīrate of Kirmān by a zone of extremely inhospitable and difficult terrain, the haunt of savage and predatory peoples like the Kūfichīs and Balūch.[4]

We possess a valuable survey of the towns and districts of the truncated Ghaznavid empire as it was in the second half of the 5th/11th century under Ibrāhīm b. Mas'ūd. In an anecdote of Fakhr-i Mudabbir Mubārak-Shāh's *Ādāb al-ḥarb wa-sh-shajā'a*, the lands under the superintendence of the royal treasurer, the Sharīf Abū l-Faraj, foster-brother to the sultan, are enumerated. In the western sector of the empire are mentioned the lands from the gates of Ghazna to Tigīnābād, Bust, Mastang, Quzdār, Kīj or Tīz,[5] Makrān, the Garmsīr,[6] Narmāshīr (? near Bam, in Kirmān), the shores of the Indian Ocean, Sīwīstān or Sībī, Daibul, Sūraj (? Broach),[7] Cambay and the whole of the adjacent Indian littoral. In the eastern (i.e. inland Indian continental) sector are mentioned Arōr or Alōr and Bhakkar in Sind, Sīwārī (? Sībī again), Bhattiya or Bhatinda in the Panjab,[8] Davā (?), Gujarbīla (?),[9] Uchh, Multān, Karōr and Bannū, up to the gates of Ghazna again.[10]

The above list shows that once the crisis of the middle years of the century was surmounted, the Indian conquests of Sebüktigin and his successors were firmly held, and with the achievement of a virtual stalemate with the Seljuqs in the west, the sultans could concentrate on what might well be regarded as the historic mission of the Ghaznavid state, sc. the extending of Muslim arms into the north-western parts of India and the laying of foundations for the later spread of the Islamic faith there under the Ghūrids and their epigoni. Hence with the great provincial centres of Khurasan—Nīshāpūr, Merv, Herat and Balkh—by then lost to the Seljuqs, Ghazna itself and Lahore, the seat of administration for the Indian provinces, became the two main centres of the later Ghaznavid empire.[11] It may well be that the reduction of the sprawling early Ghaznavid empire to a more manageable size was a source of strength rather than of weakness; the sultanate survived in Ghazna for some 120 years after the cataclysm of Dandānqān, and in the Panjab for 20 years further. The sultans were still able to tap the rich resources of India, in the shape of temple treasures, tribute exacted from Hindu rulers and slave manpower derived from the sub-continent. The importance of the spirit of Muslim *jihād* in this period should not be underestimated, even if secular motives for the spoliation of India loom more largely in our minds today than in those of the traditional Islamic sources on the Ghaznavid campaigns in

India. All those sultans whose reigns were of any length or who were not distracted by pressing internal problems seem to have led campaigns into India, although these raids are generally more poorly-documented than are those of Maḥmūd and Masʿūd in the earlier part of the 5th/11th century. The intensity of this spirit of *jihād* is seen in the florescence of the post-Firdausian Persian epic genre in eastern Afghanistan, the region of Ghazna and Zābulistān; in this, the poems of authors like Asad-i Ṭūsī and ʿUthmān Mukhtārī to a considerable extent reflect contemporary struggles with the pagans of India, equated with the enemies of the knights of ancient Iran (for ʿUthmān Mukhtārī's *Shahriyār-nāma*, see below, Ch. 3, p. 89). The spoils of India enabled the later Ghaznavid sultans to maintain the earlier traditions of their courts as centres of patronage for scholars and literary men and also to build splendid public buildings and palaces, such as the palace of Masʿūd III b. Ibrāhīm at Ghazna, recently excavated by Italian archaeologists, in which objects of clear Indian provenance have been found (see below, Ch. 3, pp. 87–9).

2.

The last months of Masʿūd's reign and his retiral to India

Masʿūd regained Ghazna, with the remnants of his forces, after a journey through the mountains of Gharchistān and Ghūr to the headwaters of the Heri Rud and thence to the capital, on 7 Shawwāl 431/21 June 1040. He was doubtless already meditating the act of vengeance and execution wrought only in the next month on the luckless Turkish generals Begtoghdï, Sübashï and ʿAlī Dāya, whom he considered to have failed him at Dandānqān,[12] and it was not long after he had been back in Ghazna that the cloud of melancholy and despair which had descended on him became worse and he made his decision to retire to India, as is described below.

For the moment, however, there was an urgent necessity to establish a firm front, if that were possible, against a feared Seljuq advance through Ṭukhāristān to the Hindu Kush and the Kabul River valley, whence an attack on the capital itself would present few problems. In particular, reinforcements for the bastion of Balkh had to be organised in face of Seljuq raids through the surrounding countryside and in face of a growing lack of confidence in the Ghaznavid cause amongst the population of Khurasan; a large proportion of these last, weary of the tramplings and extortions of the

Ghaznavid armies and of the incursions of the Türkmens into oasis and agricultural land, were in the process of peacefully surrendering their towns and rural districts to the Seljuqs. It was probably this disaffected element in the urban population of Balkh, who would have ultimately tried to come to an accommodation with the incomers, to whom Masʿūd's vizier Aḥmad b. ʿAbd aṣ-Ṣamad referred when he spoke of the large number of 'corrupt persons, evil-wishers and malevolently-inclined people' within Balkh; at the same time, the *Ṣāḥib-Barīd* or Chief of Intelligence of Balkh was writing to Ghazna about the damaging activities of the *ʿayyār*s swarming in from the countryside. The strategic importance of Balkh for the defence of the upper Oxus region and northern Afghanistan was patent to the sultan and his advisers; as the *Ṣāḥib-Barīd*'s letter said, 'All Khurasan is bound up with this town, and if our opponents are able to seize it, all the power and glory will immediately become theirs'.[13] The governor of Khuttal on the Ghaznavids' behalf—he is unnamed by Baihaqī, but he may have been the descendant of an ancient ruling family there, like the Banījūrids or Abū Dā'ūdids[14]—had evacuated the town and had presumably returned to his own principality on the right bank of the Oxus, which was itself eventually to come within the Seljuq sphere of influence.

The real organiser of resistance in Balkh against pressure from Chaghrī Beg Dā'ūd's Türkmens proved to be the *Ṣāḥib-Barīd* Abū l-Ḥasan Aḥmad b. Muḥammad ʿAnbarī, called Amīrak Baihaqī. According to the section on the ʿAnbariyyān family in Ibn Funduq's local history of the town of Baihaq, Amīrak subsequently held out in the fortress of Tirmidh for fifteen years, refusing to surrender it to the Seljuqs; this period of time is clearly exaggerated, since this same author states that Amīrak eventually headed the *Dīwān-i Risālat* or Correspondence Department for Maudūd and ʿAbd ar-Rashīd, also serving Farrukh-Zād as a secretary and dying during that sultan's reign in Shawwāl 448/December 1056. That Amīrak in fact surrendered Tirmidh in Maudūd's reign, perhaps in the mid-1040s, is confirmed by the historian of the Seljuqs Ṣadr ad-Dīn al-Ḥusainī. This author relates that, after the failure of Maudūd's expedition to Khurasan of 435/1043–4, Chaghrī Beg and his son Alp Arslan appeared before the fortress of Tirmidh and demonstrated to the *kōtwāl* or castellan Amīrak the hopelessness of his position and the unlikelihood that the Ghaznavids would ever be able to afford him any relief. Amīrak therefore accepted the offer of an honourable surrender, made over his estates at Baihaq to Chaghrï Beg's vizier Abū ʿAlī b. Shādhān, and departed for Ghazna.[15]

Ibn al-Athīr refers to the beleaguered position of Balkh after Masʿūd's retreat from Dandānqān, but is confused over the details. He states that Altuntāq Ḥājib (the Altuntash of Baihaqī) was the Ghaznavid governor in Balkh at this time and was accordingly besieged in the town when Chaghrï Beg advanced on it at the same time as his kinsman Bïghu or Paighu[16] was attacking Herat. It was the army under Maudūd and the vizier Aḥmad b. ʿAbd aṣ-Ṣamad that the sultan then sent to relieve Altuntāq in Balkh in Rabīʿ I 432/November-December 1040 (two months later than Maudūd's force actually left Ghazna for Ṭukhāristān, according to Baihaqī's detailed, day-by-day chronology); but the vanguard of Maudūd's army, so this account goes, was worsted by Chaghrï Beg's forces, so that Maudūd had to retreat and Altuntāq had willy-nilly to surrender Balkh to the Seljuqs.[17]

A much more detailed sequence of events is given by Baihaqī. Either at the end of Shawwāl or early in Dhū l-Qaʿda 431/end of July or early August 1040, Masʿūd despatched a force of 1,000 cavalry to Balkh under the Ḥājib Altuntash, promising that a larger army would follow on its heels and that he would then come personally to organise the defence of that region. The demoralisation and indiscipline characteristic of the Ghaznavid troops at Dandānqān was still in evidence; after leaving Baghlān, Altuntash's troops gave themselves up to plundering the countryside there, with the result that the wretched populace fled to the Seljuqs and warned Chaghrï Beg of the enemy's approach. The Seljuq amīr was consequently able to lure the Ghaznavid soldiers into an ambush, out of which Altuntash escaped to Balkh with only 200 men.[18]

Hence in Muḥarram 432/September 1040 Masʿūd had, as a pressing obligation, to prepare a more powerful expeditionary force to retrieve the position in northern Afghanistan. The commander of this force was Masʿūd's son Maudūd, who had recently distinguished himself on the battlefield at Dandānqān, where he had ridden round, sword in hand, trying vainly to inspirit and rally the flagging Ghaznavid soldiers.[19] To accompany him, and to provide weighty military experience, Masʿūd detailed the Turkish generals Ertigin, commander of the palace ghulāms or slave troops, and the *Ḥājib-i Buzurg* or Supreme Commander Badr (both of whom had just respectively acquired these elevated positions after the dismissal and disgrace of Begtoghdï and Sübashï), and also appointed his own vizier Aḥmad b. ʿAbd aṣ-Ṣamad as Maudūd's *kadkhudā* or adjutant. But symptomatic of the declining faith of the sultan's servants in their master, whose obstinacy and capriciousness seemed to have affected the balance of his judgment, was the fact that Aḥmad insisted on obtaining from Masʿūd a *muwāḍaʿa* or formal contract of service for this expedition, wherein the vizier's position and rights *vis-à-vis* the *Dīwān-i ʿArḍ* or Department of the Army were carefully defined, and wherein his duties and responsibilities were unequivocally laid down.[20]

A powerful and well-equipped force of élite soldiers was now assembled in Ghazna. The sultan held a splendid farewell feast in the Fīrūzī Garden, and the troops were reviewed on the greensward of the 'Golden Field'. First came prince Maudūd's personal force of 200 palace ghulāms, armed with breastplates and spears, and with numerous horses, which were to be led to the scene of battle and then used for fighting in the actual encounter (the technical term for such a horse being *janībat*), and swift riding camels; this force bore the prince's ceremonial parasol (*chatr*) and ample standards. After these came a body of infantry, again with flowing standards, and a group of 170 ghulāms, heavily-armed and with richly-caparisoned horses. The Ḥājib Ertigin had over 80 of his own personal ghulāms, after whom came another body of palace ghulāms and twenty senior officers (*sarhangs*), the greater part of them splendidly uniformed and again with horses for conveying them to the battlefield, plus riding camels. Finally, there came a further group of *sarhangs*. The total force of cavalrymen, according to Gardīzī, amounted to 4,000. The original arrangement was for the sultan to follow closely behind with the main Ghaznavid army, but by this time Masʿūd was already meditating his move to India.[21]

Maudūd's army set off northwards for the Hindu Kush passes in the middle of Muḥarram 432/later September 1040,[22] and then encamped at a place *Hībān or *Hupyān, which was evidently of some note, although it has not so far been identified with certainty. The name occurs several times in Baihaqī and Gardīzī in connection with Maudūd's expedition, and also in Ibn Bābā's *Kitāb Ra's māl an-nadīm* in connection with the events leading to ʿAbd ar-Rashīd's killing (see below, p. 141); but the consonant ductus of the name varies, as does the dotting. ʿAbd al-Ḥayy Ḥabībī, the most recent editor of Gardīzī, has preferred *Hupyān, on the grounds that a village of this name still exists in the Parwān area, and certainly Baihaqī in one place links Parwān and *Hupyān together as the initial goals of the expedition.[23] The general strategy envisaged was that the Ghaznavid forces at Balkh, comprising the original garrison plus the survivors of Altuntash's troops, would march out of Balkh and unite with Maudūd's army, and the combined force would then clear the Türkmens out of Ṭukhāristān. These designs proved abortive, since the sultan altered his original plan to go to Balkh and decided to leave for India, where he was deposed and murdered; the news of these last events reached Maudūd when he was still encamped at *Hupyān.[24]

At this time of general crisis for the Ghaznavid state, there was a further need for Mas'ūd to attend to certain spasms of unrest in the heartlands of the empire and along the inner frontiers of the realm, which had been for some time neglected through the preoccupation with events in Khurasan. Hence within days of reaching Ghazna from Dandānqān, Mas'ūd in Shawwāl 431/early July 1040 sent out to Bust his former palace slave Nūshtigin Naubatī, with instructions to hold that region firmly; the sultan realised that Türkmen raids into Sīstān or perhaps beyond were almost inevitable now that they held western Khurasan. Shortly afterwards, it transpired that a rebellious *Ṣāḥib-Barīd* of the Ghaznavids, one Bū l-Faḍl Kurnikī,[25] who had been allegedly in treacherous correspondence with the Seljuqs, had escaped to the region of Bust, and at the end of Dhū l-Qa'da 431/early August 1040 the head of the *Dīwān-i Risālat*, Abū Sahl Zauzanī, was sent to Bust in pursuit of Bū l-Faḍl. Baihaqī observes at this juncture that, although Abū Sahl Zauzanī had aroused the sultan's wrath by allowing Bū l-Faḍl Kurnikī to escape, if he had not been away at Bust he would have accompanied Mas'ūd's column to India and have been caught up in the mutiny of the army at Mārīkala; moreover, Muḥammad would certainly have had his old enemy Abū Sahl put to death as his very first act of vengeance.[26]

Soon after Abū Sahl was sent on this mission, in Muḥarram 432/September 1040 an expedition was despatched against the rebellious Afghans in what Gardīzī calls 'the foothills of the mountains adjacent to Ghazna', sc. of the mountains of the modern Afghan Gardīz and Pakhtiya provinces running eastwards to the Pakistan border; whereas Gardīzī describes these dissidents as 'Afghans', Baihaqī interestingly calls them 'Khalaj'.[27] The leader of this expedition, the *kōtwāl* or garrison commander of Ghazna, Abū 'Alī returned victorious from this punitive expedition in Rabīʿ I 432/November 1040.[28]

The most momentous decision made by Masʿūd in these last months of his reign was that of the move to India in order, as he proclaimed, to spend the coming winter in the Indus valley fortresses of Waihind (Sanskrit Udabhānda, modern Hund, on the Indus banks 15 miles north of Aṫak or Attock), M.r.manāra (probably the Maʿbar Mahanāra 'Ford of [the village of] Mahanāra' mentioned by Bīrūnī in his *India* as a ford across the Kabul River just above its confluence with the Indus), Peshawar, and Gīrī (probably Shāhbāz-Gīrī or Kapur-da-Gīrī 40 miles north-east of Peshawar, a place of great antiquity on the ancient Kabul-India route).[29] The vizier Aḥmad b. ʿAbd aṣ-Ṣamad divined what was really in the sultan's mind at the same time as the latter was proclaiming his intention to follow Maudūd to Balkh, but the decision was announced to the sultan's advisers at the end of Muḥarram–beginning of Ṣafar 432/October 1040. The northern provinces of the empire were in effect to be written off, and Balkh and Ṭukhāristān ceded to the Qarakhanid Böritigin Ibrāhīm b. Naṣr, son of the Ilig Naṣr (d. 403/1012–13) who had been Maḥmūd of Ghazna's rival over the partition of the Sāmānid lands, and the later Tamghach or Tabghach Khan (d. 462/1068).[30] Böritigin had been consolidating his position in the mountains north of the upper Oxus valleys and using such fierce mountain peoples there as the Kumījīs in order to harry the valleys of Khuttal and Chaghāniyān; it was Masʿūd's hope that, through the cession to him of territories on the south bank of the Oxus, Böritigin would be set against the Seljuqs. Although an envoy had been sent to the other leading Qarakhanid prince Arslan Khan Sulaimān as soon as the sultan had regained Ghazna, Masʿūd knew that the Seljuqs would lose no time in informing the Khan of the real magnitude of their victory at Dandānqān and that he could consequently expect little direct military or diplomatic help from that quarter.[31]

A force of 2,000 cavalry was sent around this time (the exact date is not recorded) under the prince Majdūd b. Masʿūd to secure Multān in the middle Indus valley, which we know to have been chronically disaffected under Ghaznavid control, and which had a substantial Ismāʿīlī population that was shortly to break out in rebellion during Maudūd's sultanate (see below, p. 31).[32] That the tentative plan of a transfer to India had been maturing in the sultan's mind for some time seems proven by the fact that on 1 Ṣafar 432/11 October 1040 the prince Īzad-Yār b. Masʿūd arrived back from the fortress called by Baihaqī Naghar and by Gardīzī Barghund, which was clearly not too far from Ghazna.[33] Īzad-Yār brought back with him sultan Masʿūd's deposed brother Muḥammad b. Maḥmūd (exactly when Muḥammad had been transferred to Naghar/Barghund from his earlier imprisonment in the fortress of Mandīsh in Ghūr is unknown) and Muḥammad's four sons Aḥmad, ʿAbd ar-Raḥmān (or ʿAbd ar Raḥīm), ʿUmar and ʿUthmān. All these former captives were now accorded a warm welcome at court. Muḥammad was awarded the *mukhāṭaba* or form of address of 'The Exalted Amīr, Brother',[34] and his sons were given robes of honour and presents of 1,000 dīnārs each; the eldest, Aḥmad, was married to the princess Ḥurra-yi Gauhar. In return, Muḥammad's sons had each to take oaths of allegiance (*aimān al-baiʿa*), verbal and written, to Masʿūd. It seems that in this time of vulnerability for the empire during the aftermath of the Khurasan disasters, Masʿūd was hereby endeavouring to conciliate the dispossessed branch of his family and to restore dynastic solidarity, although it would in any case have been dangerous to leave Muḥammad and his sons in Afghanistan, as possible rallying-points for disaffection, whilst he himself retired to India.[35]

The sultan's ministers, led by the vizier, protested that the situation in Afghanistan was not so desperate as to warrant the abandonment of the original Ghaznavid heartland. A strong military force could secure Balkh and Ṭukhāristān against the Seljuqs. It was unwise to assume that the Indians had any affection for the dynasty and would provide a safe haven for them. Nor could the Ghaznavids' slave soldiers, probably still demoralised and disgruntled after Dandānqān and perhaps even fearing for the continuance of the dynasty's power, be trusted with the safe conveyance of the Ghaznavid treasuries and possessions to India. In the words of Aḥmad b. ʿAbd aṣ-Ṣamad,

> If my master decides on this transfer to India simply because the enemy are fighting at the gates of Balkh, this enemy nevertheless has insufficient strength to reduce the town, since our defending force there is so superior to them in martial ardour that they are making sorties from the town and engaging the Türkmens. If my master will only give the order for his servants to go forth and clear our opponents from these regions, what need is there to depart for India? It is better to spend this winter in Ghaznī,

> since the position here is quite secure, praise be to God. On the other hand, it is certain that if our master leaves for India and transfers all his family and treasures thither, and the news becomes generally known to friend and foe alike, the glory of this illustrious house will be wholly dissipated, to the extent that every enemy will become greedy for a share in it. Nor should any reliance be placed on the Indians in transporting so much of your family and treasures to their land, for we ourselves have not acted all that well towards the Indians. Furthermore, what confidence can one have in the slave troops, to whom the treasuries will have to be entrusted on the journey through the open country?

Adding further weight to these arguments, the *kōtwāl* Abū ʿAlī expressed the view of the military that, even if Ghazna itself were threatened, it would be safer to guard the state treasuries and the royal family in the fortresses of Afghanistan than to send them on the uncertain journey to the plains of India.[36]

But such sound advice was of no avail, and the sultan's self-will, the *istibdād* so often denounced among themselves by his advisers, would not allow him to be swayed by reason. His melancholia included a fatalistic despair that the position in the west could ever be retrieved. When the commander of the *ghāzī*s in the Ghaznavid army, the seasoned general ʿAbdallāh Qaratigin, had offered to raise in India a large army of cavalry and infantry and to bring it back for offensive operations in Khurasan, Masʿūd had condemned the plan as pointless, since it had been fore-ordained that 'We rose to power at Merv [alluding to Maḥmūd's victory over the Sāmānids in Khurasan], and the power has gone from us at Merv'. He now gave his ministers and officials in Ghazna formal permission to enter the service of the Seljuqs when they should arrive, noting that Abū l-Qāsim Kathīr, for instance, had money enough for purchasing the office of vizier, and Abū Sahl Ḥamdūnī enough for the office of ʿ*Āriḍ* or Head of the Department of the Army under the putative new régime.[37]

By now, treasures and precious possessions from such outlying fortresses of central and eastern Afghanistan as Dīdī-Rū (?), Mandīsh in Ghūr, Nāy-Lāmān in Wajīristān (the later place of imprisonment of the poet Masʿūd-i Saʿd-i Salmān, see below, p. 66), Maranj (also known as a castle where Masʿūd-i Saʿd was once incarcerated), and one other fortress whose name is not comprehensible from Gardīzī's text,[38] had been concentrated on Ghazna. Four days after the failure of the sultan's advisers to dissuade him from his plan, early in Rabīʿ I 432/November 1040, all the stores of precious metals, ornaments, fine clothes, etc. (detailed by Ḥusainī as comprising 3,000 loads of Nīshāpūrī, Herātī, Maghribī and Maḥmūdī coinage, various kinds of bullion, jewels, precious vessels, etc.), together with members of the sultan's *ḥaram*, were loaded on camels and the whole assemblage departed for India. Also in the column were Muḥammad's four sons and Muḥammad himself, just brought back from Barghund, according to Gardīzī; Baihaqī says that he was intially kept in the citadel of Ghazna under the care of the *Amīr-i Ḥaras* or Commander of the Guard Sangūy.[39]

At this point of time, Baihaqī closes the ninth volume of his *Mujalladāt* and interrupts his continuous narrative of happenings at the Ghaznavid court to begin his tenth volume with accounts of events in Khwārazm under Ghaznavid rule and of events in Ray and Jibāl during Masʿūd's reign; unfortunately, the part beyond the history of Khwārazm is no longer extant. We are now accordingly dependent on Gardīzī as the sole contemporary source, supplemented by the quite detailed accounts of Masʿūd's deposition, Muḥammad's brief second sultanate and Maudūd's vengeance in Ibn Bābā and Ibn al-Athīr, and the more cursory mentions in Ḥusainī and Jūzjānī.

3.
The deposition of Masʿūd and Muḥammad's second sultanate

Masʿūd's force presumably made its way across the mountains from Ghazna, probably via Peshawar, to the Indus banks. The first section of what must have been a lengthy column crossed the river, with Masʿūd in the van, when the remaining part of the army, led by the Turkish eunuch commander Anūshtigin Balkhī and a group of the palace ghulāms, mutinied and plundered the royal treasuries. The rebels then set up Muḥammad as sultan during the night of 13 Rabīʿ II 432/20–21 December 1040, although only after Muḥammad had been threatened and possibly even forced physically to cooperate (according to Mīrkhwānd, he was even threatened with death); his sons, at least, had of course given their solemn oath of allegiance to Masʿūd only a short time previously.[40] Using hindsight, it was obviously an unwise decision of Masʿūd's to leave Muḥammad and his sons with the main body of the army whilst he went on in front and crossed the river with a smaller force of soldiers. He clearly misjudged the temper and morale of his army at this time, already seen in his over-reaction to the defeat in Khurasan. The soldiers had not only lost confidence in Masʿūd's powers as a successful war-leader in the field, but also in his overall judgment, and not even the prospect of *ghazw* against the infidels of India and the possibilities of plunder there could persuade them to retain their allegiance. With the sultan's virtual abandonment of Ghazna—whatever excuses he might adduce of merely going to India in order to collect troops for a revanche in Khurasan—it must have seemed to the soldiers that the once-mighty Ghaznavid empire had broken up. In effect, a *sauve-qui-peut* followed, for the rebellious troops cannot have seen in Muḥammad, whose tastes were predominantly literary and studious[41] and who had already failed once in his bid for the sultanate in 421/1030, a military saviour who would restore the empire to its ancient glory. Muḥammad was therefore nothing but a figurehead, raised to the throne in an attempt to give respectability and, it was hoped, ultimate legitimacy through military success, to the rebellion.

That Muḥammad could never have been more than the puppet of ambitious generals and other self-seekers would certainly have been the case if the reports in certain sources of his blindness were true. However, this question is obscure. There is no mention in the contemporary sources (Baihaqī, Gardīzī), nor in the accounts of Ḥusainī, Ibn al-Athīr or Shabānkāra'ī in his *Majmaʿ al-ansāb* that Masʿūd had Muḥammad blinded immediately after his deposition. Indeed, there is evidence from Baihaqī that Muḥammad was perfectly able to see when Masʿūd consigned him to captivity in the fortress of Mandīsh in 421/1030;[42] he read the letter written by Masʿūd to him in his own hand, notifying him of the fate of the treacherous Turkish general ʿAlī Qarīb or Khwīshāwand, and he is described as seeing from afar the arrival of the swift camel bearing this letter from the sultan in Herat.[43] Nor does the contemporary Gardīzī state specifically that Muḥammad was blind when he was raised to the throne a second time; the mention of Muḥammad as having been blinded (*masmūl*, *makḥūl*) comes only in such later sources as Ibn Bābā, Ḥusainī, Ibn Funduq, Ibn al-Athīr, Jūzjānī, Shabānkāra'ī and Firishta. The information that Muḥammad was blind should accordingly be treated with a certain amount of reserve, though it is possible that Muḥammad had gone blind during his ten years' period of captivity, and one could thereby harmonise the sources.[44]

Ibn Bābā says that Masʿūd crossed the Indus at Waihind just before the troops mutinied.[45] Masʿūd and the troops still loyal to him took refuge in the *ribāṭ* or fortress of Mārīkala, modern Marigala, situated in a pass of the low hills between Attock and Rawalpindi, a few miles to the east of Ḥasan Abdāl; according to Raverty, these hills were notoriously full of robbers and brigands, whence apparently a folk-etymology *mārrī-kala* 'fortress to protect travellers'.[46] Fighting took place between the besieged and the attacking rebels, and the superiority was clearly with the latter. Ibn al-Athīr's account has the anecdotal touch here that Masʿūd surrendered himself voluntarily on his mother's advice; Gardīzī says that the besiegers, with their troops and elephants, broke into Mārīkala, fetched out Masʿūd and bound him. Muḥammad enjoined good treatment for his brother, and in the middle of Rabīʿ II 432/late December 1040 conveyed him and his wife Sāra Khātūn, daughter of the Qarakhanid Qadïr Khan Yūsuf, to the fortress of his own choice, that of Gīrī, frequently mentioned by Baihaqī as one of the principal Ghaznavid strongholds of northwestern India.[47] There for the moment Masʿūd remained, lamenting, according to Ibn al-Athīr, the contrast between his former state and his present one.[48]

Actual power during Muḥammad's short second sultanate was largely in the hands of his sons, and above all, in those of Aḥmad, whose behaviour is described in the later sources (though not in Gardīzī or Ibn Bābā) as unbalanced (Ḥusainī and Ibn al-Athīr, 'reckless and unbalanced' and even *maʿtūh* 'mad'); of course, these later sources may well have been influenced by the picture subsequently formed of Masʿūd as the martyr-sultan. Aḥmad was backed by Anūshtigin Balkhī and other leaders whose families had suffered discrimination or disfavour during Masʿūd's reign and were now able to taste the sweetness of revenge. These included Sulaimān b. Yūsuf b. Sebüktigin, whose father had been removed from power by Masʿūd in 422/1031 and imprisoned till he died, and the son of the general ʿAlī b. Il Arslan, called Qarīb or Khwīshāwand, whose father had been initially a prominent supporter of Muḥammad's during the latter's first sultanate, had then betrayed his master, but had been very soon jailed and killed for his treachery by Masʿūd.[49] That Masʿūd had already drawn upon himself lasting hatreds by his vendetta against the *Maḥmūdiyān* or *Pidariyān*, the leading figures of his father's reign whom Masʿūd wished to remove from positions of influence in the state, had already been shown by the desertion to the Seljuqs during the Dandānqān campaign of former ghulāms of Yūsuf, of ʿAlī Qarīb and of the two other Turkish generals ruined by Masʿūd, sc. Eryaruq and Asïghtigin Ghāzī.[50]

The deposed Masʿūd remained at Gīrī for about a month, and then was killed at Aḥmad b. Muḥammad's instigation, either unbeknown to Muḥammad himself after a forged execution order had been sent to the custodian of the fortress (Gardīzī) or after Aḥmad had persuaded his father to agree to the deed (Ḥusainī and Ibn al-Athīr, both of whose accounts have many anecdotal touches). According to these latter two sources, Masʿūd was either killed and then his body thrown into a well which was then sealed up, or else thrown into the well alive and buried there; according to Ibn Bābā, his head was simply chopped off. The date of Masʿūd's death is given by Gardīzī as 11 Jumādā I 432/17 January 1041 (erroneously as Ṣafar 433/October 1041 in Ibn Bābā, see below, Appendix A, p. 140). Gardīzī's date was apparently also that given by Baihaqī in the lost part of his *Mujalladāt*, on the evidence of the marginal gloss in one of the manuscripts of Ibn Bābā's *Kitāb Ra's māl an-nadīm*, who must have had access to Baihaqī's work (see further, below, p. 22). Jūzjānī states that Masʿūd was forty-five when he died.[51] Muḥammad subsequently wrote to Maudūd in Ṭukhāristān that his father had been killed as an act of private vengeance by the sons of Masʿūd's former commander-in-chief in India, Aḥmad Inaltigin, who had unsuccessfully rebelled there against the sultan in 424/1033.[52]

4.
Maudūd's vengeance

Whoever may have been the prime mover in Masʿūd's slaying, the fact remained that he was dead and that his son Maudūd had at his disposal a sizeable military force in northern Afghanistan; he was accordingly bound to constitute himself his father's avenger and the punisher of those who had broken the oath of fealty to Masʿūd so recently taken.

From sporadic mentions in the pages of Baihaqī, it is possible to piece together something of Abū l-Fatḥ Maudūd's career before he gained the throne in 432/1041. He was indeed closely associated with his father in various military enterprises and was entrusted with several responsible tasks. Thus he accompanied Masʿūd on the expedition which left Ghazna at the end of Shawwāl 425/mid-September 1034 and went via Bust, Herat and northern Khurasan to Gurgān and Ṭabaristān, and during the course of the fighting in Gurgān, he commanded a detachment of 4,000 cavalrymen.[53] At the Mihrgān festivities at the end of 427/autumn 1036, it was decided to send Maudūd and the general ʿAlī Dāya with a strong army to Balkh, after disturbing reports of Türkmen activities in the Ray area had come in; the two commanders did not return to Ghazna till the middle of Jumādā II 429/end of March 1038.[54] His name was put forward by the sultan in Muḥarram 430/October 1038 as the possible commander of a powerful force destined for Khuttal, where the Qarakhanid Böritigin (see above, p. 14) was laying waste the upper Oxus valleys to such an extent that Masʿūd described his depredations as worse than those of the Türkmens; but the prince's name was withdrawn, on the advice of the vizier Aūmad b. ʿAbd aṣ-Ṣamad, who was in any case opposed to the diversion of such great resources to Khuttal when the Türkmen menace in Khurasan was so pressing.[55] As noted above, p. 11, Maudūd fought valiantly but vainly at Dandānqān.

As the eldest son, Maudūd was always one of Masʿūd's favourites; hence he is named with his brothers Majdūd, ʿAbd ar-Razzāq and Saʿīd as enjoying a specially-favoured closeness with Masʿūd at the Shābahār army review festivities of 428/1037. When the sultan's official heir and favourite son, the amīr Saʿīd (unless this is not a personal name at all, but a designation, *Amīr-i Saʿīd* 'the Fortunate Amīr', on the lines of former Sāmānid practice?[56]), died in Rabīʿ I 430/December 1038, Maudūd was made *walī ʿahd* or heir in his place, regaining the position which he had held at the beginning of Masʿūd's reign but had apparently lost at some point subsequent to then.[57]

What we lack is any clear indication of Maudūd's date of birth and therefore age, though Baihaqī states that he was the eldest son (see above, n. 56). There is in Baihaqī considerable information about the protracted negotiations over Maudūd's projected marriage to a Qarakhanid princess, part of Masʿūd's grand strategy in securing Qadïr Khan Yūsuf of Kāshghar and Khotan as an ally and dividing him from his brother and rival in Transoxania (and also enemy of the Ghaznavids), ʿAlī b. Ḥasan or Hārūn Bughra Khan, known as ʿAlītigin.[58] As early as 422/1031 negotiations were begun for the marriage of Mas'ūd himself with the Khan's daughter Shāh Khātūn and of Maudūd with the daughter of the Khan's eldest son and heir Bughratigin Sulaimān (the later Arslan Khan, frequently mentioned in the later pages of Baihaqī, see above, p. 7). Matters dragged on for a long time, and Maudūd's intended bride eventually died en route for Ghazna in 425/1034.[59] Children could of course be betrothed before puberty and married at an early age, but Maudūd's military charges during the course of his father's reign indicate that he had reached adulthood by the early years of Mas'ūd's sultanate. Accordingly, we should probably accept the statement of Jūzjānī that Maudūd was thirty-nine when he died, that is he was born in 401/1010–11 or 402/1011–12, rather than that of Ibn al-Athīr that he died at the age of twenty-nine only.[60]

The news of all these events reached Maudūd in Ṭukhāristān. All thoughts of reinforcing the Ghaznavid forces at Balkh and of undertaking operations against the Seljuqs had for the moment to be abandoned. He first of all returned to the base of *Hupyān in the Hindu Kush, and then, on Aḥmad b. 'Abd aṣ-Ṣamad's advice, crossed the mountains swiftly to secure Ghazna; it could be expected that Muḥammad and the rebel army would march on the capital once the finer spring weather came round. Maudūd was accorded an enthusiastic reception in Ghazna, hence he spent the latter part of the winter (mid-432/early 1041) there, holding the requisite ceremonies of mourning for his father (whose designation henceforth was invariably to be that of the *Amīr-i Shahīd* 'Martyr-King') and assembling his forces.[61]

The opposing armies did not therefore clash in battle until the spring, the date of the actual battle being given as 13 Rajab 432/19 March 1041 by Ibn Bābā, and 3 Sha'bān/8 April (a discrepancy of 20 days) by Ḥusainī and Ibn al-Athīr. The two surviving manuscripts of Gardīzī's *Zain al-akhbār* break off immediately at the end of the historian's description of the battle and of Maudūd's vengeance on his father's murderer's, and doubtless his noting of the date of the battle came just at the beginning of the lost part. In so far as Ibn Bābā seems to have had access to the lost sections of Baihaqī's *Mujalladāt*, more credence should perhaps be attached to the earlier date.[62] Muḥammad's forces had established themselves in vicinity of Peshawar for the winter, but Muḥammad was helpless in the face of their indiscipline and of their excesses. Ibn al-Athīr records in this connection that

> Muḥammad's army raised all sorts of demands against him, and he lost all kingly authority. They made tyrannical confiscations of the people's property and plundered it, so that the land became ruined and its inhabitants fled, this above all at the town of Peshawar, whose populace was massacred and their goods despoiled. A slave was sold there for a mere dirham, whereas this same sum bought a *man* of wine.

He then goes on to record that Muḥammad's forces left Peshawar on 28 Rajab/3 April, according with his later date for the battle with Maudūd's army.[63]

The most detailed account of the battle is given by Gardīzī, although it is only the much later source of Jūzjānī who mentions where it actually took place, sc. in the district of Nangrahār (the modern, post-1964 re-organisation Afghan province of that name, lying along the middle reaches of the Kabul River, with Jalālābād as its centre).[64] It seems that there was a third figure who might potentially have become involved in the clash, in addition to the two protagonists Maudūd and Muḥammad. Present near the battlefield—either having come with one of the opposing armies or else having arrived independently with a force of his own—was Maudūd's uncle ʿAbd ar-Rashīd, who had in fact also been present with Maudūd and Masʿūd on the field at Dandānqan.[65] As the sole surviving son—so far as we know—of the great sultan Maḥmūd, ʿAbd ar-Rashīd had obviously a powerful claim to the headship of the Ghaznavid dynasty, and was indeed ultimately to become sultan shortly after Maudūd's own death. Maudūd had therefore at least to secure ʿAbd ar-Rashīd's neutrality, if he could not gain his active support. Maudūd accomplished this, firstly by promising ʿAbd ar-Rashīd a dominant share in the exercise of power and bestowal of honours, if he himself successfully obtained the throne, and secondly, by reminding his uncle of the solemn oath which the latter had given to his brother Masʿūd that he would not harm the interests of Masʿūd's sons. ʿAbd ar-Rashīd's neutrality was thus gained, and the danger that he might conceivably come to an agreement with Muḥammad and join up with his forces, or even perhaps that he might watch the two opposing sides destroy each other and then step in, as a *tertius gaudens*, to seize the fruits of victory for himself, was averted.[66]

Feeling now safe from such possibilities, Maudūd led personally an assault on the enemy line which proved decisive; Muḥammad's army crumbled, and the general Ertigin and the palace ghulāms battered them in an attack from the rear. Muḥammad, his sons, and the rebel generals Anūshtigin Balkhī and ʿAlī Qarīb's son all fell into Maudūd's hands. The latter now took exemplary vengeance on those whom he deemed responsible for his father's death. Ibn Bābā names only Anūshtigin Balkhī, the son of Amīr Yūsuf b. Sebüktigin, a son of Muḥammad's (presumably Aḥmad) and three other commanders, as suffering death. Other sources, however, speak of a more general slaughter of the military leaders and of the whole of Muḥammad's family (including, by implication, Muḥammad himself), with only ʿAbd ar-Raḥmān (or ʿAbd ar-Raḥīm) being spared because he had shown compassion towards the imprisoned Masʿūd in Gīrī and had condemned his brother Aḥmad's leading rôle in the killing.[67] To mark the site of the battle and to commemorate his victory, Maudūd now built there a settlement (*qarya, qaṣaba,* what Raverty in the notes to his *Ṭabaqāt-i Nāṣirī* translation calls a 'Bāzār and emporium') and a *ribāṭ,* and named the place appropriately as Fatḥābād before returning in triumph to Ghazna. Fakhr-i Mudabbir states that Fatḥābād, which was in the same area as a *ribāṭ* built by Sebüktigin to celebrate his victory in Lāmghān over the Hindū-Shāhī Rājā Jaipāl, subsequently prospered and became noted as a resort for *ghāzī*s (perhaps for warfare against the pagans of the adjacent Kāfiristān?). The place is mentioned by the early nineteenth-century traveller Charles Masson as being situated four miles south of Bālābāgh and twelve miles from Jalālābād, and 'Futtehabad' was also occupied by the British forces advancing towards Jalālābād under Sir Robert Sale during the First Afghan War.[68]

Ibn al-Athīr gives the date of Maudūd's state entry into Ghazna as 23 Shaʿbān 432/28 April 1041, and Ibn Bābā has Shaʿbān [4]33 (read 432)/April–May 1041 as Maudūd's official accession date.[69] According to Gardīzī's information, Maudūd bore the honorific titles of Shihāb ad-Dīn wa-d-Daula and Quṭb al-Milla, and these are confirmed by his coins. Some of Maudūd's bring the further titles of Jamāl ad-Daula and Fakhr al-Umma, with the variant Quṭb ad-Dīn for that given in the literary source of Gardīzī. Since Maudūd on his coins acknowledges the supreme overlordship of the Abbasid caliph al-Qā'im, it may be assumed that these titles were obtained from Baghdad; some of them may possibly have been acquired by him during his father's lifetime.[70]

Internal threats to his position from within the Ghaznavid family had ostensibly been scotched by the defeat of Muḥammad, but Maudūd was taking no chances; in defiance of his solemn promise to ʿAbd ar-Rashīd of a share in the royal power, as mentioned above, he immediately had his uncle arrested and imprisoned in the fortress of Mandīsh, where he remained all through Maudūd's sultanate.[71]

5.
Maudūd re-establishes the position in the west

The tasks facing the new sultan were nevertheless formidable. There was still the Türkmen threat in northern Khurasan which Masʿūd had faced with such a lack of vigour, together with a new fear that the Seljuqs might take over Sīstān and outflank the Ghaznavid dominions from the south. There had been intermittent unrest in Ghaznavid India during Masʿūd's reign, seen in the serious rebellion of Aḥmad Inaltigin; Muḥammad had drawn support from there during his brief second sultanate; and we shall see that Maudūd had very soon to face further rebellions in India.

We have seen that Maudūd's intended campaign into Ṭukhāristān was rendered abortive by his need to return and secure the succession; as a result, the Ghaznavid general Altuntash was unable to defend Balkh any longer, and it now suffered a severe plundering by the Türkmens. Herat also fell to the Oghuz, but with Maudūd's firm establishment on the throne of his fathers after the Nangrahār victory, confidence in the Ghaznavids revived to some extent in eastern Khurasan. The people of Herat rose against their occupiers and restored the town once again to Ghaznavid allegiance, although by 434/1042–3 we hear of it again as besieged by Chaghrï Beg Dā'ūd; in the end it fell to the Seljuqs, and Herat and the surrounding region of Bādghīs passed definitively into the Seljuq orbit. There is further evidence of a residuum of pro-Ghaznavid feeling in the report of Ṣadr ad-Din Ḥusainī that Chaghrï Beg had to send an expedition against the local leaders of Farāzbaj or Qarābāj (?), where people were still paying taxes to the Ghaznavids; one of these local lords had to be attacked and besieged before he agreed to recognise the Seljuqs.[72] Maudūd may have recovered Balkh for a while, and Tirmidh on the Oxus certainly held out under Amīrak Baihaqī till after 435/1043–4 (see above, p. 10).

Maudūd's energetic policies and his determination not to accept that the former Ghaznavid territories in the west were irretrievably lost gained for him an access of prestige among contemporaries at this time; it must have been difficult for these last to accept that so mighty an edifice as the empire of Maḥmūd and Mas'ūd could be permanently damaged by a horde of nomadic barbarians from the Central Asian steppes. It is said that, early in his reign, Maudūd received an embassy and offers of allegiance from the 'King of the Turks' in Transoxania, obviously a Qarakhanid and probably Böritigin, who on numismatic evidence was already ruling in Bukhara in 433/1041–2 as Co-Qaghan of his brother Arslan Khan 'Ain ad-Daula Muḥammad b. Nasr of Özgend, with the corresponding title of Bughra Khan, and in Samarqand by 438/1046–7; concerted Ghaznavid-Qarakhanid military action against the common foe of the Seljuqs did not, however, materialise till the very end of Maudūd's reign, see below.[73]

In 435/1043–4, hearing that Chaghrï Beg Dā'ūd had fallen ill, Maudūd sent an army into Ṭukhāristān. This attack was parried by the Seljuq amīr's son Alp Arslan, who was at that time based on Balkh; in the ensuing battle, the Ghaznavid forces were defeated with considerable losses, and the remnants returned to Ghazna. It seems to have been this reverse which finally convinced the castellan of Tirmidh, Amīrak Baihaqī, that it was hopeless to hold out any longer against the encircling Seljuqs. Chaghrï Beg could legitimately assume from this failure of Maudūd's that the Ghaznavid sultan now lacked the resources ever to mount a serious and sustained war for the recovery of Khurasan, and Ḥusainī records that at this point, Chaghrï Beg formally made over the governorship of all north-eastern Khurasan as far as the Oxus headwaters, comprising Balkh, Tirmidh, Ṭukhāristān, Qubādhiyān, Wakhsh and Walwālij, to his son Alp Arslan.[74]

Even so, Maudūd still dreamed of regaining the lost territories, and towards the end of his reign he tried to organise a military coalition against the Seljuqs, expending large sums of money in subsidies and promising rule over the different regions of Khurasan, under a general Ghaznavid suzerainty, to various anti-Seljuq powers of eastern Islam to whom he now made approaches. These last included the Dailamī prince from the Kākūyid dynasty of Jibāl, Abū Kālījār Garshāsp b. 'Alā' ad-Daula Muḥammad, who had in 437/1045–6 finally lost his appanage of Hamadān to the Seljuq leader Ibrāhīm Inal, and who spent the last years of his life in exile with his brother Farāmurz in Iṣfahān or with the Būyids of Fārs.[75] Maudūd communicated with him in Iṣfahān, and persuaded Abū Kālījār Garshāsp to raise an army and march eastwards; but the army perished in the Great Desert, and the Kākūyid returned, ill, to western Persia. Maudūd further made approaches to the Qarakhanids, to 'the Khāqān, King of the Turks', probably Tamghach Khan Ibrāhīm b. Naṣr, the former Böritigin, again. The Khan sent a contingent from Bukhara to the vicinity of Tirmidh and plundered and devastated the district (this fact confirms the indications of Ḥusainī and Ibn Funduq that Tirmidh had by now lapsed from Ghaznavid control), and another force under his general Qashqa was sent against Khwārazm, which had been abandoned by Mas'ūd's old ally Shāh Malik and taken over by the Seljuqs. However, both these attacks were repulsed, and Chaghrī Beg and Tamghach Khan Ibrāhīm eventually met on the banks of the Oxus and made peace. By this time, Maudūd himself may well have been dead. He had set out from Ghazna with an army, but was immediately taken ill, returned to the capital and died, so that all his grand strategy came to naught.[76]

Nor could Maudūd in the end retain Sīstān within the Ghaznavid sphere of influence, as it had been in the days of Maḥmūd and Mas'ūd, and by the end of his reign, the ruling family of Ṣaffārid amīrs had constituted Sīstān as a largely autonomous unit, although subject now to ultimate Seljuq suzerainty. This was nevertheless a reasonably favourable outcome of affairs for the Ghaznavids, since the Ṣaffārid amīrate did at least form something of a buffer-state, reducing the danger of Türkmen incursions through southern Afghanistan against Ghaznavid Bust and Zamīn-Dāwar and possibly even against Ghazna itself, a fear shown by Mas'ūd's despatching his general Nūshtigin Naubatī and then his official Abū Sahl Zauzanī immediately on his return from Dandānqān to secure the region of Bust (see above, p. 13).

Until Mas'ūd's last years, the Ghaznavids had sent out officials to Sīstān in order to collect the tribute and taxes due to the sultan as suzerain of Sīstān. These officials operated latterly side-by-side with the Ṣaffārid amīr Abū l-Faḍl Naṣr b. Aḥmad, who had been appointed regent in Sīstān by Sultan Maḥmūd just before his death in 421/1030.[77] Mas'ūd for a time worked through officials of his own appointed to collect the taxation from Sīstān, but at the opening of 429/October 1037 he dismissed the two officials responsible and replaced them by amīr Abū l-Faḍl once more, who now became directly responsible to the sultan for the *ʿamal* or financial yield of the province.[78] The social and political situation in Sīstān had been since the time of the Arab governors of the caliphs, predecessors of the Ṣaffārids, a complex and divided one, in which the bands of *ʿayyār*s and *sarhang*s, who in general expressed local patriotic Sagzī feeling and opposition to outside domination, frequently played a dominant rôle.[79]

Early in 432/autumn 1040 a Sagzī rebel called Aḥmad-i Ṭāhir raised a revolt at Karkūya against the authority of amīr Abū l-Faḍl, and summoned in the Türkmens as allies. Abū l-Faḍl sought military assistance from sultan Masʿūd in Ghazna, but this request came at a highly unfavourable time, when the Ghaznavid was preparing for the move to India. He did, however, finally in Rabīʿ I 432/November–December 1040 send a force of 5,000 cavalrymen under Bā Naṣr (presumably the Ḥājib Bū n-Naṣr mentioned in various places by Baihaqī, for example, as being amongst the combatants at Dandānqān and amongst the sultan's group that fled through Ghūr back to Ghazna)[80] to relieve Abū l-Faḍl, by now beleaguered in the capital Zarang by the rebels and by the Seljuq leader Ertash, who is described as the brother of Ibrāhīm Inal and a cousin of Toghrïl Beg. Abū l-Faḍl saw no way out but capitulation to the Seljuq, and he came to an agreement with Ertash that the *khuṭba* in Zarang should be made for the more senior Seljuq chief Bïghu or Paighu.[81] Bā Naṣr's force could only withdraw to Bust. Bïghu appeared personally in Sīstān in Rabīʿ II 432/December 1040, and the united Türkmen bands advanced on Bust and laid waste the countryside there; however, differences arose between Ertash and Bïghu, and these compelled a retreat from Bust. In the end, the Türkmens evacuated the province of Sīstān and returned to Khurasan.[82]

Thus the position at Maudūd's accession was that Sīstān, under amīr Abū l-Faḍl, was temporarily clear of outside forces, but Maudūd resolved immediately to send an army to restore Ghaznavid influence and to establish there a barrier against further Türkmen raids. A force under the leadership of the commander Qaimās was sent later in 432/spring–summer 1041, but it was, however, defeated, and Abū l-Faḍl later intercepted letters from Maudūd to various notables in Sīstān; hence in Jumādā II 433/February 1042 Abū l-Faḍl arrested and imprisoned a number of Ghaznavid sympathisers, including men of religion, *faqīh*s and an *imām*, and military commanders. It may well have been that the religious classes in Sīstān were especially favourable to the Ghaznavid connection because of the sultans' reputation as upholders of the *Sunna* and because of fears of Türkmen anarchy. In Rajab of the same year/March 1042 a Ghaznavid army, numbering 2,000 cavalry and 10,000 infantry, re-appeared in Sīstān and joined forces with various dissident elements there, including the partisans of the earlier rebel Aḥmad-i Ṭāhir and the *ʿayyār* group of the Shangaliyān.[83] Fierce fighting ensued, with Abū l-Faḍl besieged in the citadel of Zarang for four months, till the latter wrote to Ertash for help. A relieving force eventually appeared, defeated the Ghaznavid coalition forces, killing many of their leaders and pursuing the fugitives through the desert of the Dasht-i Margo back to Bust, where the soldiers of Ertash and Abū l-Faḍl plundered the region before returning to Sīstān in Rabīʿ I 434/October–November 1042. It may well be this expedition that Ibn al-Athīr also mentions and places in Ṣafar 435/September–October 1043 (read rather Ṣafar 434, which would fit better with the *Ta'rīkh-i Sīstān*'s very detailed and exact chronology of events?), stating that Maudūd's forces repulsed from Bust an Oghuz attack at that time.[84]

The ensuing events of the year 434/1042–3 and thereafter in Sīstān are *inter alia* notable for the appearance, as a leading figure on the stage of history, of the Ghaznavid Turkish slave commander Toghrïl, who was to play such a maleficent rôle in ʿAbd ar-Rashīd's sultanate. At this juncture, Toghrïl left Bust with 2,000 troops and marched towards Sīstān, having the good fortune to capture en route a member of the Ṣaffārid family, the amīr Abū n-Naṣr or Bā Naṣr b. Manṣūr b. Aḥmad, at the valley of H.n.dānqān. He then entered Sīstān in Jumādā II 434/January–February 1043, occupying Karkūya and causing there indiscriminate slaughter amongst the Muslim and Zoroastrian population. Abū l-Faḍl, however, sent a body of troops to defend the citadel of Karkūya, and Toghrïl decided to return to Ghazna, taking with him the amīr Abū n-Naṣr. This last was later to be exchanged by Abū l-Faḍl for a son of the great Ghaznavid vizier Aḥmad b. Ḥasan Maimandī[85] and other captured Ghaznavid commanders, and he continued thereafter to play a part in the tortuous, often internecine strife of Sīstān. The *Ta'rīkh-i Sīstān* records under 437/1045–6 a further clash of Ertash and Ghaznavid troops, in which the Seljuq leader was defeated and fled for safety to the citadel of Zarang; he was killed at Ṭabas three years later, having been no longer mentioned in connection with events in Sīstān.[86]

Maudūd's reign thus closed with a reasonably favourable and

stable position on his southern flank. Abū l-Faḍl—who continued to reign as Amīr of Sīstān till his death in Jumādā II 465/March 1073[87]—was now balancing himself between the two rival great powers, although he gradually became more and more drawn into the Seljuq orbit as the Seljuqs consolidated their power in Khurasan and Kirmān; by Rajab 439/December 1047–January 1048 he felt secure enough to release most of the Ghaznavid sympathisers whom he had arrested six years before.[88] Bust still remained as the bulwark of Ghaznavid power in southern Afghanistan, and was never in fact to be relinquished by the Ghaznavids till the rise of the Ghūrids in the following century (see below, Ch. 4, p. 122).

6.

The campaigns in India

After the suppression of Aḥmad Inaltigin's revolt in India, Masʿūd had in Dhū l-Qaʿda 427/August–September 1036 appointed his son Majdūd to be commander-in-chief there, fitting him out with a robe of honour appropriate for the viceregal office, and attaching to him three military commanders and a splendidly-equipped army, a secretary from the *Dīwān-i Risālat* for chancery business and a *mustaufī* or accountant as his financial clerk (the latter is named by Baihaqī as Saʿd-i Salmān, obviously the father of the poet Masʿūd-i Saʿd-i Salmān, and this may well have been the origin of the family's settling in the Panjab). Majdūd thus began an association with India, doubtless building up there a power-base for himself with an entourage of officials and troops personally loyal to him. He is, however, mentioned as being back in Ghazna on occasion, for example for the ʿĪd al-Fiṭr celebrations in 428/1037, and Gardīzī (though not Baihaqī) says that he was in the autumn of early 432/1040 sent by sultan Masʿūd to secure Multān (see above, p. 14).[89]

Majdūd was thus in India when his father was deposed and murdered. What his attitude was to Muḥammad's elevation to the throne is unknown, but he refused to recognise the succession of his brother Maudūd in Ghazna. He raised the standard of revolt in both Multān and Lahore, but was mysteriously found dead three days after the ʿĪd al-Aḍḥā (presumably of 432, when this festival fell on 11 August 1041). Majdūd's revolt thereupon collapsed, and Maudūd was able to make firm his authority throughout Ghaznavid India. The army which he had already despatched from Ghazna to quell Majdūd's revolt must be that mentioned in an anecdote of Fakhr-i

Mudabbir's *Ādāb al-ḥarb wa-sh-shajāʿa* as being under the command of the Sālār Aḥmad b. Muḥammad as *Ḥājib-i Buzurg*, with the Faqīh Salīṭī nominated as governor of Lahore (it is very likely that these two names conceal, under other forms, personages mentioned in the pages of Baihaqī, but exact identification is impossible). The tale recounts how this force reached Lahore, where Maudūd's authority was recognised by the army there.[90]

Having joined up with the Lahore garrison, the Faqīh Salīṭī left a deputy in Lahore, and the combined Ghaznavid army undertook a campaign against Multān. In the course of the 4th/10th century, the extremist Shīʿī Ismāʿīlī *daʿwa* or propaganda movement had enjoyed a signal success amongst the Muslims of the old Arab colonies in Sind and Multān; these regions had recognised the supremacy of the Fāṭimid caliph in North Africa and Cairo, al-Muʿizz (341–65/953–75), and the famous idol-temple of Multān, dedicated to the Sun-God Āditya, had been destroyed by one of the Ismāʿīlī *dāʿīs* or missionaries.[91] Maḥmūd of Ghazna, the zealot for orthodoxy and upholder of the *Sunna*, had in 396/1006 attacked the local Ismāʿīlī ruler of Multān, Abū l-Fatḥ Dā'ūd b. Naṣr, stormed the town and conducted a savage massacre of Ismāʿīlī sympathisers.[92] Thereafter, we hear nothing particular about events in Multān, but Ismāʿīlism there was clearly not dead, and rebellion broke out there, probably in 432/1040–1 when the news of Masʿūd's deposition and capture at Mārīkala became generally known in India, and Ghaznavid authority was at a low ebb. Once Lahore was secured for Maudūd, the Faqīh Salīṭī marched against the rebels, who were headed by Abū l-Fatḥ Dā'ūd's son, whom the Ismāʿīlīs (*Qarāmiṭa* in contemporary Ghaznavid phraseology)[93] addressed as their *Shaikh*. The Ismāʿīlī forces were unable to withstand the powerful Ghaznavid professional army, and withdrew to Manṣūra in southern Sind. Multān itself was compelled to surrender, and the *khuṭba* there was now made for the Abbasids and Maudūd (implying that it had been made by the rebels for the Fāṭimids once again). The Faqīh Salīṭī then appointed Muḥammad-i Ḥalīmī[94] as governor of Multān before returning to Lahore, harrying the Jhats and other infidels of the middle Indus region en route.[95]

The news of Masʿūd's end likewise emboldened various Indian princes into launching an attack on the Muslims, and Fakhr-i Mudabbir goes on to say that the army returning from Multān to Lahore was attacked by a coalition of Indian rulers, 'Rāys, Rānas and Thakkurs of the hill tracts', under Sandanpāl, described as the grandson of the Kābul-Shāh (read Hindū-Shāh, sc. the Hindū-Shāhīs of Waihind, old opponents of the Ghaznavids?).[96] A battle took place at Q.d.r.j.w.r (?) in which the Faqīh Salīṭī's army routed the infidels and in which Sandanpāl was killed.[97]

Despite his unavoidable concerns with the Seljuqs in northern Khurasan and with Sīstān, Maudūd found some time to fulfil the traditional role of the Ghaznavid sultans as hammers of the pagan Hindus and as bringers into circulation within the eastern Islamic economy of the temple treasures of India. After the loss of a rich province like Khurasan, warfare in India was now especially vital for financing the administration of the Ghaznavid empire and for providing the standing army with plunder and with an outlet for its energies. Maudūd had shown himself personally as a brave fighter during his father's lifetime, and is said to have been particularly skilful with the bow. The invention of a particular kind of arrow-head, the *paikān-i Maudūdi* one, is ascribed to him, this being allegedly made from gold so that anyone shot by an arrow thus tipped could either have his shroud bought out of the value of the arrow-head or have treatment for the wound out of its value. Perhaps we have here a reminiscence of the costly equipment and bejewelled weapons used on ceremonial occasions, such as official receptions, by the Ghaznavid palace ghulāms, although the legend of Maudūd's golden arrow-heads, if legend it was, did engender the verses

The sultan of the age, Shāh Maudūd, the one who makes arrow-heads of gold for his enemy,
So that whoever is killed by it can thereby obtain his shroud, or if wounded, can get treatment through it.[98]

The principal passage in the Islamic historians relating to Maudūd's activities in India is a regrettably vague passage of Ibn al-Athīr's (substantially repeated, but with some embroidery, in Mīrkhwānd), with no topographical information and with the names of two Indian princes in corrupt form. This passage states that, in 435/1043–4, three Indian princes attacked Lahore and besieged it for a considerable period of time. The governor there (whether this was still the Faqīh Salīṭī of Fakhr-i Mudabbir's anecdote is unknown) sent to Maudūd for help and received reinforcements, by means of which the Ghaznavid army then took the offensive. One of the Indian princes had by then returned to Ghaznavid allegiance. One of the remaining two, D.w.bāl (Devapāla) H.r.bāta (?) was besieged in one of his fortresses till he surrendered; the other, Tāb.t (?) Rāy, was slain in battle with 5,000 of his men, and the fates of these persuaded other Indian rulers of doubtful allegiance to reaffirm their loyalty to the Ghaznavids. It seems that we have reference here to the confederacy of Indian potentates who at this time reconquered from the Muslims Hānsī and Thānesar to the north-west of Delhi, Nagarkōt and other places, and who besieged Lahore for seven months. One of the leading members of this coalition was the great Paramāra Rājā of Mālwā, Bhoja; the Devapāla mentioned by Ibn al-Athīr is probably the Kachchhapaghāta Rājā of that name, son of the ruler of Gwalior Kīrttirāja who may have been the prince who submitted to Maḥmūd of Ghazna in 413/1022.[99] Explicit confirmation of this is, however, lacking.[100]

To supplement this, we have only some additional information from the Deccanī historian Muḥammad Qāsim Hindū-Shāh, called Firishta, who wrote his *Gulshan-i Ibrāhīmī* at the beginning of the 11th/17th century and is accordingly a very late source. Exactly whence Firishta derived his information is unknown, and the authenticity of his information cannot be checked through earlier sources; it does not, for instance, figure in Mīrkhwānd. According to Firishta, when Masʿūd was murdered, his son Majdūd, at the instigation of his adviser Ayāz Khāṣṣ, marched from Multān and occupied for himself territory in the valley of the Indus and its tributaries as far east as Hānsī and Thānesar before his sudden and mysterious death. He then further relates how, in 435/1043–4, the Rājā of Delhi and other rulers recaptured Hānsī, Thānesar and their dependencies from Maudūd's governor in India and besieged Nagarkōt for four months. The Rajput princes of the Panjab were stirred up, and three of them attacked Lahore, but were beaten off. These latter details fit *grosso modo* with those of Ibn al-Athīr, but Firishta is nevertheless even vaguer than his predecessor in that no names are given at all for the Indian princes involved in these events.[101]

7.

The internal functioning of the empire

Lacking as we do for Maudūd's reign such a detailed account of the day-to-day working of the *dīwāns* as we derive from the pages of Baihaqī for the bureaucracy during Masʿūd's sultanate, we must perforce assume that the essential continuity in personnel over the two reigns implied little significant change in governmental ethos or in the practical running of the empire after Masʿūd's death. Certainly, the wise and experienced Abū Naṣr Aḥmad b. Muḥammad b. ʿAbd aṣ-Ṣamad Shīrāzī,[102] who had been Maudūd's adviser in Ṭukhāristān at the time of his father's murder and whose counsels had probably contributed much to Maudūd's eventually securing the throne for himself, continued in office as vizier for the early part of the new reign. Aḥmad had been *kadkhudā* (chief executive or adjutant, in effect vizier) to Maḥmūd's governor in Khwārazm, Altuntash, and then after the death of Aḥmad b. Ḥasan Maimandī in 424/1032, he became vizier to Masʿūd, exercising a moderating influence on the sultan's erratic ways without, however, being able to restrain him in the end from the ill-starred decision to retire to India, described above.[103] It was from this time onwards, sc. his appointment as vizier, that he became the *mamdūḥ* of such of the great contemporary poets as Manūchihrī, who praises him as

> The sun of viziers, Aḥmad-i ʿAbd aṣ-Ṣamad, the one who is not merely the sun of viziers but the sun of both the heavy creations [sc. of men and jinn].
>
> He is the oustanding leader of all the outstanding leaders of the world, just as the iron point is the foremost part of a *khaṭṭī* spear.
>
> He is superior to all mankind through his possession of two small things, sc. through his [stout] heart and his [eloquent] tongue.[104]

After these eight years as Masʿūd's vizier, Aḥmad served Maudūd for two years, but then fell into disfavour through the jeajousy of the military commanders; Baihaqī states that he died only a short time after dismissal, but the much later biographical sources state that his enemies had him poisoned.[105]

Maudūd now appointed to the vizierate Ṭāhir, who had been accountant (*mustaufī*) in the *Dīwān-i Istīfā'*, the accounting section of the *Dīwān-i Wazīr*. Baihaqī mentions him as being still in charge of this department in 424/1033, and when Masʿūd departed for India just before his deposition and death, he gave Ṭāhir formal permission to take office under the Seljuqs, whom he fully expected would occupy Ghazna after his retiral to India (see above, p. 16). However, it soon transpired that narrow financial expertise was not enough for the onerous job of vizier, for Ṭāhir was a complete failure as chief minister and, after only two months, Maudūd dismissed him.[106]

The sultan was more successful with his third vizier, ʿAbd ar-

Razzāq b. Aḥmad b. Ḥasan Maimandī, for ʿAbd ar-Razzāq served Maudūd for the remainder of his reign; he then played a decisive part in setting up ʿAbd ar-Rashīd as sultan and served him as chief executive during his brief tenure of power (see pp. 39–40). There was, of course, always a preference for someone like ʿAbd ar-Razzāq, whose family background was one of service to the dynasty, for it was widely held that the arcana of such professions as secretary or financial official were handed down within families; whence both the Maimandī and the Shīrāzī families were active in the Ghaznavid administration for at least three generations. It seems that ʿAbd ar-Razzāq had fallen from grace together with his father in the later part of Maḥmūd's sultanate, for when the new ruler Masʿūd ordered the release of Aḥmad b. Ḥasan from jail, ʿAbd ar-Razzāq was likewise set free at the beginning of 422/1031 from incarceration in the fortress of Nandana or Nārdin on the Jhelum river in the Panjab. Thereafter he is mentioned sporadically by Baihaqī, and must have served in the central administration; he was also present at Dandānqān. Although he did not apparently serve Farrukh-Zād as vizier, he was still active then, for Baihaqī speaks of him as still in official employment when he himself was writing in 450/1058, and he served as an informant for Baihaqī over various items of information handed down from his father Aḥmad b. Ḥasan's time.[107]

Having the spoils of India at their disposal, the Ghaznavids were great builders of palaces and kiosks and enthusiastic layers-out of gardens and polo-grounds.[108] Unfortunately, we know nothing of Maudūd's efforts in this direction, although it is likely that he endeavoured to follow in his predecessors' footsteps here. Similarly, it seems that the court continued to be organised on the familiar formal and hierarchical pattern of Perso-Islamic monarchs, with a household of court officials and eunuchs and a group of boon-companions around the sultans for entertaining him during leisure periods and drinking-sessions. We know that the prince Kai Kā'ūs b. Iskandar b. Qābūs, from the Ziyārid family of Gurgān and Ṭabaristān, spent seven or eight years at his kinsman Maudūd's court as a commensal (*nadīm-i khāṣṣ*); in his 'Mirror for Princes', the *Qābūs-nāma*, he mentions the wine-drinking sessions of Maudūd and the vizier ʿAbd ar-Razzāq.[109] We may further assume that Maudūd kept up the traditions of his house in encouraging poets and literary men, although once again, specific information is lacking; the great poetic figures of Maḥmūd's and Masʿūd's reigns, such as ʿUnṣurī, Farrukhī and

Manūchihrī, were either dead or silent by Maudūd's sultanate. The great scientist and polymath Abū Raiḥān Bīrūnī was nevertheless alive until after 442/1050–1, dying an octogenarian, probably at Ghazna; his treatise on mineralogy, the *Kitāb al-Jamāhir fī maʿrifat al-jawāhir*, was certainly written during Maudūd's reign, and perhaps also his last major work, on pharmacology, the *Kitāb aṣ-Ṣaidala fī ṭ-ṭibb*.[110]

As noted above, p. 27, Maudūd died when about to lead a revanche against the Seljuqs in Khurasan. According to Ibn Bābā, he was struck down by an internal disorder (*qūlanj*) shortly after leaving Ghazna; he had only time to despatch the vizier ʿAbd ar-Razzāq to Sīstān in order to avert a threat there before he died. Firishta, alone of the sources, has the information that Maudūd had set out via Sakāwand and the Lōghar valley making for a fortress called Sānkōt (?), where he intended to collect some treasure stored up there, when he was taken ill.[111]

The data on the date of Maudūd's death and the duration of his sultanate are incomplete and somewhat contradictory, and are further confused by uncertainty in the sources over the reigns of his two ephemeral successors Masʿūd II b. Maudūd and ʿAlī b. Masʿūd. Of the standard reference books, S. Lane Poole's *The Mohammadan dynasties* (London 1893), 289, adopted 440/1048–9 as the date for Maudūd's death, the two short reigns after him and ʿAbd ar-Rashīd's accession. E. de Zambaur, in his *Manuel de généalogie et de chronologie pour l'histoire de l'Islam* (Hanover 1927), 282, placed Maudūd's death in Rajab 440/December 1048–January 1049, the two short reigns in this same year 440 and ʿAbd ar-Rashīd's accession in 441/June 1049–May 1050. The present author, in his *The Islamic dynasties, a chronological and genealogical handbook* (Edinburgh 1967), 181, basing himself on Ibn al-Athīr's information, chose 441 as the year of Maudūd's death, the two short reigns and ʿAbd ar-Rashīd's accession, but as will emerge from what is said below, this dating is controversial.

Ibn al-Athīr states that Maudūd died on 20 Rajab 441/18 December 1049 at the age of twenty-nine, agreeing to within a day with Ibn Bābā's date of 21 Rajab 441/19 December 1049, but Ibn al-Athīr's information here that Maudūd reigned for nine [lunar] years and ten months is too long, and we should probably read eight years and ten months. Building upon the date of 23 Shaʿbān 432/28 April 1041 for Maudūd's victorious entry into Ghazna and his formal accession to power (see above, p. 24), we arrive at a duration for his reign of approximately eight lunar years, eleven months / eight solar years, seven months, three weeks. Ḥusainī gives no exact dates, but states that Maudūd ruled for seven [lunar] years, ten months and two days; this would place his death on 25 Jumādā II 440/5 December 1048.[112] We thus have two possible dates for Maudūd's death, with a disparity of just over one year. The dates given by Ibn Bābā and Ibn al-Athīr have about them the ring of definiteness; the dating based on a calculation involving Ḥusainī's figure for Maudūd's period of rule involves the computation of a date of death not directly confirmed by any written source. Nevertheless, in favour of the second date is a piece of numismatic evidence to which D. Sourdel has drawn attention. He points out that two dīnārs of ʿAbd ar-Rashīd are extant, one in the British Museum (it was presumably because of this coin that Lane Poole, the cataloguer of the British Museum's Islamic coin collection, gave in his *Muhammadan dynasties* the year 440 as that of ʿAbd ar-Rashīd's accession) and the other in the Kabul Museum, which both clearly have the date 440, and these seem therefore to confirm the dating based on Ḥusainī.[113] If one adopts this last system, the brief reigns of Masʿūd II and ʿAlī will have to be placed in the third quarter of 440/winter of 1048–9 in order to allow ʿAbd ar-Rashīd to begin his reign in say the last quarter of 440/spring 1049.

8.
Succession difficulties and the accession of ʿAbd ar-Rashīd

We do not possess much firm information about Maudūd's two immediate successors. Many of the later sources do not even mention their existence.[114] According to Jūzjānī, he left behind three sons. Ibn Bābā says that when on the point of death, Maudūd appointed his five-year-old son (named elsewhere as Masʿūd) as successor, but Masʿūd reigned only for five days before the great men of state raised to power Maudūd's brother Abū l-Ḥasan ʿAlī b. Masʿūd. The latter is an obscure figure, unmentioned by Gardīzī and Baihaqī, for instance—at least in the extant part of their works—as having played any earlier part in affairs. According to Ibn Bābā again, he reigned for only forty-five days before the army leaders deposed him and consigned him to imprisonment in a fortress, but during this time he assumed the honorific title of Bahā' ad-Daula, if the literary sources are correct; no coins of his are known.[115] Jūzjānī has the information that Masʿūd (erroneously called here Muḥammad) b. Maudūd and ʿAlī b. Masʿūd ruled in concert (*bi-sh-shirka*), which may perhaps relate to some regency provisions for the child Masʿūd; but once their ineptitude was revealed, they were removed from power.[116]

It may have happened that ʿAlī b. Masʿūd showed signs of being a potentially strong ruler, and was therefore deposed in favour of one whom the military considered more pliable; but it is more probable that the indolence of harem life and subsequent incarceration had rendered ʿAlī little fitted for the exercise of power. Indeed, the traumatic experiences of the succession disputes in 421/1030 and 432/1040, added to the general climate of fear and suspicion prevailing in a despotic state like the Ghaznavid one,[117] seem to have brought about the adoption of a policy rather like that of the later Ottoman *qafes* or 'cage', the precautionary jailing of all male relatives who might have designs on the throne. As Ibn Bābā notes, the three successive sultans ʿAbd ar-Rashīd, Farrukh-Zād and Ibrāhīm all had to be fetched out of the fortress where they had been imprisoned and then raised to power. This state of affairs forms a clear contrast to the position in the early, formative stages of the Ghaznavid empire, when brothers or uncles of the sovereign, such as Maḥmūd's brothers Abū l-Muẓaffar Naṣr and ʿAḍud ad-Daula Yūsuf, were regularly employed as military commanders or in provincial governorships.

It is difficult to know what to make of the information of Firishta, who despite his lateness as a source has interesting material on these two reigns not found in the much earlier authorities. Thus he speaks of what seems very probable, that the real power during Abū Jaʿfar Masʿūd b. Maudūd's brief reign was exercised by the great Turkish military commanders, amongst whom he names two rival parties headed by ʿAlī b. Rabīʿ Khādim and Aitigin Ḥājib,[118] respectively (neither of these generals seems to be mentioned in other sources like Gardīzī, Baihaqī and Ibn Bābā, although Aitigin is described as a former ghulām of Sultan Maḥmūd's). When Aitigin's faction emerged as dominant, he deposed Masʿūd and placed his own candidate, ʿAlī b. Masʿūd, on the throne on 1 Shaʿbān 441/20 December 1049. ʿAlī married his brother Maudūd's widow, but the Indian provinces of the empire fell away under the leadership of the rebellious ʿAlī b. Rabīʿ. ʿAlī b. Masʿūd reigned for just over two years, till a movement in favour of his uncle ʿAbd ar-Rashīd b. Maḥmūd placed the latter on the throne, with ʿAlī then imprisoned in the fortress of Dīdī-Rū (mentioned by Gardīzī, see above, p. 16). Once ʿAbd ar-Rashīd was firmly in control at Ghazna in 443/1051–2, ʿAlī b. Rabīʿ in India returned to the Ghaznavid allegiance, and Anūshtigin Ḥājib (sc. the personage who was later to play an outstanding part in the overthrow of the usurper Toghrïl and the raising to power of Farrukh-Zād, see below, p. 46) was appointed governor there.[119]

These details seem far too circumstantial to be wholly figments of the historian's imagination, and the paucity of information from the earlier sources on the events of the transition from Maudūd's to ʿAbd ar-Rashīd's sultanate prevents us from dismissing them as unhistorical. It is, for instance, highly unlikely that Firishta could have invented the further detail that at one point ʿAlī b. Masʿūd had his brothers Mardān-Shāh and Īzad-Yār released from their captivity in Dār-Dāmān and treated with honour, for we know from Jūzjānī in the first case and also from Baihaqī and Gardīzī in the second case that these two princes undoubtedly existed.[120] On the other hand, Firishta's dates cannot be accepted, for we have just seen that the testimony both of the earlier sources and of numismatics demonstrates that ʿAlī's reign cannot have begun only in the latter half of 441/winter 1049–50, whilst its duration must have been nearer two months than two years. It is quite feasible that some of Firishta's events grouped under ʿAlī's sultanate may belong in fact to ʿAbd ar-Rashīd's subsequent reign.

Returning to the evidence of the earlier historical sources on the events surrounding ʿAlī's deposition and ʿAbd ar-Rashīd's assumption of the supreme power, these sources relate that it was the vizier ʿAbd ar-Razzāq Maimandī who acted promptly now and prevented the Ghaznavid state from sliding into anarchy. He was en route for Bust and Sīstān when he received the news of Maudūd's death, and he then determined to set up the most senior surviving member of the dynasty, ʿAbd ar-Rashīd b. Maḥmūd, who had been imprisoned by Maudūd in the nearby fortress of Mandīsh in southern Ghūr (see above, p. 16). According to Ibn Bābā, ʿAbd ar-Rashīd's accession to power in Ghazna was on 27 Shaʿbān 441/24 January 1050 (but see above, p. 37, for the contradictory evidence on his succession).[121] ʿAbd ar-Rashīd's maturity, and the fact that he had played some part in affairs during Masʿūd's sultanate, made him a much more credible potential war-leader and preserver of the empire's fabric than his two short-reigned predecessors, and this must have made ʿAbd ar-Razzāq's *putsch* acceptable in Ghazna.

ʿAbd ar-Rashīd's sultanate was soon to end in tragedy, and his reign was accordingly too short for us to form any real impression of his character and attainments. The sources speak of him as both 'headstrong and self-willed' (*mustabidd*) and also somewhat lacking in resolution and strength of mind, but this may be an assumption by later writers in the light of Toghrïl's ascendancy over him and succeeding seizure of power. Jūzjānī does, however, speak of his lofty character and love of learning, which included a personal knowledge of historical traditions.[122] Gardīzī composed his history during ʿAbd ar-Rashīd's reign and named it the *Kitāb Zain al-akhbār* 'Ornament of histories' after the sultan, one of whose honorifics was Zain al-Milla. There survives a superbly-produced manuscript of a work on traditions that described the Prophet, written in Ghazna expressly for ʿAbd ar-Rashīd's library by a local *warrāq* or book-dealer and copyist—the subject-matter of this manuscript neatly confirms Jūzjānī's mention of the sultan's interest in tradition. The *ex-libris* of this manuscript further gives us useful information on ʿAbd ar-Rashīd's titulature. Gardīzī names him in full as the 'Sulṭān-i Muʿaẓẓam ʿIzz ad-Daula wa-Zain al-Milla, Saif Allāh, Muʿizz Dīn Allāh Abū Manṣūr ʿAbd ar-Rashīd b. Yamīn ad-Daula . . . Maḥmūd . . .'. ʿAbd ar-Rashīd's coins simply have ʿIzz ad-Daula wa-Zain al-Milla and Saif Allāh, but this *ex-libris* mentions also the more complicated *laqab*s of Muʿizz Dīn Allāh (as in Gardīzī) and Muẓāhir Khalīfat Allāh (otherwise unknown). Later authorities add further honorifics, such as Ibn al-Athīr's Shams Dīn Allāh and Saif ad-Daula (variant, Jamāl ad-Daula), and that of Majd ad-Daula; but Stern was probably right in doubting the accuracy of these reports.[123]

Despite the changes of sultans since Maudūd's death, the bureaucracy continued to operate and to provide an element of stability in the state. ʿAbd ar-Razzāq Maimandī seems to have remained as a guiding influence over the *dīwāns*—at least, we have no mention of anyone else as vizier—and it was in ʿAbd ar-Rashīd's reign that the historian Abū l-Faḍl Baihaqī became head of the *Dīwān-i Risālat*, where he had been employed since Masʿūd's reign. He lost this job, however, and was imprisoned by the Qāḍī of Ghazna over a matter concerning his alleged non-payment of the dowry due to a wife; during the usurpation of Toghrïl (see below) he was sent to a fortress, together with other former officials of ʿAbd ar-Rashīd's. However, another reason is given for Baihaqī's dismissal in an anecdote given by ʿAufī. According to this, Baihaqī removed from his position of authority a tyrannical slave of ʿAbd ar-Rashīd's called Tūmān, who had oppressed the people of the Peshawar district, but the removal proved to be only temporary; Tūmān regained the sultan's favour, and Baihaqī himself was dismissed. ʿAufī names his source for this as the *Ta'rīkh-i Nāṣirī*, presumably Baihaqī's own *Mujalladāt*; but one wonders whether the whole story has not been contaminated by the story of Toghrïl's rise to power in ʿAbd ar-Rashīd's reign, despite the difference in names between Tūmān and Toghrïl.[124] Clearly, as a loyal if not uncritical servant of the Ghaznavid dynasty, Baihaqī should have been an uncompromising foe of the usurper, and he certainly speaks of him approbriously in the only reference to him in the extant part of the *Mujalladāt*. This comes actually in his section on the history of Khwārazm, where he is writing on his favourite theme of the utility of history and the profitable examples to be found in it. He states here that

> One should take note of the episode of the arrogant and contemptible Toghrïl, who attempted to destroy this dynasty, and established himself on the throne of the amīrs Maḥmūd, Masʿūd and Maudūd, and of what became of him, and of what the officer who killed Toghrïl and his minions did; may God, He is exalted and magnified, bring affairs to a good conclusion![125]

9.
The usurpation of Toghrïl

The outstanding event of ʿAbd ar-Rashīd's sultanate, upon which such sources as Ibn Bābā, Ḥusainī, Ibn al-Athīr and Jūzjānī dwell at length, was the rise to power of the Turkish slave general Toghrïl (usually stigmatised in the sources as *kāfir-i niʿmat* 'the ingrate', or *malʿūn nā-mubārak* 'the accursed and inauspicious', or *maghrūr makhdhūl* 'the arrogant and contemptible'), culminating in the violent overthrow and death of ʿAbd ar-Rashīd and the temporary setting-aside of the Ghaznavid dynasty. However, this change proved too cataclysmic a one for the ruling class and the military leaders to stomach, and the old line was restored to the throne in Ghazna, to the accompaniment, it seems, of a feeling of relief much like that occasioned by Charles II's restoration after the Commonwealth and

Protectorate in seventeenth-century England. This traumatic event, coming as it did soon after the succession uncertainties following on Maudūd's death and the two ephemeral sultanates of that period, entitles us to regard the late 1040s and the early 1050s as a 'time of troubles', before the Ghaznavid sultanate was put on a firm basis once again during the long, stable reign of Ibrāhīm b. Mas'ūd (see below, Ch. 2).

One may note at the outset that the *Akhbār ad-daula as-saljūqiyya* and the *Ta'rīkh-i Baihaq*, alone of all the sources, attribute to Toghrïl an additional name, which the editor of the first of these two texts, Muḥammad Iqbāl, read as the improbable N.zān, correcting the manuscript's B.zān; the latter in fact looks much more Turkish (*bozan, buzan* 'destroyer', 'annihilator'?)[126] than the former, and the initial *b* seems to be secured by the second text's forms B.dān, B.r'ān.[127] Toghrïl's career clearly went back to the time of earlier Ghaznavid princes. Of possible interest, in the light of Toghrïl's subsequent display of animus against the Ghaznavid dynasty and in the light of the fact that some of Yūsuf b. Sebüktigin's personal ghulāms had deserted to the Seljuqs before Dandānqān (see above, p. 20), is Shabānkāra'ī's statement that Toghrïl had 'probably' (*ghāliban*) been a ghulām of the disgraced amīr Yūsuf. However, this may well be a confused reminiscence of the fact that Yūsuf did have a slave officer, especially dear to his heart and called Toghrïl, who betrayed his master's trust by acting as sultan Mas'ūd's *mushrif* or spy over him when he went on his expedition to Quṣdār in Baluchistan in 421 / 1030; Baihaqī expressly notes that this Toghrïl, also *kāfir-i ni'mat*, died young, and he cannot therefore be our present Toghrïl.[128]

Jūzjānī, on the other hand, says that Toghrïl had been one of sultan Maḥmūd's ghulāms, and that during Maudūd's reign he had left the Ghaznavid service and fought under the Seljuq banner for a while, thus gaining a knowledge of their fighting techniques; he then returned to Ghazna only in the early part of 'Abd ar-Rashīd's reign. There seems to be an echo of this story in the balder information of the *Akhbār ad-daula as-saljūqiyya* that Toghrïl first rose to prominence in 432 / 1041, that he subsequently fled from his Ghaznavid masters to the Seljuqs, and that he then returned with an army of Turks (i.e. Türkmens?) to attack 'Abd ar-Rashīd. Though this is at best a very jejune telescoping of events, Ḥusainī's history is the sole source—for what it is worth—which says that during Toghrïl's brief rule in

Ghazna he acknowledged the Seljuqs as suzerains and forwarded to them the surplus of taxation that he had collected and that he did not have to spend on the upkeep of his army.[129] Yet it seems improbable that Toghrïl ruled long enough for any such regular arrangments to have evolved, and the very few coins extant of Toghrïl's (see below) do not mention the Seljuqs at all, as one might expect. The whole story of these connections of Toghrïl with the Seljuqs, found only in this distinctly pro-Seljuq source, seems dubious, perhaps a later invention to provide some rationale for his usurpation; and there is an obvious possibility of confusion between the name of the ghulām Toghrïl and that of the Seljuq leader Toghrïl Beg.

It is more likely that Toghrïl achieved his reputation as a vigorous and brave general during Maudūd's reign, for the two most detailed accounts of the former's tenure of power we possess, those of Ibn Bābā and Ibn al-Athīr (the latter account under the year 444/1052–3) both record that Maudūd singled him out for special honours and even gave him the hand in marriage of one of his own sisters. When ʿAbd ar-Rashīd came to the throne, he appointed Toghrïl commander-in-chief (*ḥājib al-ḥujjāb*) of the army. Toghrïl perhaps already sensed that he could gain an ascendancy over the somewhat easy-going sultan; he urged the unwilling ʿAbd ar-Rashīd to provide him with troops and resources so that he could lead an army against the Seljuqs and clear them out of Khurasan. According to Ibn Bābā, Toghrïl had led an army into northern Afghanistan against Alp Arslan and had secured a victory over the Seljuq prince at *Hībān/*Hupyān in the Hindu Kush (i.e. the place where prince Maudūd's army had encamped during the last days of his father's sultanate, see above, p. 22). Ibn al-Athīr, however, makes ʿAbd ar-Rashīd himself the leader of this campaign, which fell in the autumn and winter of 443/1051–2, against Chaghrï Beg himself, who had come with an army from Kirmān.[130]

The account in Jūzjānī, though brief, provides a means of harmonising the two somewhat divergent accounts (as we shall see, both of these go on to recount the story of Toghrïl's invasion of Sīstān, which is described in detail below). According to the *Ṭabaqāt-i Nāṣirī*, the Seljuq contemplated a two-pronged attack on the Ghaznavid possessions, in which Chaghrï Beg was to advance through Sīstān towards Bust and his son Alp Arslan was to strike through Ṭukhāristān and attack Kabul and Ghazna from the north. ʿAbd ar-Rashīd sent Toghrïl firstly against Alp Arslan, and Toghrïl secured a victory over the Seljuq prince at a place which Jūzjānī calls 'just before the valley between hills/just before the pass of Kh.mār (*pīsh-i dara-yi Kh.mār*)'.[131] One wonders whether this is not just a corrupt orthography of *Hībān/*Hupyān, خمار — هسان; the place is otherwise unknown. At all events, if the Seljuq forces penetrated as far as the Parwān region, the situation was potentially very serious for the Ghaznavids, and Toghrïl's resolute action in probably saving the state at this juncture may well have put into his mind the idea of seizing supreme power in Ghazna if ʿAbd ar-Rashīd really was as hesitant and ineffective a ruler as Toghrïl's contemptuous words of justification for his coup, as reported by Jūzjānī, make out.[132]

Then, with the northern flank of the Ghaznavid empire thus secured, Toghrïl turned southwards towards Sīstān; since Sīstān and its amīrs had now thrown off their dependence on the Ghaznavids (see above pp. 27–30), and were now inclined rather to the side of the Seljuqs, there was a danger of their allowing the Seljuqs to penetrate through Ṣaffārid territory against Bust and the Ghaznavid lands. The *Ta'rīkh-i Sīstān* now becomes a detailed source for Toghrïl's operations in Sīstān, the immediate prelude to his seizure of supreme power in Ghazna.

Toghrïl led his army into Sīstān, and on 3 Rajab 443/10 November 1051 appeared suddenly at Ṭāq and invested the citadel there. This was defended by the amīr Abū l-Faḍl Naṣr's *kōtwāl*, Hilāl Daraqī, till his death in the fighting, and then by another commander, aided by the patriotic forces of Sīstān, the *sarhang*s and *ʿayyār*s. The substantial Ghaznavid army comprised 5,000 Maḥmūdī cavalrymen (veterans of Maḥmūd's campaigns?), five war elephants and 2,000 Sagzī and Ghaznavī infantrymen.[132] The attackers nevertheless failed to make headway, but Toghrïl detached a contingent of 1,000 cavalrymen secretly to launch an assault on Zarang. Bïghu had meanwhile come from Herat to reinforce the Ṣaffārid amīr Abū l-Faḍl in his capital, but the Seljuq force was decisively defeated by Toghrïl, and both Bïghu and Abū l-Faḍl fled in disarray back to Herat. Even so, Toghrïl could not capture Ṭāq, and on 16 Shaʿbān 443/23 December 1051 he gave up the siege and marched away towards Ghazna, triumphant over the Seljuqs at least; but Abū l-Faḍl returned to Zarang in the following month, and on 8 Muḥarram 445/30 April 1053 the local historian of Sīstān records that the *khuṭba* in Zarang was made in the first place for Toghrïl Beg the Seljuq.[134]

The story of Toghrïl may now be resumed from Ibn Bābā and Ibn al-Athīr. Flushed with his success against Bïghu and the amīr Abū l-Faḍl, Toghrïl decided to march on Ghazna and depose ʿAbd ar-Rashīd. When he reached a distance of five farsakhs from the capital he sent a deceitful message to the sultan informing him that the army was in a rebellious state and was demanding a pay increase. ʿAbd ar-Rashīd saw the writing on the wall and shut himself up in the citadel of Ghazna; Toghrïl was able to take over the royal palace and centre of administration, and apparently won over to his side a significant part of the garrison of Ghazna. He was thus able either to storm the citadel and capture ʿAbd ar-Rashīd (Ibn Bābā) or to threaten the defenders with such a dire fate that they surrendered the hapless sultan (Ibn al-Athīr, Mīrkhwānd). There then followed a bloodbath of all the male members of the Ghaznavid family in the immediate vicinity. Jūzjānī and Ḥusainī say that a total of eleven Ghaznavid princes, the sons of Masʿūd, were slaughtered, including Sulaimān and Shujāʿ (wrongly described by the latter author as ʿAbd ar-Rashīd's brothers); Ḥamdallāh Mustaufī says that nine princes, sc. Ḥusain, Naṣr, Īrān-Shāh, Khālid, ʿAbd ar-Raḥmān, Manṣūr, Humām, ʿAbd ar-Raḥīm and Ismāʿīl, were killed, and only three preserved, sc. Farrukh-Zād, Ibrāhīm and Shujāʿ. Toghrïl also forcibly married one of Masʿūd's daughters.[135]

Toghrïl now assumed the throne himself. The enforced marriage at this point with the Ghaznavid princess, just mentioned above (presumably in addition to the daughter of sultan Maudūd previously espoused) indicates an attempt to legitimise his power in a familiar way. He also began to mint both gold and silver coins. The three coins of his that are extant, a dīnār (dated 443/1051–2) and two dirhams (undated), bear his name 'Abū Saʿīd Toghrïl' and the *laqab* of Qiwām ad-Daula, and the ultimate sovereignty of the Abbasid caliph al-Qā'im is also acknowledged.[136]

Yet sentiment in the empire for the fallen dynasty was still strong, despite the damage done to the prestige of the Ghaznavids by the spectacle of several different reigns within a short time. There were still the Ghaznavid forces in India to reckon with, and when Toghrïl wrote to the commander-in-chief there, the general Khirkhīz (sc. Kirghiz)[137], asking for his support and help in a joint campaign against the Seljuqs, Khirkhīz had no mind to subordinate himself to a fellow-slave commander, and sent back a categoric refusal. He condemned Toghrïl's murder of ʿAbd ar-Rashīd, and he wrote to

Masʿūd's daughter and to the army commanders condemning them for condoning and tolerating Toghrïl's usurpation. These reproaches led to a revulsion of feeling against Toghrïl, and he was murdered by a group of conspirators (Ibn al-Athīr, Mīrkhwānd); by an obscure palace ghulām called Nūshtigin, for private reasons of revenge (Ibn Bābā); by Nūshtigin, a former slave of Sultan Masʿūd's, 'fulfilling the rights due to his former master' (Ḥusainī); or by Nūshtigin the *silāḥ-dār* or armour-bearer, in concert with one of his cronies, after which they caused Toghrïl's head to be paraded round Ghazna on the end of a pole (Jūzjānī).

Whether the deed was an isolated act of vengeance or the result of a conspiracy, the result was an end to the 'extensive injustice and tyranny' which the *Ṭabaqāt-i Nāṣirī* says he had practised. Khirkhīz arrived back from India three or five days after Toghrïl's assassination, and after consultation with the great men of state and the military commanders, they agreed to set up a Ghaznavid prince on the throne once again. According to Jūzjānī once more, only two princes remained of Masʿūd's line, Ibrāhīm and Farrukh-Zād, both of whom were immured in the fortress of Barghund (the place of Muḥammad b. Maḥmūd's imprisonment, see above, p. 15). Toghrïl had sent a detachment expressly to put them to death, but the *kōtwāl* of Barghund procrastinated over admitting the execution squad, till at the eleventh hour, couriers arrived with the news of Toghrïl's own death. The preference of the leaders in Ghazna was for Ibrāhīm, but he was ill at the time, hence Farrukh-Zād was brought forth and set on the throne. At the same time, a purge was launched of all those who had been involved in Toghrïl's seizure of power. The only other author who has much detail on this last event, the choice of a new ruler, is Firishta, whose account varies slightly from that of Jūzjānī. According to him, three of the sons of Masʿūd remained alive at this point, Farrukh-Zād, Ibrāhīm and Shujāʿ, and out of those, Farrukh-Zād was chosen by lot to be the new sultan; this seems highly improbable.[138]

The questions of the chronology of ʿAbd ar-Rashīd's reign, of Toghrïl's usurpation and of Farrukh-Zād's accession, are all interconnected. According to the *Ṭabaqāt-i Nāṣirī*, ʿAbd ar-Rashīd reigned for two-and-a-half years and died at the age of thirty, whilst Farrukh-Zād succeeded to the throne on Saturday, 9 Dhū l-Qaʿda 443/13 March 1052. Thus Jūzjānī's 'two-and-a-half years' are actually two years and two months, if ʿAbd ar-Rashīd came to power, as Ibn Bābā says, on 27 Shaʿbān 441 / 24 January 1050, i.e. Jūzjānī does not include the period of Toghrïl's usurpation in his computation, if we accept the date of Dhū l-Qaʿda 443 / March 1052 for Toghrïl's assassination. But if we adopt the chronology based on inference from Ḥusainī and on the numismatic evidence (see above, p. 37) and place ʿAbd ar-Rashīd's accession in the last quarter of 440 / spring 1049, then Jūzjānī's 'two-and-a-half years' bring us up to Jumādā I 443 / August–September 1051, and Toghrïl would have a reign of some six months. This seems quite feasible, in view of the fact that he was able to start minting his own coins, and the *Ṭabaqāt-i Nāṣirī*'s suspiciously round-looking number of 40 days for Toghrïl's reign is too short. Jūzjānī's placing of his murder and Farrukh-Zād's accession in Dhū l-Qaʿda 443 is confirmed by Ḥusainī; that it began before the end of this year, and not in 444, is secured by the existence of several dīnārs of Farrukh-Zād's with the date of 443.[139] Although Ibn al-Athīr gives a particularly detailed account of these events, he gives no dates, merely putting the whole episode under 444 / 1052–3. As for Ibn Bābā's setting of these events in 443 and part of 444, one can take the 'part of 444' as referring to Farrukh-Zād's initial period of installation and settling down on the throne.[140]

10.

Farrukh-Zād's sultanate

Abū Shujāʿ Farrukh-Zād began a reign which lasted for seven lunar years, three months / seven solar years, three weeks, quite a long one by the standard of what had been recent events in Ghazna. His honorific titles, as known from his coins, were the modest ones of Jamāl ad-Daula wa-Kamāl al-Milla, but an interesting point, to which Sourdel has called attention, is the first appearance, on a dirham described by Markov and now in the Hermitage Museum at Leningrad, of the title *as-Sulṭān al-Muʿaẓẓam*, so characteristic of the titulature of the later Ghaznavids. Certainly, Baihaqī normally refers to Farrukh-Zād as *Sulṭān-i Muʿaẓẓam* or *as-Sulṭān al-Muʿaẓẓam.*[141] The whole question of this title, and its definitive adoption by Farrukh-Zād's successor Ibrāhīm, is considered below, Ch. 2; p. 55f.

Farrukh-Zād remains personally a somewhat shadowy figure, although he is praised for his justice and benevolent rule, which did something to infuse an atmosphere of tranquillity into the state after the *Sturm und Drang* of the preceding years. Baihaqī mourns that he died comparatively young, when his exercise of power was so beneficent;

in Ibn Bābā's words, 'through his coming to the throne, the flow of water which had dwindled away and the splendour which had departed, came back once more'. According to Jūzjānī, he restored prosperity to the various parts of the empire, remitting the taxes of the province of Zābulistān, which had suffered from extraordinary tax-levies and impositions (*ʿawāriḍ wa muʾnāt*).[142]

The Ḥājib Khirkhīz, to whose prompt action Farrukh-Zād owed his throne, inevitably had a large say in the regulation of affairs during the early part of the reign at least, although after his repulse of the Seljuq attack mentioned below, Khirkhīz is not specifically mentioned in the sources.[143] The former vizier of Maudūd and ʿAbd ar-Rashīd, ʿAbd ar-Razzāq Maimandī, continued in official service under Farrukh-Zād, though not as vizier (see above, p. 35). On his accession, Farrukh-Zād made Ḥusain b. Mihrān his vizier. The latter had been adjutant (*nāʾib wa katkhudā*) to prince Muḥammad in sultan Maḥmūd's time, but had made a timely transfer to the service of the victorious Masʿūd, becoming overseer (*mushrif*) of the treasury for him. He served Farrukh-Zād for two years, but was then dismissed and imprisoned. His successor (presumably at the end of 445–beginning of 446/spring-summer 1055) was Abū Bakr b. Abī Ṣāliḥ, an experienced warrior as well as administrator, who had for thirty years acted as a governor in India, where he left behind many public and charitable works. He remained vizier for the rest of Farrukh-Zād's reign and then became Ibrāhīm's first vizier, before coming to the violent end characteristic of the careers of so many viziers (see Ch. 2, below, p. 71).[144]

Of the sultan's other high officials, we learn that Abū Sahl Zauzanī, familiar from the pages of Baihaqī, acted as head of the Correspondence Department, whilst Farrukh-Zād's ʿ*Āriḍ* or head of the Army Department was Masʿūd Rukh(kh)ūdī (i.e. from Rukh(kh)ud or Rukhkhaj, classical Arachosia, the alternative name for the region of Zamīn-Dāwar), who had already held this post under Maudūd.[145] Baihaqī himself must have emerged from imprisonment with the overthrow of Toghrïl, and in his retirement started to put together his *Mujalladāt*, beginning to write his administrative diary-cum-history just when Farrukh-Zād and Ibrāhīm came to the throne in Ṣafar 451/April 1059; but, as noted below in Ch. 2, p. 52, he was brought out of his retirement in order to display his secretarial expertise in drawing up the peace treaty which ended the warfare in northern Afghanistan between the Ghaznavids and Seljuqs.[146]

Farrukh-Zād's reign fell before the period of literary activity on the part of the great poets of Ibrāhīm's sultanate and after, but we do have mention of the sultan's outstanding panegyrist Ḥakīm Jauharī; 'Aufī names him in full as Abū l-Maḥāmid Maḥmūd b. 'Umar al-Jauharī aṣ-Ṣā'igh al-Harawī, and quotes a long *qaṣīda* of his dedicated to Farrukh-Zād.[147]

Of external relations during Farrukh-Zād's reign, we have only the barest details. Chaghrï Beg was, not surprisingly, emboldened to take advantage of the cataclysm which had struck the Ghaznavid state in the form of Toghrïl's usurpation and then assassination, and when the news of these events reached the Seljuq ruler, he sent a force against Ghazna which was, however, halted and then defeated by Khirkhīz.[148] Concerning Farrukh-Zād's personal prowess as a warrior, Fakhr-i Mudabbir says that his favourite weapon was the battle-axe.[149] Towards the end of his sultanate, when stability within the empire seemed to be assured, he launched an expedition against the Seljuqs in Ṭukhāristān, which had some success; the opposing Seljuq commander, the Atabeg Quṭb ad-Dīn Kul-Sarïgh, was captured, and his forces fled. But Alp Arslan then led a fresh Seljuq force against the Ghaznavid army, which was this time itself defeated, with several of its commanders made prisoner. A peace agreement and an exchange of prisoners was obviously the next step to be envisaged, but Farrukh-Zād's death must have supervened around this time, since the only comparatively early sources mentioning these events, Ḥusainī and Ibn al-Athīr, are uncertain as to whether peace was made by Farrukh-Zād or by Ibrāhīm just after his accession (see on this question Ch. 2, below, pp. 51–2). Whoever were precisely the principals involved here, Ḥusainī's words express the favourable outcome, that 'the Sebüktigīnī and Seljūqī judgments agreed together that each power should be sovereign and independent within its own dominions, and that each should leave off attacking the other'.[150]

Farrukh-Zād's death came on 17 Ṣafar 451/4 April 1059 (the exact date in Ibn Bābā) at the age of thirty-four years. His reign had not been free latterly of the chronic turbulence and greed shown by the palace ghulāms, given fresh stimulus by the rule of weaker sovereigns after Maudūd's death. In 450/1058 these slaves had attempted to assassinate him in the baths, and although Farrukh-Zād had escaped, a mood of world-weariness and distaste for life came over him, until he died naturally of *qūlanj* a year later.[151]

TWO

The Reign of Ibrāhīm: Retrenchment and Continuity

1.

Ibrāhīm and the Seljuqs

The fullest account which we possess of the circumstances of Ibrāhīm's accession is that of the *Ṭabaqāt-i Nāṣirī*. We have seen that at the time of the Ghaznavid restoration after Toghrïl's usurpation, both Farrukh-Zād and Ibrāhīm had been found imprisoned at Barghund, and that Farrukh-Zād had been brought forth and acclaimed as sultan in Ghazna. So far as we know, Ibrāhīm remained at Barghund for some time, but was then transferred by Farrukh-Zād to the fortress of Nāy in Wajīristān or Ajīristān, the region to the west of Ghazna on the headwaters of the Arghandāb and the Helmand (not to be confused with the modern district of Waziristan in the North-West Frontier region of Pakistan);[1] this was a favoured stronghold for detaining Ghaznavid princes, and later it formed one of the places of the poet Mas'ūd-i Sa'd-i Salmān's first period of imprisonment (see below, p. 66). When Farrukh-Zād died, there was a general consensus among the great men of state in Ghazna that Ibrāhīm should be raised to the throne; it appears that Abū l-Muẓaffar Ibrāhīm was the last surviving son of political significance, and may well have been the senior member of the Ghaznavid royal family (nothing is heard now of the other son who is said to have survived Toghrïl's massacre of Ghaznavid princes, Shujā', see above, Ch. 1, p. 45). The military leader (*Sarhang*) Ḥasan went with an escort to fetch Ibrāhīm, the procession returned to Ghazna, and on Monday, 19 Ṣafar 451/6 April 1059 (the date being given thus by Baihaqī),[2] homage was done to Ibrāhīm as Amīr and Sultan.

Concerning Ibrāhīm's earlier life, we only know that he was born in 424/1033 during the campaign led by his father Mas'ūd into Gurgān and Ṭabaristān to collect the arrears of tribute due from the local Ziyārid prince Manūchihr b. Qābūs, that is he was twenty-seven lunar years or twenty-six solar years old at his accession. He proved to be extremely prolific in regard to offspring. The *Ṭabaqāt-i Nāṣirī* lists forty sons, bearing names which display a mixture of Islamic components, epic Persian names and Turkish ones. It further mentions that Ibrāhīm had thirty-six daughters, all of them given in marriage to well-born sayyids and ulema; one of these was actually married to the great-great-grandfather of the historian Jūzjānī, sc. to ʿAbd al-Khāliq Jūzjānī, who migrated from Gūzgān to Ghazna as the result of a dream in order to marry this princess.[3]

The most pressing tasks facing the new ruler were first, the restoration of social tranquillity and economic prosperity within the Ghaznavid dominions, a process already begun by Farrukh-Zād (see above, Ch. 1, p. 46); and second, the achieving of a lasting peace with the Seljuqs, or at least, a *modus vivendi* between the two great empires. Concerning the first task, Jūzjānī mentions that Ibrāhīm adopted a vigorous policy aimed at bringing back the empire's prosperity, including the rebuilding of towns devastated in the civil warfare of the preceding decade and the building of new settlements; of these last, he mentions specifically Khairābād, Ḥ.r.zābād (read by Raverty as Jatrābād / Chatrābād) and Aimanābād. Unfortunately, none of these can be identified, and what florescence they enjoyed may only have been temporary.[4]

Concerning the second task, Ibrāhīm seems to have been a realist and not to have been seduced by irredentist visions of regaining the lost territories of his father and grandfather, as appears clearly from the words imputed to him by Ibn al-Athīr or his sources (concerning which, see below, p. 61f.), 'If only I had been in my father Masʿūd's place, after the death of my grandfather Maḥmūd, then the lynch-pin of our dominion would not have fallen out. But now I am impotent to recover what others have taken, and monarchs with extensive realms and numerous armies have conquered our land'.[5] The Seljuq amīrs of the east, sc. Chaghrï Beg Dā'ūd and Alp Arslan, appear for their part to have recognised that they had expanded as far eastwards into Afghanistan as geographical factors permitted, and that the western spurs of the Paropamisus, the mountains of Ghūr and the Hindu Kush, constituted a reasonable natural frontier with the Ghaznavids.

As noted in Ch. 1 in the section on Farrukh-Zād's sultanate, the sources are unclear about the peace negotiations between the

Ghaznavids and the Seljuqs, whether the conclusion of hostilities fell just within the closing days of Farrukh-Zād's reign or in the opening ones of Ibrāhīm's. Ḥusainī, who is well-informed about Seljuq affairs, states that Farrukh-Zād made an agreement with Chaghrï Beg. The Ghaznavid sultan agreed to return with full honours the prisoners captured from the Seljuq army, including the amīr Quṭb ad-Dīn Atabeg Kul-Sarïgh, and both sides promised to remain within the confines of their own empire. The actual peace treaty (*kitāb aṣ-ṣulḥ*) was written out by the historian Abu l-Faḍl Baihaqī, who was called out of retirement (he had lost his job as head of the *Dīwān-i Risālat* under ʿAbd ar-Rashīd, see above, Ch. 1, p. 40) and away from his work on the compilation of the *Mujalladāt*, which he was to carry down to 451/1059.[6] Ibn al-Athīr, however, attributes the achieving of peace to Ibrāhīm, and states that after careful, reasoned analysis by 'the intelligent persons of both sides', leading to the conclusion that neither party could gain any further territorial advantage but would merely expend treasure and devastate territory to no worthwhile result. Ibrāhīm and Chaghrï Beg agreed to make peace on an *uti possidetis* basis.[7] It may be that negotiations spanned the end of Farrukh-Zād's reign and the beginning of Ibrāhīm's one, or simply that the peace treaty had to be ratified again by the new Ghaznavid ruler, who could not be expected automatically to abide by the agreements of his predecessor.

So far as we know, Ghaznavid-Seljuq relations remained peaceful during the last year or so of Chaghrï Beg's amīrate and the reign of Alp Arslan, but we hear of warfare during Malik Shāh's sultanate. Malik Shāh only gained his father's throne in 465/1072–3 after a sharp struggle with his uncle Qāwurd of Kirmān, who considered that by the tribal right of seniorate he should have supreme power within the Seljuq dominions, and certain of Malik Shāh's own brothers were known to be ambitious for power. These internal discords seem to have tempted Ibrāhīm to depart from the pacific policies towards the Seljuqs of the first fourteen years of his reign and to attempt the recovery of the former Ghaznavid territories around Balkh, Qunduz or Walwālīj and Ṭalaqān, sc. the provinces of Ṭukhāristān and Badakhshān. In Jumādā I 465/January–February 1073—at the moment when Qāwurd was occupying Ray and raising the standard of revolt—Ibrāhīm sent an army against Sakalkand. This was a small place just south of Baghlān and to the north of the Hindu Kush and the Chahārdār Pass leading to the Ghōrband and

Kabul River valleys, and it must have lain near the Ghaznavid-Seljuq frontier, which probably approximated roughly to the Kabul River basin–Oxus basin watershed.[8] The Seljuq governor here was Malik Shāh's uncle, the *Amīr al-Umarā'* 'Uthmān b. Chaghrï Beg, who was now captured with his treasury and retinue and ignominiously carried off to Ghazna. However, a force under the Seljuq amīr Gümüshtigin Bilge Beg and including Anūshtigin Gharcha'ī, the subsequent founder of the line of Khwārazm-Shāhs, appeared in the area, pursued the Ghaznavid forces and devastated Sakalkand.[9]

The only other episode known to us of Ghaznavid-Seljuq friction also took place in Malik Shāh's reign, but cannot be dated more exactly; the references to it are of an anecdotal nature rather than sober history, but there may nevertheless be some historical basis for the information. Ḥusainī and Ibn al-Athīr record that Malik Shāh at one juncture—perhaps after the fighting in Badakhshān described above and after the sultan had finally subdued Qāwurd's rebellion—marched on Isfizār. Isfizār or Asfizār lay to the south of Herat on the Sistan road, and is the modern Sabzavār-i Herāt. This place, however, was a long way from the nearest Ghaznavid territory; the sultan would have had to march through Sīstān against Bust and then Zamīn-Dāwar before he could have struck at the heart of the Ghaznavid empire. It may be that Ibrāhīm's spies brought him news of Seljuq troop concentrations at Isfizār. At all events, the historical sources state that Ibrahim coped with the threat by a clever piece of psychological warfare. He wrote letters to the commanders of the Seljuq army thanking them for their help in a conspiracy to lure Malik Shāh into this expedition against the Ghaznavid territories, in the course of which they would at an opportune moment seize and depose the Sultan and defect to the Ghaznavid side. The Ghaznavid envoy to these supposedly treacherous commanders allowed himself to be captured by Malik Shāh. Learning thereby of the fictitious plot, but attaching credence to it, the Seljuq sultan withdrew to his capital Iṣfahān without informing his commanders about his suspicions as to their loyalty.[10]

Whatever the truth of these historical reports, the dissuading of Malik Shāh from his planned attack forms the subject of a lengthy anecdote of Fakhr-i Mudabbir Mubārak Shāh, in which the hero is Ibrāhīm's courtier Mihtar Rashīd and in which the stratagems employed are much more elaborate than in the reports of Ḥusainī and Ibn al-Athīr. This Mihtar Rashīd must be the Jamāl al-Mulk

Abū r-Rushd Rashīd b. Muḥtāj (a scion of the line of former amīrs of Chaghāniyān, the Āl-i Muḥtāj?) who was the *mamdūḥ* of the poets Masʿūd-i Saʿd-i Salmān and Abū l-Faraj Rūnī; there exists, in fact, a poem of Masʿūd-i Saʿd's congratulating him on his return from this mission, and the imprisoned Masʿūd-i Saʿd tried to get Abū r-Rushd Rashīd to intercede with Sultan Ibrāhīm on his behalf.[11] Fakhr-i Mudabbir says that a well-endowed madrasa founded by Abū r-Rushd Rashīd and adjacent to Sultan Maḥmūd's tomb near Ghazna still remained in his own time.

In the anecdote, Mihtar Rashīd takes to Malik Shāh's camp a munificent array of presents, calculated to impress the Seljuq monarch, including camels' loads of fine clothes; a hundred ass loads of the superlative 'elephant' pears (*pīl-amrūd*) from the districts round Ghazna of (?) Nūgh, Khamār, Lamghān and Shāhbahār; remarkable animals and birds, including an elephant, monkeys, ostriches, peacocks, parrots and a bird of the *shārak* species which could not only talk but also recite the Qur'ān; and so forth. After displaying all these, Mihtar Rashīd advises the bemused sultan to desist from his misguided intentions, if he wishes to preserve peace between the two great empires: 'The first condition of peace is that you should give up your plan of marching on Ghaznīn, for your army does not have the courage and strength of its Ghaznavid counterpart; you have only one kind of troops in your army, whereas we have ten different ones'.[12] He then proposes a marriage alliance between the two houses, which is duly arranged with a daughter of Chaghrï Beg, who is subsequently escorted ceremonially from ʿIrāq [ʿAjamī] to Ghazna. Finally, Mihtar Rashīd employs the trick detailed in the historical sources of pretending to suborn the Seljuq military commanders and of secretly sending them sums of money, thus casting fears about their loyalty into the hearts of Malik Shāh and his minister Niẓām al-Mulk, who advises a timely withdrawal to ʿIrāq ʿAjamī, sc. to western Persia.[13]

The anecdote contains some palpably inaccurate details, such as the confusion between the marriage of Malik Shāh's daughter, the famous Mahd-i ʿIrāq, and Masʿūd b. Ibrāhīm, and this supposed marriage with Chaghrï Beg's daughter, but it seems probable that there is a kernel of historical truth here: that of Malik Shāh, poised with an army on the fringe of eastern Khurasan, of peace negotiations inaugurated by Ibrāhīm and carried out by Abū r-Rushd Rashīd, and of a détente between the two empires, sealed by the marriage alliance. This last was not the first such link, since the marriage of Alp Arslan's son Arslan Shāh to a daughter of Ibrāhīm is mentioned in the year 456/1064, the year of the Seljuq sultan's accession, when at the same time Alp Arslan married his other son Malik Shāh to a Qarakhanid princess.[14] We do not have a definite date for Mas'ūd b. Ibrāhīm's marriage with Jauhar Khātūn bint Malik Shāh, the Mahd-i 'Irāq 'bride from 'Irāq ['Ajamī]', though it is mentioned that Mas'ūd had been previously married to a daughter of Alp Arslan (perhaps this first marriage is the source of Fakhr-i Mudabbir's information that a marriage was arranged between Mas'ūd and a daughter of Alp Arslan's father Chaghrï Beg?).[15]

At all events, it is clear that the two great empires of the eastern Islamic world treated with each other on equal terms, and although the Seljuqs were supplanters of the Ghaznavids, they regarded the elder dynasty with the respect often accorded to old-established houses. Later sources mention that, such was the respect for Ibrāhīm of the Seljuq sultans that they used to address him as *Pidar-i buzurg* 'Exalted father', and Mustaufī adds that when the Seljuqs wrote to him, they did not affix their *tughra* or emblem to the letter, out of respect for him again. Ḥusainī says that in the following century (sc. the 6th/12th), the supreme Seljuq sultan Muḥammad b. Malik Shāh was reluctant to countenance his brother Sanjar's intervention in Ghazna in support of Bahrām Shāh b. Mas'ūd against his brother Arslan, out of his great respect for the Ghaznavid house.[16]

There was undoubtedly some social and cultural interaction between the courts of the two powers, beginning in the reign of Ibrāhīm and continuing under his successors. Poets and literary men passed to and fro between Ghazna and the courts of the Seljuqs and their tributaries in eastern Persia. Thus among the poems of 'Uthmān Mukhtārī we find odes addressed to the amīrs of the Seljuq vassal state of Ṣaffārid Sīstān (in particular, to the amīr Tāj ad-Dīn Abū l-Faḍl or Abū l-Fatḥ Naṣr b. Khalaf, who succeeded to the throne in Sīstān *ca.* 496/1103) and to the Seljuq amīrs of Kirmān, at whose court 'Uthmān stayed for a while, and their viziers.[17] Ḥakīm Sanā'ī addressed panegyrics to Sanjar; and he wrote two odes for, and kept up a cordial exchange of correspondence with, the Seljuq official Qiwām ad-Dīn Abū l-Qāsim ad-Darguzīnī al-Ansabādhī, vizier to sultan Maḥmūd b. Muḥammad b. Malik Shāh and then to Sanjar, and addressed an ode to Sanjar's vizier Mu'īn ad-Dīn Abū Naṣr Aḥmad b. Faḍl.[18] The Ghaznavid sultans' formal assumption around this time (e.g. on coin legends) of the typically Seljuq title of *as-Sulṭān al-Muʿaẓẓam* 'Highly-exalted Sultan' has been seen as an aspect of Seljuq influence in the field of royal titulature. Ibrāhīm adopted the title of *Sulṭān* during the caliphate of al-Qā'im, hence before 467/1075, and it seems to appear on a Ghaznavid dīnār of his in the Hermitage Museum at Leningrad, which was not properly described by Markov but which probably dates from 462/1069–70.[19] However, the Ghaznavids had of course long been addressed informally and described in documents as sultans, as well as amīrs and maliks, as the historical and literary sources amply show. The formula *as-Sulṭān al-Muʿaẓẓam* first appears unambiguously on a dirham of Farrukh-Zād's, and under Ibrāhīm and his successors, the formulae *as-Sulṭān al-Muʿaẓẓam* and *as-Sulṭān al-Aʿẓam* 'Most exalted Sultan' become standard on the coinage.[20]

It may be appropriate at this point to mention that coins are particularly valuable as evidence for the very rich titulature enjoyed by Ibrāhīm, one which doubtless grew as his prestige accrued from such a long tenure of power, the longest of any Ghaznavid ruler. As well as these formulae *as-Sulṭān al-Muʿaẓẓam/al-Aʿẓam* mentioned above, we find in the numismatic and literary sources the honorifics Ẓahīr ad-Daula, Ẓahīr al-Milla, Nāṣir (or Naṣīr) al-Milla, Niẓām ad-Daula, Raḍī ad-Dīn, Sayyid as-Salāṭīn, Malik al-Islām, Fakhr al-Umma (?), Qāhir al-Mulūk and Mu'ayyid Amīr al-Mu'minīn, to which epigraphic evidence from the neighbourhood of Ghazna adds those of Mu'ayyid ad-Dīn, Muʿīn al-Muslimīn and Malik Riqāb al-Umam. One of the sources for these honorifics, the anonymous *Mujmal at-tawārīkh wa-l-qiṣaṣ*, also states that Ibrāhīm's *tauqīʿ* or official motto was *Bi-llāh al-Karīm yathiq Ibrāhīm* 'Ibrāhīm puts his trust in God, the Bountiful One'.[21]

Another practice of Ibrāhīm's which may have been influenced by that of the Seljuqs, and by Ibrāhīm's connections with Malik Shāh, is the Ghaznavid sultan's having a lion device on his banner (*rāyat*), if a line of Abū l-Faraj Rūnī is to be believed:

> Like the lion device on a banner, the bold braggart has no heart; like a gazelle's horn, the branch of his tree is without fruit.

The Persian poets of the Seljuqs certainly make frequent reference to the lion device on their masters' flags, for example in the odes of Anwarī addressed to Sanjar and his military commander epigoni in Khurasan.[22]

Further, in regard to possible Seljuq influence in the Ghaznavid state at this time, the Turkish historian Fuad Köprülü suggested some thirty years ago that the system of land grants (*iqṭā*ʿs), which evolved in Iraq and western Persia in the 3rd–4th/9th–10th centuries and which was taken over by the Seljuqs in the ensuing period and extended into eastern Persia, found its way into the Ghaznavid dominions by the late 5th/11th and early 6th/12th centuries. From the silence of such early Ghaznavid authorities as ʿUtbī, Baihaqī and Gardīzī on the presence of hereditary *iqṭā*ʿs in the empire, it does not seem that the system existed there before the middle of the 5th/11th century at the earliest; the ability of the Ghaznavid sultans to tap the rich resources of India meant that they could go on paying their troops substantially in cash for much longer than the military régimes in the lands further west had been able.[23] Köprülü adduced some lines of Sanāʾī, addressed to sultan Bahrām Shāh and therefore written after 512/1118, in which the poet complains that the Turkish soldiery have taken people's lands unlawfully:

[*Sanāʾī*] *recited this poem on the theme of the reversal of men's estate and the changes of fate*

O Muslims, people have changed the nature of things, and have wrought disgraceful acts, changing what was ordained as good into what is considered bad.

Instead of paying attention to the commandments of the Eternal One in listening obediently and accepting wise counsel, they have made the eye of heeding divine warnings blind and the ear of sagacity deaf.

The material circumstances and the prestige of the religious leaders have become laid low, since the evil-doers have raised their heads from every corner.

Powerful rulers have erected at their courts barriers, as strong as Alexander's wall to keep out Gog and Magog, against oppressed seekers of justice.

They have given the property of all and sundry [lit. ʿAmr and Zaid] to the Turks, and they have exposed to view the flowing blood of widows' eyes.

They have brusquely set aside the divine law of Islam for distinguishing good from evil, and have adopted as articles of faith the views of Ptolemy and Galen.

Learned scholars, lacking position and livelihood, and impelled

> by an excess of covetousness and desire for rewards, have let themselves become the despised butts of the military leaders.
>
> One sees, at this time, a time-serving flatterer intriguing for a religious endowment [*waqf*] or the granting of an office, and they place every tyrannical oppressor on a level with ʿUmar as a dispenser of justice.

Köprülü accordingly speculated that the *iqṭāʿ* may have spread within the Ghaznavid lands as a response to the warfare with the Seljuqs during the first decades of the 6th/12th century, starting with Sanjar's intervention of 510/1117 in favour of Bahrām Shāh against his brother Arslan Shāh.[24] If this spreading of the *iqṭāʿ* system really took place, the process might well have begun earlier, during Ibrāhīm's reign, when Ghaznavid-Seljuq connections were close, and when one might expect a process of interaction to be felt in the sphere of social organisation as well as that of culture.[25]

2.

The Ghaznavid army in the later period

The question of land grants held by the Ghaznavids' Turkish and other soldiery leads us to a consideration of the importance of the army during Ibrāhīm's reign. In the absence of information in such detail as we find in ʿUtbī, Gardīzī and Baihaqī for the early Ghaznavid period, we have to assume that the military traditions and practices of the later sultans were essentially the same as those of their forebears.[26] Even if the expansionism characteristic of early Ghaznavid policy under Maḥmūd and Masʿūd no longer operated and a largely static position had been reached on the western borders, India still remained as a prime field into which military energies could be diverted with great profit. As part of the image of Ibrāhīm as a pious and just ruler (see further on this, below, pp. 74–5), the sources stress his love of *ghazw* and *jihād*, the holy war, in effect, expansion into India; and although we know little about personal leadership in battle there, Fakhr-i Mudabbir mentions that the spear and the bow were the sultan's favourite weapons.[27]

A valuable source of information in military matters lies in the works of the poets, although the accounts of campaigns are usually somewhat impressionistic and dates are usually lacking, so that it is not always possible to assign episodes and details to specific reigns, given the fact that the literary activity of several poets spanned a long period, in some cases from Ibrāhīm to Bahrām Shāh. The corpus of later Ghaznavid verse demands a closer study and analysis than is possible here, but it is nevertheless possible to cite some relevant points from it.

It seems that the army continued to be directed administratively from the *Dīwān-i ʿArḍ*, which had been of such importance in the early Ghaznavid period when the whole might of the state had been geared to conquest and the maintenance of a powerful war-machine.[28] We have various poems dedicated to officials described as *ʿĀriḍ*s, such as to Manṣūr b. Saʿīd b. Aḥmad b. Ḥasan Maimandī, the amīr Abū l-Fatḥ and an unnamed *ʿĀriḍ-i Lashkar*, by Masʿūd-i Saʿd-i Salmān, and to Manṣūr b. Saʿīd by Abū l-Faraj Rūnī; but we do not, for instance, know whether these officials functioned from the central administration in Ghazna, as in earlier times, or from the centre of government in India, sc. Lahore.[29]

From the point of view of ethnic composition, the army under Ibrāhīm continued to be a multinational one, as the boast of Mihtar Rashīd to the Seljuq Malik Shāh, that his master had ten different types of troops (see above, p. 54), shows. Within the army at large, moreover, these continued to be a special élite force of the palace ghulāms; Masʿūd-i Saʿd mentions the *sarā'iyān u ghulāmān* as being in the thick of the fighting at Āgra when prince Maḥmūd b. Ibrāhīm led his expedition thither (see below, p. 66).[30] In the past, the corps of *ghulāmān-i sarāy* had traditionally been a preserve of the Turks, but it is probable that by this time, Indians also formed part of it, as they had always done within the army at large, though we have no direct information about this.[31]

The later Ghaznavids no longer had direct access to the sources of supply for Turkish slaves, sc. Central Asia, as had had their predecessors until the death of Masʿūd, whose influence had come to extend beyond the Oxus into Khwārazm and the upper Oxus principalities of Chaghāniyān and Khuttal, and who had had friendly relations with some branches at least of the Qarakhanids in Transoxania, ensuring a stream of recruits from the Turkish steppes for the Ghaznavid armies.[32] Hence we do not know exactly how Turkish military slaves found their way into the Ghaznavid territories during Ibrāhīm's reign, but it is very likely that they still formed a considerable proportion of the army. To balance Sanā'ī's condemnations of the spoliations and exactions of the Turks in the Ghazna area, cited above, we find praise of the Turks as warriors in the army of Arslan Shāh b. Masʿūd in an ode addressed by Masʿūd-i Saʿd-i

Salmān to the sultan, in which he speaks of them (in a passage which is especially interesting as one of the rare places where the names of specific Turkish tribes are mentioned) as

> Like the raging tempest in dashing forward, like a firmly-compacted mountain in solid strength,
>
> With the nature of champions in the fray, with the attack [reading here *ḥamla* for the printed text's *jumla*] of heroes eager for battle,
>
> Clustered around his [sc. the sultan's] banner, a man each from the Yaghmā, from the Qāy and from the Tatār.[33]

Masʿūd-i Saʿd further has a long ode in which he praises sultan Masʿūd b. Ibrāhīm and the Turkish soldiery:

> The Turks, who are the backbone and the right arm of the kingdom and of the age, are the outstanding ones on the battle-field at the time of launching a charge.
>
> They are proud and restless warriors, courageous and expert; they are like lions of the thicket and panthers of the mountains.
>
> In their hands, bows are like clouds; when the tips of their arrows penetrate the target, they are like destructive down-pours.
>
> In the eyes of benevolent and well-wishing people, they look like fresh roses, but in the soul of evil-thinking people, they are like the wounding of thorns.
>
> On the field of combat, they pierce the steel with their swords; on the day of battle, their arrows darken the sun.
>
> They spur their mounts forward, emerging from the fire of the battle-field; they loose their twin-barbed arrows from the iron defences of the fortress.
>
> God's mercy be upon these heads, which are raised up straight as a cypress-tree, yet in the king's palace, on ceremonial occa-sions, they humble themselves like vines.
>
> God's mercy be upon these brave heroes, who on the battle-field will withstand an attack like lions of the thickly-growing undergrowth.
>
> With their belts girded on tightly, and ready for destroying the enemy, devoting their lives to the service of the world-dominating monarch, with his absolute power!

The dedications of the verses of the poets give us information about the names of the high officers and generals of the army, variously designated by such titles as *amīr*, *sarhang* or *sipahsālār*, yet surprisingly, there are few definitely Turkish names amongst these officers. More typical are Iranian names like Bahrām, Māhū and Kai Kā'ūs,[34] or Islamic ones like Muḥammad b. Khaṭīb Harawī the governor of Sind, Maḥmūd Rūbāhī, Muḥammad b. Faraj Nawābādhī, and various members of the Shaibānī family (on whom see below, p. 85) such as Najm ad-Dīn and ʿImād ad-Daula Sarhang Muḥammad b. ʿAlī.[35] It is true that ʿUthmān Muktārī addressed a poem to the amīr ʿAḍud ad-Dīn Lāchīn (Turkish *lachïn* 'falcon') Khāzin, although it is not certain whether this officer was in the Ghaznavid service anyway; Masʿūd-i Saʿd has a poem addressed to a Sulaimān Inanj Beg; Abū l-Faraj Rūnī dedicated an ode to 'the amīr Badr ad-Dīn Ayāz al-Malikī' (not apparently to be identified with sultan Maḥmūd's famous catamite, who died in 449/1057–8); and Jūzjānī names the Ḥājib Togha(n)tigin as leading the Ghaznavid raiders across the Ganges and as penetrating far into the Dōab during Masʿūd b. Ibrāhīm's reign.[36] It may be that Turkish soldiers, or their offspring, were increasingly adopting non-Turkish names, with a decreasing sense of their Turkish ethnicity; or it may be that, in the light of the ending of direct access by the Ghaznavids to the Central Asian steppes, the proportion of Turks in the army decreased, and they had to share the top commands with officers of Tājīk, Afghan and Indo-Muslim origin.[37]

The spectacular rôle in battle of the war-elephants, which had played a significant part in Ghaznavid military organisation from the outset,[38] attracted the poetic genius of writers. Masʿūd-i Saʿd, for instance, more than once gives vivid descriptions of their fearsomeness in the Indian battles; whilst in another couplet, he praises the sultan's battle-axe (*nāchakh*) (which, as we have seen above, Ch. 1, p. 49, had been the favourite weapon of sultan Farrukh-Zād).[39]

3.

Ibrāhīm's campaigns in India and in Ghūr

In considering Ibrāhīm's Indian campaigns, we have only one relevant passage in the historical sources proper, that of Ibn al-Athīr, who under the year 472/1079–80 inserts a general survey of Ibrāhīm's Indian campaigns because, he says, the first one fell within that year.[40] It is inconceivable that Ibrāhīm should have reigned for twenty years before leading an expedition into India, and Ibn al-Athīr confesses that very little about Ibrāhīm's campaigns had reached him as he wrote in Iraq; and unfortunately, although

Ibrāhīm certainly had his poets, he had no ʿUtbī, as had his grandfather, to record his exploits in scintillating prose. Ibn al-Athīr's account appears to have been the basis for later Indo-Muslim historians writing about Ibrāhīm's Indian campaigns, such as Firishta, and thence by more modern writers.[41] Since Ibn al-Athīr's information is unique of its kind, a translation of the passage is given below *in extenso*:

[Year 472/1079–80]

Mention of the Indian conquests of Ibrāhīm, ruler of Ghazna

In this year, the monarch Ibrāhīm b. Masʿūd b. Maḥmūd b. Sebüktigin raided into India. He then laid siege to the fortress of 'j.w.d, which is 120 farsakhs from Lahore; it is extremely well-fortified and inaccessible, and great in size, holding 10,000 warriors. They fought back at him, and kept up a prolonged fight below the fortress. The sultan led several dogged attacks on them, and their hearts were filled with fear and trembling from what they observed of his determination in battle. They accordingly surrendered the fortress to him on 11th Ṣafar of this year [= 13th August 1079].

In the outlying regions of India there was a fortress called that of Rūbāl [var. W.bāl], situated at the summit of a lofty hill, with tangled jungle beneath it and the river [*al-baḥr*] behind it. The only way of attacking it was by a narrow defile, and this was filled with war elephants. The fortress was garrisoned by several thousand warriors. The sultan launched successive attacks on them, and kept up the pressure of battle against them with all sorts of methods of warfare; finally, he captured the fortress and brought out of it all the defenders.

In a certain place called D.r.h N.w.r.h there was a people of Khurasanian origin, whose forefathers had been established in ancient times by Afrāsiyāb the Turk. No ruler had ever managed to attack them at all. But Ibrāhīm marched on them; first of all, he summoned them to Islam, but they refused, and gave battle with him. Nevertheless, he gained the victory over them, wreaking great slaughter amongst them; those who escaped scattered throughout the land, and Ibrāhīm captured as slaves 100,000 of the womenfolk and children. There was in this fortress a water cistern about half-a-farsakh wide and of unfathomable depth, from which the fortress garrison and all their beasts used to drink, without any perceptible diminution of the water's level being apparent.

Also in India is a place called W.r.h, which is a tract of territory between two stretches of water. The monarch Ibrāhīm led an expedition against it, and reached it in Jumādā I, having passed en route for it through many steep and difficult places and through dense jungles. He remained there for three months, his army suffering considerable hardships from the winter, and did not relax his attack until God had given His servants the victory and had sent down humiliation on His enemies. He then returned, unharmed and victorious, to Ghazna.

I do not know the full story of these expeditions. The first raid took place in this year, and consequently I have placed all the raids consecutively under the entry for this year.

Ibn al-Athīr's passage is clearly vague and impressionistic, and contains little firm topographical or historical information. The only reasonably sure identification appears to be that of 'j.w.d with Ajōdhan (the modern Pāk-Patan, a ferry point over the Sutlej river in the southern Panjab, which lay on the route westwards from Multān to the Delhi region and which was in post-Ghaznavid times famed for the shrine of the Suhrawardī Ṣūfī saint Farīd ad-Dīn Ganj-Shakar), and the historian places this particular victory of Ibrahim's in 472/1079. For the rest, we can make no clear identification of places or dates. One can only assume, for instance, that *W.r.h, described as a *barr bain khalījain*, lay in the hill country of north-eastern Panjab, between the confluence of two rivers; only in such terrain would the attacking Ghaznavid army have suffered from the winter cold.

The middle years of the 5th/11th century, with its succession crises and short-lived sultans in Ghazna, were inevitably unfavourable to the progress of Ghaznavid arms in India. After Maudūd's death, none of the succeeding sultans of the following decade left any reputation as conquerors in India, although it is recorded that in ʿAbd ar-Rashid's reign, the Turkish general Nushtigin managed to recapture Nagarkot or Kāngrā, first taken by sultan Maḥmūd in 399/1099,[42] but regained by a coalition of Hindu Rājās in 434/1043. There had, indeed, arisen in northern India since the time of sultan Masʿūd b. Maḥmūd two powerful Hindu dynasties, the Paramāras of Mālwa and the Kalachuris of Tripuri in modern Madhya Pradesh, under their forceful respective rulers Bhōja (*ca.* 1000–55) and Karṇa or Lakṣmīkarṇa (between 1034 and 1042 until 1070). These monarchs had pushed back the Ghaznavid position in the eastern Panjab, and it was not until after the death of Karṇa that the Muslims were able to undertake prolonged offensive operations from their base at Lahore.[43]

Lahore really functioned as a second capital for the Ghaznavid empire. The administrative offices for India were situated there, and the town was the concentration-point for the *ghāzīs* and other enthusiasts for the holy war, who hoped for rich plunder from the *Dār al-Kufr*. The sultans had to exercise particular care in appointing trusted officials and commanders to Lahore, for once installed there, with hordes of troops at their disposal and rich financial resources behind them, governors had many temptations to rebel; thus money kept back from the Hindu princes' tribute, plus the spoils of an expedition against Benares, had in 424/1033 led Masʿūd's commander in India, Aḥmad Inaltigin, to rebel.[44]

We have noted above the paucity of strictly historical data about the campaigns of Ibrāhīm, but the *dīwāns* of contemporary Ghaznavid poets provide us with certain items of information on the raids of Ibrāhīm and his two sons Saif ad-Daula Maḥmūd and ʿAlāʾ ad-Daula Masʿūd (the future sultan), for these poets wrote many odes on the occasions of their patrons' victories. D. C. Ganguly attempted to utilise information from Masʿūd-i Saʿd-i Salmān's poems, and he noted that the poet commemorates victories of Ibrāhīm and of the deputy governor in the Panjab during Ibrāhīm's last years and the early ones of Masʿūd III, Abū Naṣr-i Fārsī (see below).[45] Yet the value of Ganguly's attempt is almost nil because he never actually referred to the Persian text of the *Dīwān*, although at least two printed editions of it were available when he wrote. Instead he used only the English prose paraphrases, drastically condensed, made by Sir Henry Elliot of a few of Masʿūd-i Saʿd's poems or of parts of them.[46] The first two of these poems translated by Elliot may be identified in the printed *Dīwān* edited by Yāsimī as the one addressed to Abū Naṣr-i Fārsī at pp. 169–76 and the one addressed to sultan Ibrāhīm at pp. 370–3.

In the first of these poems, the writer describes a night raid led by Abū Naṣr-i Fārsī on Jālandhar or Chālandhar (sc. Jullundur, in the sub-Himalayan hill country of the northeastern Panjab, a region which had already been raided in 408/1017–18 by sultan Maḥmūd's general Qaratigin and a force of *ghāzīs* from Transoxania[47]), when the Ghaznavid general marched from the place Dhagān (Yāsimī's text, D.h.gān) and defeated and killed a local ruler, named by Elliot and, following him, Ganguly, as Sāīr Sambrā; Yāsimī's text simply has S.y.rrā.[48] In the second poem, Masʿūd-i Saʿd praises Ibrāhīm's leadership of an expedition to a place that Elliot and Ganguly read as Tabarhinda (? Sirhind, in the former Patiala State of the eastern Panjab, according to Elliot's suggestion), and to Būriya, on the Jumna river in the Ambāla District; at this latter place, the local Rājā was killed, being drowned with his troops in the river. Yāsimī's text, however, does not allow so confident a reconstruction of these events; for Tabarhinda we have F.r.h.n.da, and for Būriya, B.w.d (? n.k.r.da].[49] There is no correspondence of the names here with those, for instance, in the passage of Ibn al-Athīr translated above; and since Yāsimī's text of Masʿūd-i Saʿd has no *apparatus criticus*, only an examination of the manuscripts of the *Dīwān*, combined with a first-hand acquaintanceship with the topography of northern India and a knowledge of the internal politics of the Hindu dynasties there, could determine whether any significant information can in fact be derived from either Masʿūd-i Saʿd or Ibn al-Athīr. For the present, many of the conclusions drawn here by Ganguly can only be regarded as highly speculative.[50]

There are, in any case, difficulties in utilising the native Indian sources on account of their imprecision, especially in their lack of firm dates, their blanket designation of the invading Muslims as Turuṣkas and Hammīras (for these terms, see below) or by other vague and opprobrious terms, and their failure to mention any specific names of Muslim rulers or generals. Thus Dasharatha Sharma was probably correct in equating the Mātaṇgas or Mlechhas of the Sanskrit chronicle of the *Pṛthvīrājavijaya* with the Muslim forces that attacked what is now eastern Rajputana at some point in sultan Ibrāhīm's reign, killed the Chāhamāna ruler of Śākambharī, Durlabharāja III, and attacked Pṛthvīpāla of Ṇāḍol; but the Sanskrit text is distressingly vague, and Sharma's reliance on Firishta's history (with information stemming from Ibn al-Athīr or his source) for pinpointing the date as 1079 is wholly unjustified.[51]

One of the few firm dates in all these questions is that of 469/1076–7, when Ibrāhīm appointed Saif ad-Daula Maḥmūd, who had already proven his mettle in the Indian fighting, to be governor in India. Masʿūd-i Saʿd celebrates this act in fine ode, describing the rich presents and the insignia of office that the sultan bestowed on the prince; it is this poem which contains a chronogram giving the date 469. Abū l-Faraj Rūnī likewise has a poem commemorating this event.[52] It was during Masʿūd-i Saʿd's period of service with Prince Maḥmūd that he first fell from grace, being imprisoned by sultan Ibrāhīm in the fortress of Nāy for some ten years. It seems to have been his connection with Maḥmūd that brought this about, since Niẓāmī ʿArūḍī states that malicious rumours had reached the sultan that his son Maḥmūd was in treasonable communication with the Seljuq monarch Malik Shāh and was contemplating moving to the Seljuq lands; accordingly, Ibrāhīm imprisoned Maḥmūd in Nāy, together with various of the latter's retainers. We have no confirmation of this alleged dubious behaviour on the part of Maḥmūd in any historical source; these sources are, indeed, wholly silent about Maḥmūd, and we know nothing of the circumstances in which he relinquished the governorship of India, why he did not succeed his father in 492/1099, or what his subsequent fate was. But it is by no means improbable that Maḥmūd's successes in India should have tempted him into some form of disloyalty, for such things had happened before more than once. Qazwīnī was inclined to accept some degree of Masʿūd-i Saʿd's culpability here, in the light of Ibrāhīm's unrelenting attitude towards those who interceded for the poet's release, although he pointed out that Niẓāmī ʿArūḍī's date of 472/1079–80 for all these events was impossibly early and should probably be amended to 480/1087–8. In reality, given what we know about Maḥmūd's campaigns around this time in what is now Uttar Pradesh and in Central India, as described below, even this date must be somewhat too early.[53]

Two of Masʿūd-i Saʿd's poems deal specifically with prince Maḥmūd's victories at Āgra (spelt '.k.ra). At some time between 479/1086 and 483/1070, Maḥmūd led an army of *ghāzīs* and 40,000 cavalrymen (if this suspiciously round number be credited) into the heart of modern Uttar Pradesh. Having reached Āgra, Maḥmūd's troops attacked the Rājā Jaipāl (thus spelt in the first poem), and for several days were involved in fierce fighting with the defenders of the fortress, who rained down fire and missiles on the attacker's heads. In the end, the fortress was taken. The submission of several other local potentates followed, and they brought rich presents of treasure and of elephants for Maḥmūd; these last beasts were committed to the keeping of Chand Rāy (thus spelt in the poem) at Kanauj.[54]

The name of the ruler of Āgra, Jaipāl, has been plausibly identified by Ganguly with that of Gopāla of the Rāṣṭrakūṭa dynasty. This family ruled the region of Pānchāla, stretching from the Himalayas to the Chambal river, the right-bank affluent of the Jumna, and this would include Āgra and Kanauj; their capital seems to have been at Vodāmayūtā, modern Badā'ūn in the Bareilly division of Uttar Pradesh.[55] The Chand Ray of Kanauj was further identified by Ganguly with Chandradeva, son of Mahīchandra or Mahītala, of the Gāhaḍavāla dynasty. Chandradeva seems to have entered into friendly relations with prince Maḥmūd, taking charge of the captured elephants and those received as tribute, and he utilised Ghaznavid support in order to extend his own power over Kanauj, till then held by Gopāla. The appearance of Ghaznavid forces in the kingdom of Kanauj must have caused considerable disturbance and upsetting of existing political relationships, and this chaos allowed a transfer of power within Kanauj at this time, sc. shortly before 1090. Interesting, too, is the fact that the inscriptions of the Gāhaḍavālas, dating from 1090 onwards, mention a tax called the *Turuṣkadaṇda*, which may have been a defence tax to meet the costs of resisting Muslim raids, but was more probably meant to raise the tribute which Chandradeva had agreed to pay the Ghaznavids in return for help in securing the throne of Kanauj.[56]

If prince Maḥmūd did fall from favour towards the end of Ibrāhīm's reign (see above), then there must have been a replacement for him as governor in India, and this was probably his brother Mas'ūd; hence some at least of the eulogies addressed to Mas'ūd by the poets would fall within the period before his accession to the sultanate in 492/1099. When he did become ruler, he appointed his own son 'Aḍud ad-Daula Shīr-Zād (the future ephemeral sultan, 508–9/1115–16) as governor in India.[57] Mas'ūd-i Sa'd-i Salmān, now released from his incarceration at Nāy, became one of Shīr-Zād's intimates in India, and especially of Shīr-Zād's deputy governor there, Qiwām al-Mulk Niẓām ad-Dīn[58] Abū Naṣr Hibatallāh Fārsī, famed as administrator, warrior and poet (for his literary rôle, see below, p. 77).[59] There are in Mas'ūd-i Sa'd's *Dīwān* a considerable number of poems addressed to Abū Naṣr-i Fārsī, and the latter appointed the poet—who as a native of Lahore must have had valuable local knowledge of the Panjab—to be governor (the term employed by Mas'ūd-i Sa'd himself in one of his poems is *qahrawān*) of Jālandhar or Chālandhar, as several references in the poems show.

But once again, the poet was dragged down by his association with the fortunes of an ill-starred master, and when Abū Naṣr-i Fārsī fell from power, Masʿūd-i Saʿd then suffered his second term of imprisonment, this time at Maranj in India.[60]

India was thus the principal target of Ghaznavid military activity at this time, and the only other sphere of action known to us (apart from what was basically a holding operation against the Seljuqs in the west) was that of Ghūr, the mountainous and inaccessible region of central Afghanistan; we know of Ibrāhīm's policy regarding Ghūr mainly through the information of the historian Jūzjānī's *Ṭabaqāt-i Nāṣirī* and through one reference in a poem of Masʿūd-i Saʿd's addressed to sultan Ibrāhīm and lauding his conquests in India and Ghūr.

Ghūr had been brought into a loose vassal status *viv-à-vis* the early Ghaznavid empire by sultan Maḥmūd and his son Masʿūd, who in 401/1011, 405/1015 and 411/1020 had both led expeditions into Ghūr, establishing the beginnings of Islam there in lieu of the indigenous paganism, and who had set up one of the petty chieftains there, Abū ʿAlī b. Muḥammad b. Sūrī of the Shansabānī family of Āhangarān on the upper Heri Rud, as a Ghaznavid nominee.[61] When the Seljuqs took over Khurasan and western Afghanistan, Ghūr was then in the buffer-zone between the two empires (and accordingly of some strategic importance, since raiders from the heart of Ghūr could harry the routes which skirted the fringes of their region), but seems to have kept up its connection with Ghazna. Alone of the sources, Firishta states that in 438/1046–7 Maudūd sent his general Barstigin (this name, 'prince-tiger' in Turkish, seems to be the best interpretation of the consonant ductus of the manuscript used here) into Ghūr with a force to assist the son of Yaḥyā Ghūrī against Abū ʿAlī. Barstigin captured Abū ʿAlī's fortress there, and had both Abū ʿAlī and the son of Yaḥyā Ghūrī sent back to Ghazna, where they were both executed. We have no mention at all of these events in the *Ṭabaqāt-i Nāṣirī*, which is our most detailed and reliable source for affairs in Ghūr during the 5th/11th century, nor is the 'son of Yaḥyā Ghūrī' otherwise known at all. It is possible that the story of Maudūd's treacherous execution of the two Ghūrī chiefs is an echo of events of the following century, when the Ghaznavid Bahrām Shāh certainly did attempt to curb the rising power of the Shansabānīs by encompassing the deaths of certain of their chiefs, as described below, Ch. 4, pp. 113–15.[62] At all events, the degree of control over Ghūr exercised from Ghazna in the 5th/11th century doubtless varied according to the strength of the sultans' personal authority; one source says that Ghūr and Gharchistān fell away completely during the reign of ʿAbd ar-Rashīd and the period of Toghrïl's usurpation.[63] When he was able, Ibrāhīm endeavoured to restore a degree of control over Ghūr; unfortunately, we have no dates at all for these Ghaznavid-Ghūrid dealings. The Shansabānī amīr Abū ʿAlī had been overthrown in an internal upheaval by his nephew ʿAbbās b. Shīth b. Muḥammad b. Sūrī, again at a date that is unspecified but which must have been in the middle years of the 5th/11th century. ʿAbbās proved himself a strong and tyrannical ruler; his exactions and confiscations aroused widespread discontent within Ghūr, and a group of the local chieftains appealed to sultan Ibrāhīm to intervene in their country. Ibrāhīm therefore marched in with an army, and with the support of local interests, deposed and imprisoned ʿAbbās, setting up in his stead his son Muḥammad b. ʿAbbās. It is this expedition to which Masʿūd-i Saʿd alludes in his eulogy of Ibrāhīm, where he speaks of 'the conquest of Ghūr and the case of Muḥammad-i ʿAbbās [Yāsimī's text, ʿ.lāsh]', and where he describes the inaccessibility of ʿAbbās's fortress and the difficulties of storming it; in the attack, the palace guards (*sarā'iyān*) were to the fore, and so much blood flowed that 'the mountains of Ghūr all became filled with the crimson of anemones'.[64] Muḥammad b. ʿAbbās is praised by Jūzjāni for his virtues and humanity, qualities contrasted with the vices of his father, and is said to have remainad the faithful vassal of Ibrāhīm, periodically coming to do homage and regularly paying the stipulated tribute.[65] How far Ghaznavid control was exercised over the whole of Ghūr, as distinct from the principality of the Shansabānīs, is unknown; Jūzjānī, as in effect the official historian of the Ghūrid dynasty, tends to inflate the importance and the extensiveness of the Shansabānīs' sphere of influence, but it is probable that Ghūr remained until the early 6th/12th century politically fragmented, with several local chieftains controlling various of its isolated valleys.

4.
The internal administration of the empire

Concerning the internal administration of the empire under Ibrāhīm, we again have little information relating specifically to his reign. We must therefore fall back on the assumption that the administrative system of Maḥmūd and Mas'ūd's reigns, as known to us from the detailed account of Baihaqī, continued substantially to operate.[66] Its sphere of operation was of course somewhat reduced from the days when Ghazna was the capital of an empire stretching from Lahore to Hamadān, although the internal espionage and postal system, the *barīd* and *ishrāf*, retained its importance as a means of linking together within the empire the highland areas of eastern Afghanistan and the plains of northwestern India; as Fakhr-i Mudabbir notes, under the Ghaznavids many *Ṣāḥib-Barīds* subsequently became viziers to the sultans or other very high ministers.[67] We learn from this same author that Sultan Ibrāhīm's treasurer and confidant, the Sharīf Abū l-Faraj Ṣiddīqī, used to undertake annual progresses round the empire to watch over its condition, going in alternate years first to Zamīn-Dāwar and Bust and then through Baluchistan to Multān and the Panjab and back round to Ghazna, and then in the following year over the same route but in the reverse direction.[68]

This Sharīf Abū l-Faraj was a veritable Pooh-Bah in the number of offices—a total of twenty-one, according to Fakhr-i Mudabbir—which he is said to have held, being high in the sultan's favour as his foster-brother and school-fellow, and as the sharer in Ibrāhīm's previous imprisonment in the fortress of Nāy. His responsibilities included those of overseer (*kadkhudā*) of the royal palace, the harem and the princes; official deputed to have charge (*nawwāb*) of the palace supplies and stores, including charge of feeding the poor (? *kandūrī istiẓhār*); overseer of the Ghaznavid family estates in mortmain (*auqāf*); master of the mint and the *ṭirāz* or textile embroidering manufactory; and treasurer and keeper of the royal wardrobe.[69] The sultan's favour to him was such that he had a retinue of 400 (according to the India Office manuscript of the *Ādāb al-ḥarb*) or of 70 (according to the British Museum one) Turkish ghulāms, sumptuously attired and accoutred and with their salaries and allowances paid directly by Ibrāhīm; in Fakhr-i Mudabbir's own time (sc. later 6th/12th century–early 7th/13th) there was still in Ghazna a 'quarter of the golden-belted ones' (*kūy zarrīn-kamarān*) where they had been billeted.[70] As a reward for the Sharīf Abū l-Faraj's wise counsel in coping with a local dearth of grain in Ghazna—this being the core of Fakhr-i Mudabbir's anecdote, which occurs in a chapter on the kindness and compassion of rulers towards their subjects—Ibrāhīm rewarded him further with the exceptional gift of seven robes of honour (one for each three of his offices), a palanquin, a bed, the right to have drums beaten before his house, a banner (*ʿalam*), an elephant, a shield, a battle-axe and an *ʿalāma* (? a standard again, or a blazon).[71]

Outside the anecdotal literature, we have mentions of several of Ibrāhīm's viziers and ministers in the works specifically devoted to the biographies of viziers, sc. those of Nāṣir ad-Dīn Kirmānī, Saif ad-Dīn ʿUqailī and Khwāndamīr, and in works of literary biography like ʿAufī's *Lubāb al-albāb*, which has a special section on viziers and great men of state who were also poets. The dedications of laudatory poems, and sometimes the subject-matter of the poems themselves, in the *dīwāns* of contemporary poets provide us with further items of information. One notes first of all a factor which must have made for administrative continuity with the early Ghaznavid system, namely the presence in the bureaucracy of the sons and grandsons of the great officials who had served Maḥmūd and Masʿūd. This was only natural, and in accordance with the generally accepted belief in mediaeval Islam that such skills as those of the vizier, the financial official of the chancery secretary often developed and flourished within particular families and groups through the hereditary transmission and the accumulation of particular forms of expertise and of wisdom.

Nāṣir ad-Dīn Kirmānī and the sources dependent upon him list three persons who acted as vizier for Ibrāhīm. The first was Abū Bakr b. Abī Ṣāliḥ, who stayed on as vizier from Farrukh-Zād's reign, see above, Ch. 1, p. 48. However, whilst in office he was killed early in the new sultan's reign by the Turkish military commanders and the palace ghulāms; possibly Ibrāhīm, having only recently acceded to the throne and feeling still dependent on the army leaders who had brought him to power, felt unable to protect his minister. The second vizier mentioned is Abū Sahl Khujandī, who had been a secretary in the central administration since the time of sultan Masʿūd b. Maḥmūd; but he fell from favour, and Ibrāhīm had him blinded.

Finally, there is mentioned in these particular sources ʿAbd al-Ḥamīd b. Aḥmad b. ʿAbd aṣ-Ṣamad Shīrāzī, described as vizier to Ibrāhīm for twenty-two years and to Masʿūd b. Ibrāhīm for sixteen years. No dates are given for any of these vizierates, but if ʿAbd al-Ḥamīd served Ibrāhīm for twenty-two years before passing into his son's service, he must have begun his ministry for Ibrāhīm in 470/1077–8. ʿAbd al-Ḥamīd exemplifies the contemporary preference for ministers stemming from established official families. His father

Aḥmad b. ʿAbd aṣ-Ṣamad had been, as we have seen in Ch. 1 above, vizier to Masʿūd and then his son Maudūd. The family background was of service under the Sāmānids of Transoxania and Khurasan, although the ultimate origins of the family lay in western Persian as the *nisba* of 'Shīrāzī' implies; a verse of Masʿūd-i Saʿd-i Salmān's indicates that the family further claimed descent from the Baghdad Abbasids:

> ⁂ Khwāja ʿAbd al-Ḥamīd, the glory of the stock of the children of ʿAbbās.

This claim is further echoed by sultan Bahrām Shāh's court poet Sayyid Ḥasan when he describes 'Abū l-Maḥāsin- ʿAbd aṣ-Ṣamad' (apparently referring to ʿAbd al-Ḥamīd) as *zi gauhar-i ʿAbbās* 'of Abbasid origin'.[72] ʿAbd al-Ḥamīd's secretarial skill and his learning are highly praised, and Kirmānī and the later sources dependent on him quote as almost proverbial a verse by Abū l-Faraj Rūnī to the effect that

> ⁂ ʿAbd al-Ḥamīd-i ʿAbd-i Ṣamad firmly established the rule of excellence, the upholding of religion and the system of justice.[73]

Masʿūd-i Saʿd-i Salmān addressed poems to him from prison, seeking his intercession with the sultan, and there are actually four odes in his *Dīwān* written to ʿAbd al-Ḥamīd.[74] Kirmānī states that ʿAbd al-Ḥamīd died at the beginning of Bahrām Shāh's reign (sc. shortly after 512/1118), a martyr; perhaps he had been too closely identified with the fortunes of the previous sultan, Malik Arslan, and was killed by Bahrām Shāh in a purge of his brother's supporters.[75] It would appear that the Abū l-Maʿālī Naṣr or Naṣrallāh b. Muḥammad b. ʿAbd al-Ḥamīd Shīrāzī, the famed translator into elegant Persian prose of Ibn al-Muqaffaʿ's Arabic version of *Kalīla wa-Dimna* and later vizier to Khusrau Shāh b. Bahrām Shāh, was the grandson of ʿAbd al-Ḥamīd b. Aḥmad b. ʿAbd aṣ-Ṣamad.[76] Also apparently from this same Shīrāzī family, although with the precise degree of relationship unknown, was the Qāḍī ʿAbd al-Wadūd b. ʿAbd aṣ-Ṣamad, Chief Qāḍī of Ghazna under Masʿūd b. Ibrāhīm and the *mamdūḥ* of Sanāʾī.[77]

A problem in considering this question of Ibrāhīm's viziers is that we have unequivocal information in certain sources about a fourth vizier of this sultan, unrecorded by Kirmānī, ʿUqailī and Khwāndamir. This is Muḥammad b. Bihrūz b. Aḥmad, or Bihrūz b. Aḥmad as the name sometimes appears (it seems highly improbable that we are dealing with a father and a son who both became viziers yet are not mentioned in the biographies of viziers nor in the historical sources[78]). Muḥammad b. Bihrūz is praised by Masʿūd-i Saʿd-i Salmān, whilst we possess a couplet from an elegy by ʿUthmān Mukhtārī and two fragments from elegies by Sanāʾī on his death, one of them composed for his tombstone; from these fragments it appears that Muḥammad b. Bihrūz's *laqab* was Niẓām al-Mulk. Under the name of 'Khwāja Bihrūz b. Aḥmad', he is also the subject of an anecdote in ʿAufī's *Jawāmiʿ al-ḥikāyāt,* in which he has a dream foretelling his rise to the heights of the vizierate. Muḥammad b. Bihrūz's son was also praised in a poem by Sanāʾī as 'the Khwāja-ʿAmīd Mardān Shāh b. Muḥammad-i Bihrūz', and achieved high office under Masʿūd III. We have no dates for Muḥammad b. Bihrūz, but presumably his period of office fell within the first nineteen years of Ibrāhīm's reign, before ʿAbd al-Ḥamīd b. ʿAḥmad b. ʿAbd aṣ-Ṣamad's assumption and long tenure of the vizierate. We possess only two poems addressed to him in Masʿūd-i Saʿd-i Salmān's *Dīwān,* compared with the many odes to subsequent officials and dignitaries; both this poet and the vizier's elegist ʿUthmān Mukhtārī must have been only at the beginnings of their poetic careers when Muḥammad b. Bihrūz left office and / or died.[79]

Various others of Ibrāhīm's chief ministers and secretaries are mentioned in the anecdotal collections and were the dedicatees of verse by the contemporary poets. Thus the Maimandī family continued to hold high office after the death of Aḥmad b. Ḥasan in 424/1032. As noted above in Ch. I, p. 35, his son ʿAbd ar-Razzāq served Maudūd as vizier for seven years, in effect as successor to the fallen Aḥmad b. ʿAbd aṣ-Ṣamad, and then sultan ʿAbd ar-Rashīd, whom he in 440 / 1049 or 441 / 1050 brought out from the fortress of Mandīsh and set up as ruler. In turn, a grandson of Aḥmad b. Ḥasan's, Abū Naṣr or Abū l-Muʾayyid Manṣūr b. Saʿīd b. Aḥmad b. Ḥasan, was ʿ*Āriḍ* or minister for war during Ibrāhīm's reign, and is addressed by the poets as 'Khwāja-ʿAmīd'. There are poems addressed to him by Abū l-Faraj Rūnī, Sanāʾī, ʿUthmān Mukhtārī and Masʿūd-i Saʿd-i Salmān (the latter two poets giving him the honorific of ʿImād ad-Dīn); he seems to have died in the reign of Masʿūd III, since the latter two poets have elegies on his death.[80]

Also possibly from a famous Ghaznavid official family was Thiqat al-Mulk Ṭāhir b. ʿAlī, whose genealogy Niẓāmī ʿArūḍī alone of authorities then takes back to Mishkān, thus making him the putative nephew of Abū Naṣr-i Mishkān, head of the Correspondence

Department under sultan Mas'ūd b. Maḥmūd.[81] Thiqat al-Mulk Ṭāhir's father 'Alī had been the sultan's treasurer, and he himself was an influential figure in Ibrāhīm's reign, with the title of *Khāṣṣ*, confidant of the ruler; certain authorities, such as 'Aufī, say that he served as vizier to the next sultan Mas'ūd III, and in the headings of poems addressed to him by Sanā'ī he is described as 'the Khwāja 'Amīd'. He must have died at some point in the decade 500–10/1107–17. All four of the great poets of the time addressed odes to him, those by Mas'ūd-i Sa'd-i Salmān being especially numerous, since the poet made many appeals to him from jail, and it was Thiqat al-Mulk Ṭāhir's intercession with sultan Mas'ūd which procured his release from his second period of eight years' imprisonment in India, in *ca.* 500/1106–7.[82]

Finally, one might add here that an anecdote of 'Aufī's describes as one of Ibrāhīm's trusted advisers Abū l-Qāsim Ḥuṣairī, who makes an intriguing appearance in Baihaqī's pages, together with his father the *faqīh* Abū Bakr Ḥuṣairī, in an episode when the vizier Maimandī wrought vengeance on them for their maltreatment of one of his servants.[83]

5.
Court life and culture

Amongst all the Ghaznavid sultans, Ibrāhīm left a reputation amongst posterity as a wise and beneficent ruler, solicitous for the welfare of his subjects, pious and god-fearing. This reputation seems to have evolved within a century or so of his death, for Ibn al-Athīr in his obituary notice stresses his piety and the fact that he used to copy in his own hand a Qur'ān each year and send it, with other offerings, to Mecca.[84] The fact that Ibrāhīm seems generally to have been addressed—on the evidence of contemporary poetry—as the *Sulṭān-i Raḍī* (from his honorific of Raḍī ad-Dīn 'the One well-pleasing to religion') may indicate that the sultan himself wished to cultivate this aspect of his authority. In the anecdotal literature, the image of the wise ruler emerges especially closely. 'Aufī has anecdotes on Ibrāhīm's care to consult with his advisers over appointments to key affairs; on his compensating an old woman for the sequestration of her house; on his agreeing not to levy taxes on a certain place; and on his relieving the burden of a stone-breaker in Ghazna.[85] Fakhr-i Mudabbir has a long story about Ibrāhīm's concern over a famine in Ghazna, which was causing the emigration elsewhere of many of its citizens and which was relieved by his releasing grain from the royal granary to the bakers and fodder merchants; in what seems to be another version of the same incident, however, related by the contemporary Niẓām al-Mulk (or conceivably inserted by his editor, Muḥammad Maghribī), the sultan takes draconian measures against the royal bakers who had monopolised the purchase of flour and has them trampled to death by elephants as a warning to all other would-be profiteers.[86]

One has the usual problem here in evaluating the more hagiographical aspects of mediaeval Islamic literature. The image of their master projected by the contemporary Ghaznavid poets must have favoured this building-up of Ibrāhīm as the Hezekiah of his dynasty, and there was still fresh in the minds of the Muslims in general an image of the Ghaznavid dynasty as a whole as the scourge of infidels; because of its dazzling Arabic style, 'Utbī's *Yamīnī* circulated very widely in the central and eastern parts of the Islamic world, and Maḥmūd in particular was built up as an Islamic hero against the pagan Hindus and against such Muslim dissidents as the Ismā'īlīs and other Shī'ī groups.

There is no doubt that Ibrāhīm carried on the traditions of his forebears in making his court a centre of literary and cultural activity, whether his motives stemmed from a disinterested love of learning or from a desire to dazzle the rest of the eastern Islamic world with his munificent patronage. The level of poetic production was remarkably high, amply coming up to that of the early Ghaznavid period, the age of 'Unṣurī, Farrukhī, Manūchihrī, etc. As well as the quadrumvirate frequently mentioned and quoted in the previous pages, sc. Abū l-Faraj Rūnī, Sanā'ī, 'Uthmān Mukhtārī and Mas'ūd-i Sa'd-i Salmān, whose creative activity spanned the period from Ibrāhīm's sultanate to the early years of Bahrām Shāh, there were certainly several other good poets of whom little or nothing has survived.[87]

Thus we know little of Abū Ḥanīfa-yi Iskāfī, the friend of Baihaqī, active in the early years of Ibrāhīm's reign, beyond the odes cited by Baihaqī himself in the *Ta'rīkh-i Mas'ūdī*, two of which are dedicated to Sultan Ibrāhīm (see above, Ch. 2, p. 52), unless he is identical with the Abū Ḥanīfa Panjdihī mentioned by the literary biographer 'Alī b. al-Ḥasan al-Bākharzī.[88]

The poet Rāshidī is even more obscure, since we have no biography of him in any representative of the *tadhkirat ash-shu'arā'* works, but merely a mention of him by Niẓāmī ʿArūḍī in the list of poets who glorified the name of the house of Ghazna. His verses have disappeared, but he seems to have been one of Ibrāhīm's court poets, and was involved in poetic contests (*mushāʿarāt, munāẓarāt*) with Masʿūd-i Saʿd-i Salmān; the latter boasts in an ode addressed to his master in India, the prince Saif ad-Daula Maḥmūd b. Ibrāhīm,

> To every ode which had taken Rāshidī a whole month to compose, I immediately extemporised a better one in reply.
> But for respect to you, O Shāh, in God's truth I would have deprived him of both fame and sustenance[89]

Likewise, virtually nothing is known about a court poet whose *takhalluṣ* was Akhtarī, and to whom Masʿūd-i Saʿd addressed a eulogy containing much play on the word *akhtar* 'star' and other astronomical terms.[90]

Somewhat less obscure is the secretary Abū l-ʿAlā' ʿAṭā' b. Yaʿqūb, called Nākūk, since ʿAufī devotes some space to him; and because he left *dīwāns* of both Arabic and Persian poetry, Bākharzī has a brief mention of him in his anthology. Much of his career as a high official (he is accorded the title of "ʿAmīd') was spent in India, and for eight years he suffered imprisonment in Lahore at the hands of sultan Ibrāhīm, dying in 491/1098. This bond of suffering perhaps contributed to the great cordiality of his friendship with Masʿūd-i Saʿd, who mentions him in one of his poems and who composed an elegy on his death.[91]

The centre of government for the Ghaznavids' Indian possessions, Lahore, in many ways functioned as a second capital and a second court within the empire. Hence the court circle of the governor of India was, like that around the sultan in Ghazna, a mecca for poets and writers. Masʿūd-i Saʿd-i Salmān, himself a native of Lahore and scion of a family that had long served the Ghaznavids in India, attached himself to the prince Saif ad-Daula Maḥmūd b. Ibrāhīm, who in 469/1076–7 became governor in India (see above, pp. 65–6), and addressed to the *Shāh-i Hindustān*, as he calls him in one verse, a large number of odes[92] (the title *shāh* is frequently given to Maḥmūd by Abū l-Faraj Rūnī in his panegyrics also, and clearly did not at this time imply supreme rulership, except in so far as the governor of the Ghaznavid territories in India inevitably, because of geographical and strategic considerations, enjoyed quasi-regal status). Masʿūd-i Saʿd also enjoyed the patronage, in the later part of

Ibrāhīm's reign and in the early part of that of his son Masʿūd, of the deputy governor there, Abū Naṣr Hibatallāh Fārsī (see above, p. 67). The latter is therefore the dedicatee of several of Masʿūd-i Saʿd's poems, but he was also a fine poet in his own right; ʿAufī includes him among the viziers and high officials who were poets, and Niẓāmī ʿArūḍī states that 'Certainly, no poet has been heard of who produced so many splendid odes and precious pearls of verse, born of his fiery genius'.[93]

Other poets of this period connected with Ghaznavid India are known only fragmentarily. Bākharzī mentions a poet of Khurasanian origin but resident in Lahore who, being his own contemporary, must have flourished in the middle decades of the century and therefore in the earlier part of Ibrāhīm's reign, sc. Abū l-Qāsim Aḥmad b. Ibrāhīm. The anthologist cites an exchange of Arabic verses which Abū l-Qāsim Aḥmad had with the *faqīh* Abū l-Muẓaffar Nāṣir b. Manṣūr b. Ibrāhīm Bustī, called al-Ghazzāl 'the writer of lyrical and love poetry'; the latter is described as an *ʿĀriḍ*, and it seems likely that Abū l-Muẓaffar Nāṣir functioned in the important office of supervisor of military affairs in India at this time.[94]

In mediaeval Islam, poets and scholars moved easily from one land to another, but even if they did not care to migrate to the court of a foreign potentate, they might nevertheless address panegyrics to outside rulers and great men, in the hope of receiving reward. Hence we know of some poets who lived outside the Ghaznavid boundaries but addressed odes to the sultans, such as the Seljuq poet Muʿizzī, and the poet of Samarqand and eulogist of Malik Shāh, Abū Muḥammad b. Muḥammad Rashīdī, who exchanged verses with the imprisoned Masʿūd-i Saʿd.[95]

In his great collection of anecdotes, the *Jawāmiʿ al-ḥikāyāt*, ʿAufī mentions sultan Ibrāhīm as himself the author of a manual on statecraft, the *Dastūr al-wuzarā'*, from which an anecdote is allegedly cited about the commander of the guard in Ghazna, who explains to Ibrāhīm how the city was successfully kept in order under sultan Maḥmūd. Niẓámu 'd-Dín was inclined to accept the authenticity of this work, basing himself on Ibrāhīm's image as the restorer of good government and of Ghaznavid fortunes after the losses in the west. Possibly this work, if it existed, was a collection of the standard aphorisms on government, and not necessarily of any great originality; but in the absence of more definite proof of its existence, the adoption of a sceptical attitude is safest.[96]

6.

Relations with the Abbasid caliphate

Relations with the Abbasid caliphate in Baghdad must have been kept up by the later Ghaznavids, though we have no information about specific embassies during Ibrāhīm's reign. Maḥmūd and Mas'ūd had in the first part of the century been especially eager to maintain close relations with the Abbasids, projecting their image of defenders of Sunnī orthodoxy against extremist Shī'ism and other heresies, and announcing their declared intention of rescuing the caliphs from the yoke in Iraq of the Shī'ī Būyids.[97] In the event, it was the Seljuqs who delivered the caliphs from the Dailamīs, whilst themselves substituting a tutelage over the Abbasids which was little lighter than that of the Byūids; and the eastwards-facing empire of Ibrāhīm and his successors no longer had such close geographical contacts with Iraq as had had Maḥmūd and Mas'ūd after the conquest of Ray and Jibāl in 420/1029. However, so far as we know, the sultans continued to regard legitimation by the caliphs of their succession to the throne as important from the points of view of constitutional propriety and of the buttressing of their royal position in the eyes of their subjects. Lacking the work of a Baihaqī for Ibrāhīm's reign, we do not possess anything resembling that historian's detailed account of Mas'ūd's reception of the caliph al-Qādir's envoy at Nīshāpūr in 421/1030; this envoy brought him a *manshūr* or investiture patent and a string of honorific titles, all of them potent weapons in Mas'ūd's struggle to establish his claim to the throne against his brother Muḥammad (see further below, Ch. 3, p. 83). Nor do we possess any complete texts like sultan Mas'ūd's public proclamation of the succession to the caliphate of al-Qā'im in 423/end of 1032 and the announcement of his own declared allegiance to the new Commander of the Faithful.[98]

We do have the text of an ornate *fatḥ-nāma* or victory proclamation, sent out by al-Qā'im and written by his Christian secretary Ibn Mauṣilāyā, announcing the final defeat in Baghdad of the rebel Arslan Basāsīrī (Dhū l-Ḥijja 451/January 1060) to Ibrāhīm, but this tells us nothing about Abbasid-Ghaznavid relations beyond the fact that the caliph regarded the sultan as one of the important contemporary potentates to whom such a document should be sent. Yet leaving aside the text of the document itself, there may possibly be some diplomatic and constitutional significance in the fact that the heading of the *fatḥ-nāma*, as given by Qalqashandī, states that 'Abū Sa'īd al-'Alā' b. Mauṣilāyā wrote it on behalf of al-Qā'im bi'llāh to 'Aḍud ad-Daula Alp Arslan to Mas'ūd b. Maḥmūd [read: Ibrāhīm b. Mas'ūd], the lord of Ghazna, on the nearer fringes of India'.[99] If this is authentic, and provided that a copula has not dropped out between the names of the two Seljuq and Ghaznavid leaders, this may imply that the Seljuqs were now requiring the caliphs to communicate with the Ghaznavids only via themselves (Alp Arslan was not yet the Great Sultan, but was virtual ruler of the eastern lands of the Seljuqs in place of his sick father Chaghrï Beg Dā'ūd). A forceful ruler was often able to require of his neighbours or vassals, above all if envoys to and from these last had to traverse his own territories, that they should communicate with the seat of the caliphate only through himself. In their prime, the Ghaznavids had themselves enforced such conditions: in 404 or 405/1014 the Ma'mūnid Khwārazm-Shāh Abū l-'Abbās Ma'mūn b. Ma'mūn had been afraid to receive directly from the caliph an investiture patent, a robe of honour, honorific titles and other insignia of royalty, lest Sultan Maḥmūd be offended; in 422/1031 the caliph had undertaken to Mas'ūd that he would not negotiate or deal with the Qarakhanids of Transoxania except via the Ghaznavids.[100] The Seljuqs, of course, now controlled all the land routes across Persia connecting Iraq with Ghazna, and might well have been able to enforce restrictions at least at the Baghdad end; whether they were able to impose a similar requirement at the other end, that is on the Ghaznavids, is less likely.

Ibrāhīm had a particularly resplendent series of honorifics, gathered in the course of his lengthy reign (see above, p. 56, for details of these). In the absence of explicit information, we may assume that these were solicited by him from Baghdad in the normal way, and were sought in return for public recognition of the Abbasids in the *khuṭba* and in the *sikka* or coinage (as the extant coins of Ibrāhīm show was in fact done) and in return for rich presents to Baghdad from the Indian booty. It is in the texts of certain poems, rather than in the historical sources, that we find mention of the receiving of honorifics and other caliphal favours. Thus amongst Mas'ūd-i Sa'd-i Salmān's numerous poems in praise of Saif ad-Daula Maḥmūd b. Ibrāhīm, there are two poems composed on the occasion of Maḥmūd's acquisition—doubtless after some special military achievement in India—of the titles Ṣanī' Amīr al-Mu'minīn and ʿIzz al-Milla from either al-Qā'im (d. 467/1075) or his successor al-Muqtadī (467–87/1075–94). In one of these two poems there occur the verses

> O you upon whom the Commander of the Faithful has bestowed the title of his devoted companion[*ṣanīʿ*], may your glory increase steadily in a similar way.
>
> Previously you had the additional title of 'Sword of the state', and now the Commander of the Faithful has added to this that of 'Glory of the religious community'![101]

Likewise, and at a slightly later period, Masʿūd-i Saʿd wrote a poem in praise of the newly installed sultan Malik Arslan b. Masʿūd (presumably therefore in 509/1115, see below, p. 91), congratulating him on the receipt of the insignia of rulership from the caliph, including a standard (*liwā'*) and an investiture diploma (*ʿahd*).[102]

7.

Ibrāhīm as ruler

Despite the picture of sultan Ibrāhīm built up by his panegyrists and by the later writers of *adab* literature, the picture of him as the beau ideal of Islamic rulers, the friend of religion, the shepherd of his people and the Maecenas of the age, we can readily discern that the sultan was neither a pious simpleton nor a fanatic obsessed by the projection of his own image, but rather, a hard-headed realist. The general trend of his political policy towards the Seljuqs emphasises this, as we have seen above, as does also his matter-of-fact appraisal of the position and resources of the Ghaznavid empire in his own time compared with that of his forebears (see above, p. 51). We should probably be not far wrong in regarding him as a despotic sovereign of his father's and grandfather's stamp. He demanded the same implicit obedience and unquestioning loyalty of his servants, as is shown by his ruthlessness towards the fallen vizier Abū Sahl Khujandī and the zeal with which he watched for signs of incompetence in the administration of the Indian provinces or signs of incipient rebelliousness amongst his officials and commanders in that classic trouble spot.

Ruthless financial exploitation of the dependent provinces had been a prime reason for the rapid falling-away from Ghaznavid allegiance of Jibāl and Khurasan at the time of the Seljuq incursions during Masʿūd's reign.[103] Despite the more restricted sphere of operations of the imperial bureaucracy and the resources available by way of plunder and tribute from India, the administrative costs of running the Ghaznavid empire and its army during Ibrāhīm's reign must still have been heavy; the sultan doubtless lived opulently, with fine palaces and gardens, although we have no explicit information about these, and with an élite guard of highly-paid and richly-equipped soldiers. He certainly kept up, like his predecessors, an extensive entourage of scholars and literary men. Indeed, Jūzjānī notes that Ibrāhīm's son and successor Mas'ūd had on his accession to get rid of some harsh financial practices of the former reign, see below, Ch. 3, pp. 86–7.

Ibrāhīm's death took place on 5 Shawwāl 492/25 August 1099 at the age of sixty-eight lunar years and after he had reigned for forty-two lunar years.[104] His tomb, according to a survey of the tomb inscriptions of Ghazna and district written in 1326/1908, was 'in the northeastern part of [mediaeval] Ghazna near the tomb of Shaikh Raḍī d-Dīn 'Alī Lālā'; this information probably stems from the oral tradition which makes a fairly recent *ziyārat* or sanctuary, known as that of sultan Ibrāhīm, his last resting-place.[105]

THREE

Mas'ūd III and his Sons: Equilibrium and Incipient Decline

I.

Mas'ūd's reign

The half-century or so extending from Ibrāhīm's death in 492/1099 till the struggle for power in eastern Afghanistan between the Ghūrids and Ghaznavids which broke out in *ca.* 543/1148 (see Ch. 4 below) spans the reigns of Mas'ūd III b. Ibrāhīm (492–508/1099–1115) and his three sons, rulers successively, Shīr-Zād (508–9/1115–16), Malik Arslan (509–11/1116–17) and Bahrām Shāh (511–?552/1117–?1157). It forms a period of comparative equilibrium for the Ghaznavid empire, after the recovery of prosperity and stability by Ibrāhīm and before the protracted, but ultimately fatal, struggle with the Ghūrids. Even so, within these decades one may discern signs of incipient decline within the state once Mas'ūd's reign was over. His death was followed by four years of internecine strife amongst his sons, and the one who emerged victorious, Bahrām Shāh, achieved power only with the support of the eastern Seljuq sultan Sanjar, whose vassal he had now perforce to become. Accordingly, for the first time since Maḥmūd b. Sebüktigin had thrown off the suzerainty of the Sāmānids in 389/999, the Ghaznavid state became subject to an outside power.

As noted above at the end of Ch. 2, we know absolutely nothing about the transfer of power to Mas'ūd on his father's death in Shawwāl 492/August 1099 beyond Ibn Bābā's bare mention of fratricidal disputes at this point. It cannot, indeed, have been strange if, out of Ibrāhīm's extensive progeny (detailed, as we have seen, by Jūzjānī), someone should have disputed the succession with Mas'ūd. Prince Saif ad-Daula Maḥmūd, the victor in many Indian campaigns (see above, Ch. 2, pp. 64–6) would have been a serious rival in any struggle with Mas'ūd for the throne; the absence of any mention of him at this time indicates either that he was by now dead, or else had been shut up for the rest of his life in some fortress.

Abū Saʿd Masʿūd had the honorifics of Jalāl ad-Dīn (thus according to Ibn al-Athīr), ʿAlāʾ ad-Daula wa-d-Dīn, Sanāʾ al-Milla, Ẓahīr al-Umma (thus, for the Ẓahīr al-ʾmām of a coin as read by Rodgers), and Niẓām ad-Dīn wa-d-Dunyā. The second *laqab*, ʿAlāʾ ad-Daula wa-d-Dīn, is the one most frequently used in the literary sources, whilst the remaining ones figure mainly on his coins, together with grandiloquent phrases like Maulā s-Salāṭīn, al-Malik al-Muʾayyad al-Qādim bi-amr Allāh and al-Qāʾim bi-ḥujjat Allāh.[1] Two of Masʿūd's honorifics are referred to in a verse of an ode addressed to him by ʿUthmān Mukhtārī,

> *Khudāyigān-i salāṭīn, ʿAlāʾ-i Daula u Dīn, Niẓām-i Dunyā, maulā l-mulūk, shāh-i jahān.*[2]

The name of the Abbasid caliph al-Mustaẓhir (487–512/1094–1118) appears on his coins, indicating that the traditional Ghaznavid policy of acknowledging the religious and moral supremacy of the Baghdad caliphate was kept up by Masʿūd, a fact confirmed by the title Nāṣir Khalīfat Allāh appearing in the inscription of Masʿūd's minaret at Ghazna.[3]

Considering the sixteen years' length of Masʿūd's apparently successful reign, we are woefully uninformed about specific events falling within it. Masʿūd had early been married to a Seljuq princess, the Mahd-i ʿIrāq Jauhar Khātūn bint Malik Shāh, possibly in *ca.* 475/1082–3, although the exact date is unknown (see above, Ch. 2, p. 54f.), and the generally harmonious relations between the Ghaznavids and the eastern branch of the Great Seljuqs continued during Masʿūd's reign. The ease with which a poet like ʿUthmān Mukhtārī moved to-and-fro between the court of Ghazna, that of the Seljuqs in Kirmān and that of the Ṣaffārids in Zarang, further points to generally amicable relations. We have specific mention in the historical sources of only one potentially disturbing episode here, though even this does not seem to have ruffled the surface of the entente between Masʿūd and Sanjar.

According to the historical sources, in the most detailed fashion in Ibn al-Athīr, under the year 495/1101–2, more summarily in Bundārī, the Qarakhanid ruler of the western khanate of Bukhara and Samarqand, Qadïr Khan Jibrāʾīl b. ʿUmar, attempted to take advantage, first of Sanjar's absence at Baghdad in 494/1100–1 helping Muḥammad b. Malik Shāh against the rival sultan Berk-Yaruq,[4] and second, of a severe, almost mortal illness which afflicted Sanjar at this time. The khan was encouraged by one of Sanjar's Turkish commanders Küntoghdï, a former ghulām of the Seljuq prince Tutush b. Alp Arslan, but his attempt to invade Khurasan from Transoxania was halted at Tirmidh on the Oxus. The khan was defeated in battle, captured and then executed by Sanjar for the breach of allegiance to his Seljuq suzerain (2 Shaʿbān 495/22 May 1102), but Küntoghdï either escaped from captivity by crawling for two *farsakhs* through the underground culvert of an irrigation *qanāt*, or according to another version of the story, was allowed to depart from the Seljuq dominions. At all events, Küntoghdï appeared in Ghazna, and as an experienced officer was welcomed into the Ghaznavid army. He won sultan Masʿūd's approbation by storming and taking a stronghold of rebels in the mountains of Ūtān (? Ūnān), 40 *farsakhs* from Ghazna, after Masʿūd's own attacks on their position had been fruitless. But his rise in the sultan's favour stirred up jealousies amongst the other commanders of the Ghaznavid army, and Küntoghdï was forced to flee for his life towards Herat and the Seljuq dominions once more, where he died.[5]

The main sphere of Masʿūd's own military activities, apart from punitive expeditions against local rebels such as the unsuccessful one mentioned above, was India. We have seen above, Ch. 2, p. 67, that it was probably Masʿūd who replaced his brother Saif ad-Daula Maḥmūd after the latter's fall from grace towards the end of sultan Ibrāhīm's reign, and such a poem as the ode dedicated to Masʿūd by ʿUthmān Mukhtārī in which the Ghaznavid is addressed as *Ghāzī* may well date from the years when he was governor in India.[6] According to Fakhr-i Mudabbir, Masʿūd was a doughty warrior with the weapons of the *bilgetigīnī* variety of mace (named after the slave commander of Alptigin's, Bilgetigin, who had governed in Ghazna before Sebüktigin's elevation to power there?) and the *qalāchūrī* or long, curved cavalry sword.[7] The poets of the time were assiduous in building up the image of the sultan and of his son Shīr-Zād as mighty fighters for the faith in India. Thus ʿUthmān Mikhtārī again states of the sultan (or of the prince, if this particular poem dates from before Sultan Ibrāhīm's death):

> ⸙ If Malik Masʿūd-i Ibrāhīm, the cherisher of religion, struts proudly once more through India for the firm upholding of the faith of his God,
>
> Wreak there a work with such incisiveness and renown that

people in Khurasan will turn it into an example for all to copy.[8]

Of special interest is a long ode by this same poet, composed by ʿUthmān whilst he was staying at the court of the Seljuq amīr of Kirmān and when there reached him the *fatḥ-nāma* or proclamation announcing a spectacular victory of Masʿūd in India. The poem speaks of the conquest of a fortress there, hitherto impregnable for a thousand years, in the course of which conquest 'the moon of the Rājā's standard' was hurled to the ground and an idol-temple thrown down and burnt. The sultan's own dagger wrought there an effect comparable to the miracle of Noah's flood, by producing a sea of severed heads, and immense booty was brought back to Ghazna.[9]

Both Masʿūd-i Saʿd-i Salmān and Abū l-Faraj Rūnī allude in their verses to the capture by Masʿūd (explicit in Masʿūd-i Saʿd, by inference to be connected with Masʿūd in Rūnī) of the ruler of Kanauj, who was subsequently ransomed—but only after a long interval—by his own son. The captured ruler is named in the poems as M.h.l.y/M.l.h.y or M.t.l.y, tempting one to identify him with Mahītala/Mahīyala, the father of the Rājā of Kanauj Chandradeva (see above, Ch. 2, p. 67); but on chronological grounds this is impossible, and Ganguly therefore suggested that we have in reality to do with Chandradeva's son and successor Madanachandra or Madanapāla (ruled in Kanauj 1100–14). This ruler was ransomed from the Muslims by his own son Govindachandra (reigned from 1114 till after 1154), as appears from the evidence of inscriptions of the Gāhaḍavālas dating from 1104–9.[10]

The raids of Masʿūd's commander Togha(n)tigin (the spelling Ṭoghān-tigīn is in fact explicit in a poem of ʿUthmān Mukhtārī's addressed to Masʿūd's son Malik Arslan, where he is mentioned with another Turkish general, Alp Sonqur),[11] which reached as far as the Ganges-Jumna Dōāb, have already been noted (see above, Ch. 2, p. 61), and it is very probable that the activities in Central India of the general Najm ad-Dīn Zarīr Shaibānī, son of Bū Ḥalīm Shaibānī, fall within Masʿūd's sultanate. A poem by Masʿūd-i Saʿd-i Salmān addressed to Najm ad-Dīn Zarīr describes how the latter marches with an army against Mālwa in Central India and then against the fortress of Kālinjar (Kālañjara) in Bundelkhand by way of Narā'īn (sc. Narāyapur, in the former Alwar State), which would be on the route from the Jumna river and the Āgra district. It seems therefore possible that these raids were a pendant to, or a continuation of, those of Prince Maḥmūd against Āgra and Kanauj described above. Najm ad-Dīn Zarīr may accordingly have been detached from the main army to march against the Paramāra kings in Ujjain. An inscription from Nagpur of 1104, when the Paramāra ruler was Naravarman, reports that the ruler's brother and predecessor Lakṣmadeva (reigned at some time between 1088 and 1094) repulsed an attack by the Turuṣkas. This check may have been the reason why the Ghaznavid army was deflected from Mālwa northeastwards to Kālinjar in the territory of the Chandellas, where it came up against the Chandella king Kīrttivarman, before returning up the Jumna valley to the Panjab.[12]

From mentions in the contemporary poets, rather than from the historical sources, we know the names of one or two others of Masʿūd's officials and commanders in India. One of the *mamdūḥs* of Sanā'ī was Sarhang amīr Muḥammad Harawī, whose valorous exploits at Kanauj are mentioned by the poet.[13] Known from references in the verses of ʿUthmān Mukhtārī, Masʿūd-i Saʿd-i Salmān and Sanā'ī, is Sarhang Muḥammad Khaṭībī. This last was both scholar-poet, engaging in poetic contests with his friend Masʿūd-i Saʿd, and administrator-commander, holding at one period in Masʿūd's sultanate the governorship of Quṣdār in northeastern Baluchistan before calumniators secured his dismissal and imprisonment in the fortress of Maranj. ʿUthmān Mukhtārī dedicated a poem to him, in which he is described as 'the Ṣadr, ʿAmīd, Sarhang Muḥammad b. Khaṭīb', and as governor (*ʿāmil*) of Sind; whether he held this important office before or after his imprisonment is unknown.[14]

Masʿūd enjoyed the services of his father Ibrāhīm's vizier ʿAbd al-Ḥamīd b. Aḥmad b. ʿAbd aṣ-Ṣamad, whose tenure of office extended through the whole of the sultan's sixteen-year reign, and various others of Ibrāhīm's high officials, such as Thiqat al-Mulk Ṭāhir b. ʿAlī, seem to have continued to serve the new sultan (see above, Ch. 2, pp. 71–4). The character of the sultan himself hardly emerges from the brevity of the sources on his reign. The *Ṭabaqāt-i Nāṣirī* notes that on his accession, Masʿūd got rid of many harsh financial practices left over from the former reign:

> He suppressed the whole of the repressive dues which had been established previously; he completely abolished the extraordinary exactions levied by the *Dīwān* officials [? *ʿawāriḍ-i qalamī*; Raverty simply translates 'the contingent taxes'] throughout

> the whole of the Maḥmūdī region [? *sarband-i maḥmūdī*, perhaps referring to the heartland of the first Ghaznavids' territories, that is, the immediate district of Ghazna] and Zābulistān, and he remitted all the tolls and transit dues in all the empire.[15]

Such acts of benevolence were not unusual at the accession of a monarch, when the new broom would sweep clean for a while; but then the old abuses would often creep back, as the urgent need for fresh sources of taxation, to finance military campaigns and to maintain the opulent life-style of the sultans, became more pressing. Two anecdotes of Fakhr-i Mudabbir's, cast in a familiar mould, emphasise Masʿūd's equity and concern for the welfare of his subjects. In the first of these stories, placed in the year 503/1109–10, the sultan leaves on the ground a valuable pearl that has fallen from the beak of the hawk surmounting his *chatr* or ceremonial parasol, in order that some poor person may find it and thereby become rich; and in the second, the sultan, on the occasion of a famine and plague of locusts at Ghazna in 505/1111–12, releases grain from the royal granaries and sells it to the people at 70 per cent of the normal price.[16] Two further anecdotes are to be found in ʿAufī's collection: in the first, Masʿūd, on his accession, calls in all the debased and corrupt coinage circulating in India, and in its place releases three million dirhams' worth of new currency from the royal treasury; and in the second, he prays fervently to God that He might halt the incessant rainfall which was afflicting the neighbourhood of Ghazna.[17]

That Masʿūd continued to live like his forefathers, within an ambience of splendid palaces and gardens, is demonstrated by the recent discovery of one of his palaces at Ghazna. The site of this palace has been the subject of excavations by the Italian Archaeological Mission in Afghanistan since 1957, and lies near to the well-known minaret of Masʿūd III (formerly attributed to Sultan Maḥmūd). The attribution of the palace to Masʿūd III seems incontestable after the discovery by the Italian team of an Arabic inscription describing how Muḥammad b. Ḥusain b. Mubārak completed the construction work in Ramaḍān 505/March 112; the sultan's name appears, moreover, on a piece of stone used in the *miḥrāb* of a later oratory built on the palace site.[18] The palace was constructed, like other similar Ghaznavid buildings at Ghazna and at Lashkar-i Bāzār near Bust, out of brick (the walls round the main rectangular courtyard, each with an *īwān*, were actually of fired brick) and therefore had a short life. It may well have been abandoned by the time of Masʿūd's own son and next-but-one successor, Malik Arslan, for Bombaci has cited poetry by ʿUthmān Mukhtārī stating that Arslan built his own palace (*qaṣr*) and was crowned there, and that he chose to reside in his own palace and administrative headquarters (*daulat-khāna*).[19]

However, marble was also used in the construction of Masʿūd's palace, this being hewn from a nearby quarry, and slabs of this material were used for a dado running round the façades of the inner courtyard. The slabs were apparently inscribed with a Persian poetical text, *mathnawī* in praise of sultan Masʿūd, and these verses ran round the four sides of the courtyard. Bombaci has pieced together with great skill, from the surviving slabs, as much as possible of this poetical text. In these fragments we find praises of sultan Maḥmūd b. Sebüktigin as the upholder of the Islamic faith and of his son and successor Masʿūd I, the martyr-sultan, and these verses doubtless led up to a panegyric of the latter's grandson Masʿūd III b. Ibrāhīm himself.[20]

Bombaci has also written penetratingly about the historical and cultural significance of the palace in general and the poetic inscription in particular. The construction of the palace would be almost completely financed out of the spoils of the Indian campaigns, as the discovery of a statue of Brahma during the course of the Italian excavations shows clearly. Culturally, we have interesting confirmation of the process whereby the ethnically Turkish Ghaznavids adapted to the surroundings on the fringe of the Iranian world and whereby they enthusiastically espoused the Iranian national culture and its monarchical ethos. The poetic inscription is one of the earliest known examples of New Persian used for epigraphic purposes, and especially, of metrical forms employed for this aim. The verses must have been specially composed by some unknown author for the adornment of Masʿūd's palace. Bombaci has surmised that the poet in question was probably either ʿUthmān Mukhtārī, who returned from Kirmān to the court of Ghazna during Masʿūd's sultanate, or else Masʿūd-i Saʿd-i Salmān, who was released from his imprisonment in the early part of Masʿūd's reign and was entrusted with supervision of the royal library in Ghazna.[21] Abū l-Faraj Rūnī, on the other hand, may have been no longer alive at this time, whilst Sanā'ī had not yet proved himself.[22]

The verses on the courtyard walls are in the *mutaqārib* metre, that employed by Firdausī for the *Shāh-nāma*, and they apparently celebrate the exploits of successive members of the Ghaznavid dynasty in the same heroic fashion as Firdausī's epic celebrates the paladins of ancient Iran. Thus we have a two-fold emphasis on Maḥmūd as the protagonist of the Islamic religion and also as an Iranian warrior-hero. Such ideas were very much part of the Ghaznavid cultural environment at this time, and were fed by the feelings of *jihād* engendered by the Indian campaigns. Abū l-Faraj Rūnī in one and the same verse calls Masʿūd 'the Solomon of the age' and 'Farīdūn, son of Ābitīn', whilst Masʿūd-i Saʿd, in an ode addressed to the sultan, praises his sons as legitimate heirs to the ancient Iranian tradition:

> These princely ones, through whom the foundations of the structure of the state and the faith have become once more supremely strong,
>
> Endowed with the charisma [*farr*] and lofty estate of Khusrau Aparvīz and Kai Kubād, and with the courage and forcefulness of Rustam, Gīr and Isfandiyār.[23]

At the end of Masʿūd's reign, in 509/1115, ʿUthmān Mukhtārī completed his epic *mathnawī* poem, cast in the post-Firdausian mould, of the *Shahriyār-nāma*. Jalāl ad-Dīn Humāʾī, who has edited the surviving parts of the poem, is probably correct in suggesting that ʿAṭāʾ b. Yaʿqūb Kātib's *Barzū-nāma*, written for sultan Ibrāhīm b. Masʿūd, was in Masʿūd III's mind when he encouraged ʿUthmān Mukhtārī in this composition. We know from the surviving section that the poem is set in India, and revolves around the exploits of Shahriyār, son of Barzū, and around the struggles of the heroes of ancient Iran (in fact, to be equated with the Muslim *ghāzī*s of the poet's own time) against the infidel Hindus; the inspiration for this subject was clearly Masʿūd's own Indian campaigns.[24]

2.

The struggles for power amongst Masʿūd's sons

Masʿūd died in Shawwāl 508/March 1115, at the age of fifty-five lunar years. As was usual with the Ghaznavids, he left numerous offspring, of whom Jūzjānī names a dozen or so. It is unknown whether Masʿūd had followed the by now time-hallowed practice of imprisoning or otherwise disposing of potential rivals to the throne, in the shape of his brothers and senior male relatives; at all events, his own sons speedily fell out with each other in the years following his death.[25]

In accordance with Masʿūd's *ʿahd* or testament, his second son Shīr-Zād succeeded to the throne, but he reigned for one year only. As is the case with Maudūd's two ephemeral successors, Masʿūd II b. Maudūd and ʿAlī b. Masʿūd I (see above, Ch. I, p. 37), Shīr-Zād is not mentioned in many of the sources. It is not surprising that Ibn al-Athīr and the Seljuq sources should be unaware of Shīr-Zād's existence, but remarkable that a local historian like Jūzjānī makes no mention of him either; indeed, it is only in the comparatively late source of Ḥamdallāh Mustaufī, and in the even later sources following him, like Firishta, that we find any record of him at all. Shīr-Zād had the honorific of ʿAḍud ad-Daula when he was acting as governor in India for his father, and there is attributed to him in the sources the further *laqab* of Kamāl ad-Daula, probably adopted by him on becoming sultan; no coins of his are apparently extant. According to Mustaufī, Shīr-Zād reigned for just a year, and then in 509/1116 his brother Malik Arslan overthrew and killed him.[26] We can fill out this laconic notice by a reference from the local historian of Ṭabaristān, Ibn Isfandiyār. In his section on the Bāwandids, who were an ancient local dynasty of the Caspian region, he mentions that Shīr-Zād took refuge with the Ispahbad ʿAlā' ad-Daula ʿAlī b. Shahriyār, who gave him the means to perform the Pilgrimage to Mecca, after which Shīr-Zād was able to return to Ghazna.[27] On chronological grounds, this Pilgrimage must relate to Dhū l-Ḥijja 509/April–May 1116; the implication seems to be that Shīr-Zād was driven from the throne by Shawwāl 509/February 1116 (see below for this date), fled to the Caspian lands, made the Pilgrimage from there and then attempted to regain his throne in Ghazna, but was killed by Malik Arslan.

Malik Arslan (sometimes given in the sources the name of Arslan Shāh) was Masʿūd's third son, and was probably the child of the Seljuq princess, the Mahd-i ʿIrāq Jauhar Khātūn, since two poems by Masʿūd-i Saʿd-i Salmān addressed to Malik Arslan praise him for his dual lineage, that from Maḥmūd of Ghazna on the one hand, and that from the Seljuq Abū Sulaimān Chaghrī Beg Dā'ūd on the other. In one of these we find the verses

> I am the source of all justice and the source of all liberality,
> I am sultan Malik Arslan-i Masʿūd.
>
> My exalted judgment spreads illumination over the world just

like the sun, and my generosity has become as rain making its impress upon the earth.

I am endowed with praiseworthy [*maḥmūd*] characteristics, and am fully cognisant [reading here *dānam* for the text's *rānam*] of the ways and manners of conducting all kinds of procedure, since I am of the noble stock of Maḥmūd,

With the power and omnipotence of Solomon [Sulaimān], since I am from the origin and progeny of Dā'ūd.[28]

If Malik Arslan was, as seems most probable, twenty-seven years old when he was killed in 512/1118 (see below), he must have been born in 485/1092 and have been twenty-six years old at this point. He now succeeded to the throne in Ghazna on Wednesday, 6 Shawwāl 509/22 February 1116, according to the date explicitly given in a coronation ode composed for him by Mas'ūd-i Sa'd,[29] with the honorific of Sulṭān ad-Daula; this *laqab* appears on the few coins of his extant, together with acknowledgment of the Abbasid caliph al-Mustaẓhir.[30] His patronymic, known from frequent references in such of his eulogists as 'Uthmān Mukhtārī—who, from the considerable number of odes which he addressed to Malik Arslan during the latter short reign of three years, may be regarded as Malik Arslan's poet-laureate—was Abū l-Mulūk. The prophetic wish expressed in this *kunya*, 'Father of monarchs', was of course never fulfilled, since the last three monarchs of the Ghaznavid line, Malik Arslan's immediate successors, comprised his brother Bahrām Shāh and the latter's progeny. There is mention in the sources of only one of Malik Arslan's own sons, sc. Khusrau Malik. On the evidence of an ode by Mas'ūd-i Sa'd-i Salmān (who, like 'Uthmān Mukhtārī, enjoyed a period of royal favour and patronage in Malik Arslan's reign) greeting Malik Arslan on the birth of his son, to whom the title of Jamāl al-Milla was seemingly given, he was born during his father's sultanate. 'Uthmān Mukhtārī also has a poem in praise of the infant Khusrau Malik. Of the child's later fate, however, nothing is known.[31]

Mindful of the struggle which he had just had in order to gain the throne, Malik Arslan immediately imprisoned or blinded all his remaining brothers, with the exception of Bahrām Shāh, who was fortunately absent in Zamīn-Dāwar at the time of Malik Arslan's seizure of power.[32] His vizier was Shams al-Wuzarā' Quṭb ad-Dīn Niẓām al-Mulk Abū l-Fatḥ Yūsuf b. Ya'qūb (a brother of Abū l-'Alā' 'Aṭā' b. Ya'qūb, who had served sultan Ibrāhīm, see above,

Ch. 2, p. 76, ?); nothing is known of his executive acts, and the last Ghaznavid vizier mentioned in the biographical works on viziers is the vizier of Ibrāhīm and Masʿūd, ʿAbd al-Ḥamīd b. Aḥmad b. ʿAbd aṣ-Ṣamad, but ʿUthmān Mukhtārī addressed several odes to Abū l-Fatḥ Yūsuf, who was clearly an influential person in the state.[33] The only domestic event of Malik Arslan's reign recorded by the historians is of a destructive conflagration in the markets of Ghazna caused by a falling thunderbolt and regarded by later writers as a portent of the brevity of his reign and of the violence that filled it.[34]

Because of his difficulties in securing the throne and the threat that soon arose to his position from the rival Bahrām Shāh, Malik Arslan was never able to campaign personally in India, the sacred duty of all Ghaznavid sultans; only at the end of his reign, after Bahrām Shāh's first installation at Ghazna in his stead, sc. in 510/1117, did he retire to India in order to collect an army for a revanche. During his reign, the governorship and the military command in India were entrusted, it is deducible from one of Masʿūd-i Saʿd-i Salmān's poems addressed to Malik Arslan, to two brothers of the Bū Ḥalīm Shaibānī family, which already had a tradition of distinguished service in India (see above, p. 85): ʿImād ad-Daula Muḥammad b. ʿAlī, who bore the title of *Ispahbad* or commander-in-chief, and Rabīʿ, whose sphere of action is not specified but whose duties may have included some on the civil side. In this poem, Masʿūd-i Saʿd rejoices in the coming victories in India and the rich plunder which the two leaders will bring back for the sultan; Sarhang Muḥammad-i ʿAlī's exploits will reach as far as Ceylon, and the spoils will include a hundred elephants of a kind even better than those known as 'acceptable to monarchs' (*malik-pasand*). In another ode to Malik Arslan, this same poet describes the fabulous presents which Muḥammad and Rabīʿ send from India to the sultan on the occasions of the great Iranian festivals.[35] Both Muḥammad and Rabīʿ remained faithful to Malik Arslan after Bahrām Shāh had assumed power in Ghazna, and one of the latter's first acts, once he was firmly established on the throne, was a punitive expedition into India with the aim of bringing Muḥammad back to allegiance (see below).

Bahrām Shāh coveted the throne of his half-brother Malik Arslan and was not disposed to allow the latter to continue in possession of the imperial power. Gulam Mustafa Khan has demonstrated the unlikelihood that Bahrām Shāh was Malik Arslan's full brother, that is a son of Masʿūd III's wife Jauhar Khātūn, even though many historians (e.g. Rāwandī and Ḥamdallāh Mustaufī) state that Bahrām Shāh was the nephew and kinsman of Sanjar, himself the brother of the Mahd-i ʿIrāq. First, as already pointed out by the modern editor of Masʿūd-i Saʿd-i Salmān's *Dīwān*, Rashīd Yāsimī, in a laudatory verse of the poet, Bahrām Shāh's descent is traced back to Maḥmūd of Ghazna only, and not to the Seljuq sultans additionally, as was the case, we have just seen, with the same poet's panegyrics of Malik Arslan. Second, in an anecdote of the *Ādāb al-ḥarb*, Sanjar is pictured as reluctant to intervene in Ghaznavid internal affairs in order to place his protégé Bahrām Shāh on the throne: 'The sultan feared that if he were to supply him (sc. Bahrām Shāh) with aid and topple sultan Malik Arslan from his throne, people would say that Sanjar had helped a stranger but removed one of his own kith-and-kin from the throne'. Third, Khan suggests that if the Mahd-i ʿIrāq had also been Bahrām Shāh's mother, Malik Arslan would not have sent her, as certain sources relate, on an embassy to Sanjar, nor would he have appealed to the supreme Seljuq sultan Muḥammad b. Malik Shāh in the hope of preventing Sanjar from his projected attack on Ghazna and his plan to place Bahrām Shāh on the throne.[36]

The successive stages of the diplomatic and military struggle between Malik Arslan on the one side, and Bahrām Shāh and Sanjar on the other, can be pieced together from the detailed account of Ibn al-Athīr and from the briefer lines in Jūzjānī and the Seljuq historians, together with some anecdotal material in the collections of ʿAufī and Fakhr-i Mudabbir.

When Malik Arslan was formally hailed as ruler in Ghazna in Shawwāl 509/February 1116, Bahrām Shāh was in Zamīn-Dāwar and attempted to make a stand there in assertion of his own claims to the throne. Fighting took place at Tigīnābād, in which his forces were nevertheless worsted. With this initial threat from Bahrām Shāh thus parried, Malik Arslan was able to send troops into various parts of the Ghaznavid dominions to secure his power; these events are referred to in poems of Masʿūd-i Saʿd-i Salmān.[37] Bahrām Shāh meanwhile fled westwards, with one attendant only and with their horses shod backwards in order to elude pursuit, according to an anecdote of ʿAufī's.[38] He passed through Sīstān to Kirmān and arrived at the court of the Seljuq amīr Muḥyī d-Dīn Arslan Shāh b.

Kirmān Shāh (495–537/1101–42), who had been some years previous to this the patron of the poet ʿUthmān Mukhtārī. The Seljuq prince treated Bahrām Shāh honourably, but was reluctant to give him military support without prior reference to the head of the Seljuq family in eastern Persia, Sanjar: 'Since the supreme sultan Sanjar is now on the throne, it is not proper for me to give you an army, but I have done all within my power to help you financially'. He then sent one of his commanders to escort Bahrām Shāh safely to Sanjar's court in Merv.[39]

The fugitive Ghaznavid then proceeded to Khurasan, and speedily made himself very much *persona grata* in Sanjar's court circle, as hunting-companion and confidant of the sultan. According to an anecdote of Fakhr-i Mudabbir's, Bahrām Shāh's skill with the spear, and especially with the bow, was responsible for Sanjar's decision to provide military aid for wresting the throne of Ghazna from Malik Arslan, after he had witnessed a remarkable feat of Bahrām Shāh's in the hunting field. When asked about his decision, Sanjar replied that

> I noted that all the notables, great men of state and military commanders, had become his fervent supporters and were unanimous in his praise. Moreover, I found him exceptionally brave and courageous, and unparalleled in his skill as an archer. So I was afraid that, if he used such skill in archery, and shot just one arrow at me and took away my kingdom, there would be no-one to recover it. So, [I thought], let him do what he can with the kingdom of his father and forefathers, but not with mine![40]

Exactly how eager Sanjar was in fact to intervene in what was really a Ghaznavid internal affair is hard to discern, but he obviously made a conscious choice here in favour of an activist policy. There had been for some decades a rough state of balance between the Seljuq and Ghaznavid empires, and not since the time of sultan Ibrāhīm b. Masʿūd had the smooth course of these peaceful relations been at all ruffled. But Sanjar was now erecting for himself a powerful sultanate in the east of the Iranian world, a reconstitution of part of his father Malik Shāh's extensive empire, and his dominion was to appear all the stronger when contrasted with the comparative disarray and weakness into which the western half of the Great Seljuq empire fell after the death of Muḥammad b. Malik Shāh. In Transoxania, Sanjar already had a tributary and protégé on the Qarakhanid throne in Bukhara and Samarqand, his kinsman Arslan Khan

Muḥammad b. Sulaimān (495–524/1102–30), and he could still exact obedience from his governors in Khwārazm, the Khwārazm-Shāhs of Anūshtigin Gharcha'ī's line; the prospect of bringing the Ghaznavids into this Seljuq imperial orbit as a further dependent power must have appealed strongly to Sanjar at this time.

Nevertheless, Sanjar's attitude was not one of pure aggression. He first of all wrote to Malik Arslan urging him to compromise with Bahrām Shāh, without receiving any response, according to Ibn al-Athīr; but an anecdote of 'Aufī's describes in fact how Malik Arslan sent the Qāḍī Abū l-Barakāt on a mission to Sanjar's court, laden with rich presents, in order to undermine Bahrām Shāh's position there and to deter the Seljuq sultan from providing the claimant with military assistance. Also, according to Jūzjānī and later sources like Firishta, Malik Arslan treated his own mother, the Mahd-i 'Irāq, with indignity, and this maltreatment of a high Seljuq lady naturally incensed Sanjar against him; it seems improbable, however, that Malik Arslan would have committed such an unfilial, as well as tactically unwise, action as this.[41] But the outcome of these exchanges was certainly that Sanjar resolved to aid Bahrām Shāh. On hearing about this, Malik Arslan wrote to the supreme head of the Seljuq dynasty, Muḥammad b. Malik Shāh, in western Persia, complaining of Sanjar's unfriendly attitude. Sultan Muḥammad was reluctant to interfere in the affairs of what was an old-established, generally friendly power, and ordered Sanjar to desist. According to Ḥusainī, he said, 'O my brother, do not undertake this, for the Ghaznavid house is an ancient one, so do not attack it!' Despite this, he instructed his envoy not to pursue Sanjar in order to deliver the message if the latter had already despatched an army. This was in fact the case; a force had already left Merv under the commander Unar and accompanied by Bahrām Shāh. Arriving at Bust, these troops were joined by a contingent under Sanjar's son-in-law and tributary, the Ṣaffārid amīr Tāj ad-Dīn Abū l-Faḍl Naṣr b. Khalaf or Ṭāhir (d. 559/1164).[42]

Malik Arslan's army was initially defeated by the united forces of Khurasan and Sīstān, and the survivors straggled back to Ghazna. Malik Arslan now offered a substantial tribute to Sanjar if the latter would agree to withdraw his forces, but Sanjar now prepared to come in person to eastern Afghanistan. Malik Arslan despairingly resorted to diplomacy again, and according to the later sources such as Firishta, sent his mother, the Mahd-i 'Irāq, to Sanjar with a present of 200,000 dīnārs; but once she had arrived at her brother's court, she actually incited him against Malik Arslan in favour of Bahrām Shāh. There is, however, some doubt about this story. Jūzjānī does not mention it, and Ibn al-Athīr states that Malik Arslan's ambassadress to Sanjar was the wife of Malik Arslan's uncle Naṣr b. Ibrāhīm (a Naṣr is actually mentioned amongst the sons of sultan Ibrāhīm in Jūzjānī's enumeration of these), a Seljuq princess who had been forcibly married to Sultan Masʿūd III after the latter had killed her original husband. Yet whichever of the two princesses may have been involved in the mission, the result was the same; she urged Sanjar on against Malik Arslan, on the grounds that the Ghaznavid ruler had behaved savagely to his innocent brothers. To add fuel to Sanjar's wrath, Malik Arslan seized and imprisoned one of Sanjar's own envoys to him.[43]

The decisive battle between Malik Arslan and Sanjar took place a *farsakh* outside Ghazna on the plain of Shahrābād (the Shābahār of Gardīzī and Baihaqī, used *inter alia* for the *ʿarḍ* or review of the Ghaznavid army?). The Ghaznavid army had its usual core of war elephants, 50 according to Ḥusainī and Bundārī, 120 according to Ibn al-Athīr, on top of which archers were carried, secured by chains to their beasts.[44] These elephants usually held the centre of the line, and their charge frequently struck terror into the hearts of those troops facing them. At first, the elephants terrified the Seljuq soldiers, and they broke through Sanjar's centre, wheeling round to attack his left wing. But the commander there, the amīr Tāj ad-Dīn Abū l-Faḍl, rallied his troops and halted the elephants by personally demonstrating how their soft under-bellies, unprotected by armour, could be ripped open by daggers from below. Tāj ad-Dīn's bravery in this battle became famous; he was subsequently richly rewarded by Sanjar, and his exploits were lauded by poets of the age, such as ʿAbd al-Wāsiʿ Jabalī Gharchistānī.[45] Then, after the amīr Unar had led an attack of the Seljuq right wing and had swept behind the opposing Ghaznavid left wing, the Ghaznavid army crumbled; the elephants were scattered, and their riders and archers, impotent to disentangle themselves from the beasts, were unable to escape and were slaughtered.

Sanjar now entered Ghazna on 20 Shawwāl 510/25 February 1117 in company with Bahrām Shāh. Ibn al-Athīr's account says that Malik Arslan shut himself up in the citadel of Ghazna, which was however delivered up to Sanjar without a fight. But it seems that

Malik Arslan escaped safely to the Ghaznavid territories in northern India (specifically, to Lahore, according to Ḥamdallāh Mustaufī), where he sought the aid of the governor there, Muḥammad b. ʿAlī of the Bū Ḥalīm Shaibānī family. When Sanjar made his triumphal entry into Ghazna, Bahrām Shāh had to walk in front of the mounted Seljuq sultan. He now ascended the Ghaznavid throne as sultan, but as tributary to Sanjar, his own name only coming fourth in the *khuṭba* after those of the Abbasid caliph al-Mustaẓhir, the supreme Seljuq sultan Muḥammad b. Malik Shāh and Sanjar himself; tribute was fixed at 1,000 dīnārs a day (Rāwandī) or 250,000 dīnārs a year (Ḥusainī). The boast of the poet Sayyid Ḥasan, who is said to have recited an ode before Sanjar on the occasion of Bahrām Shāh's enthronement containing the following verse,

> The herald has arisen and has proclaimed from the seven heavens, that Bahrām Shāh is the monarch of the world![46]

was thus a singularly empty one.

The Seljuq army also began an orgy of plundering in Ghazna, looting palaces of the great men, and stripping silver plates from the walls of houses and silver irrigation ducts from the gardens, until Sanjar intervened and crucified a group of looters as an example. Despite this show of disapproval, Sanjar himself during his forty days' occupation of Ghazna carried off a great amount of treasure accumulated by the Ghaznavid monarchs, amongst which is mentioned five crowns, seventeen gold and silver thrones and 1,300 settings of precious metals and jewels. This sacking of Ghazna by the Seljuq army presaged that on a more savage scale by the Ghūrid ruler ʿAlāʾ al-Dīn Ḥusain Jahān-Sūz some thirty-five years later; as Ḥusainī and Bundārī note, previous to this, Ghazna had been a virgin city, never taken from the time of the Ghaznavids' first appearance there in the later 4th/10th century. A Seljuq *ʿāmil* or tax-collector was now left there to superintend collection of the tribute, and a *fatḥ-nāma* was composed and sent to sultan Muḥammad b. Malik Shāh, who was, however, by this time in the throes of mortal illness (he died on 24 Dhū l-Ḥijja 511/18 April 1118).[47]

Malik Arslan, meanwhile, was assembling his forces in India. When Sanjar departed from Ghazna at the end of 510/spring 1117, Malik Arslan advanced on the capital with his troops. Bahrām Shāh fled without attempting any resistance northwards to the region of Bāmiyān, whence he sent to Sanjar for help once more. The latter accordingly sent an army from Balkh; Malik Arslan knew that he could not withstand the Seljuq army, and after only a month's occupation of Ghazna, withdrew from the city and took refuge in the mountains of Ūghnān (thus in Ibn al-Athīr's text; is this the modern Urgun district on the borders of the Ghazni and Pakhtiya provinces?).[48] There he was captured by a commander of Sanjar's army. Bahrām Shāh bought the prisoner from this commander, lest Malik Arslan be carried off to Khurasan and be used as a future threat to his security. Ibn al-Athīr simply says that Bahrām Shāh had Malik Arslan strangled in Jumādā II 512/September–October 1118, Malik Arslan's age at death being twenty-seven (according to Jūzjānī, 35). Later sources state that Bahrām Shāh first imprisoned Malik Arslan, then released him, but finally had him killed after he had been plotting against the sultan; yet it seems improbable that Bahrām Shāh, after so many vicissitudes during his quest for power, would ever have been so foolish as to release a proven enemy like Malik Arslan. On his death, Malik Arslan was buried in the mausoleum of his father Masʿūd III at Ghazna.[49]

3.
Bahrām Shāh's reign: the Indian summer before the Ghūrid invasion

Abū l-Muẓaffar[50] Bahrām Shāh could now enjoy undisputed power in Ghazna, and began a reign of some four decades' length, almost equalling the sultanate of his grandfather Ibrāhīm b. Masʿūd in its long duration. As befitted a monarch who reigned for so many years, we find mentioned in the sources several honorifics of his. The one in favoured use was clearly Yamīn ad-Daula wa-Amīn al-Milla, for this is frequently applied to him in the historical sources and on coins; the implied, flattering comparison of Bahrām Shāh with his great-great-grandfather Maḥmūd, who had borne these titles also,[51] was no doubt in the minds of contemporaries. The title Muʿīn (variant, Muʿizz) ad-Daula wa-d-Dīn is the principal one given to the sultan by Jūzjānī, and several later historical sources mention that of ʿAlā' ad-Daula or ʿAlā' ad-Dīn; the latter *laqab*, not known for instance on coins, is nevertheless apparently confirmed by a reference in a verse by Sayyid Ḥasan where Bahrām Shāh is described as *ʿAlā'-i Daulat u Dīn*. In a poem of ʿUthmān Mukhtārī's apparently congratulating the sultan on the suppression of the revolt in India of the general Muḥammad b. ʿAlī of the Bū Ḥalīm family (below, pp. 102–3), the sultan is addressed both as Yamīn ad-Daula and Ẓahīr al-Milla.[52]

Other insignia of royalty enjoyed by Bahrām Shāh are mentioned in various verses of his eulogists, such as his banners, black in colour and with a lion device, identical with those known to have been used by his predecessors; and Sayyid Ḥasan further refers to a crescent symbol, the *hilāl-i rāyat*, this being either a device embroidered on his banner or else a physical similitude of a crescent moon surmounting the flagstaff, and to the black *chatr* or ceremonial parasol.[53]

All these were the insignia and symbols of powerful and independent monarchs, yet Bahrām Shāh remained during the whole of his long reign, apart from one episode of refractory behaviour to be mentioned below, the vassal of Sanjar and the Seljuqs. This dependence is expressed in concrete terms on his coins. On many of Bahrām Shāh's extant issues, the sultan's own name appears on the reverse, but those of the Abbasid caliphs (al-Mustarshid, 512–29/1118–35, and al-Muqtafī, 530–55/1136–60; the short-reigned ar-Rāshid, 529–30/1135–6, is not mentioned on any extant Ghaznavid coins) on the obverse. All these are coins presumably minted at Ghazna for circulation in eastern Afghanistan; the bullion and copper coinage intended for circulation in India bears only the name of Bahrām Shāh himself, together with the usual features of Ghaznavid Indian coinage, the Bull of Nandi and the legend *Śri samanta deva* in Nagari characters.[54] Although when Sanjar's army first entered Ghazna to place Bahrām Shāh on the throne, the supreme Seljuq sultan Muḥammad b. Malik Shāh had figured in the *khuṭba*, this acknowledgement is not reflected in the extant coinage of Bahrām Shāh (little of which, if any at all, is clearly datable). In any case, sultan Muḥammad was, as we have seen above, dead only a year or so after Bahrām Shāh's accession, and Sanjar then became the supreme Seljuq sultan; he wrote in 513/1119 to all his tributaries, including Bahrām Shāh in Ghazna, that the new sultan in the western lands of the Great Seljuq empire, Maḥmūd b. Muḥammad, was to be mentioned in the *khuṭba* of the Seljuq dominions and their dependencies only after Sanjar's own name.[55]

A further possible assertion of Sanjar's overlordship may be seen in Bahrām Shāh's despatch of his eldest son Daulat Shāh as a hostage to reside at the Seljuq court, if the interpretation by Gulam Mustafa Khan of a passage in Sanā'ī's *Ḥadīqat al-ḥaqīqa* is, as seems likely, correct.[56] This requirement of a Ghaznavid prince being held hostage at Merv must date from the earlier part of Bahrām Shāh's reign, since Sanā'ī wrote these lines in 524/1130, when Daulat Shāh had already returned to Ghazna; he was subsequently slain in the fighting with the Ghūrids at Tigīnābād in 545/1150, see below, Ch. 4, p. 116.

What is also somewhat intriguing is the mention in an anecdote of the *Ādāb al-ḥarb*, concerning the illness of one of Bahrām Shāh's slave-girls and her being cured by a visiting Christian physician, of a certain Mihtar Jauhar in the sultan's retinue and described as his Atabeg. The office of Atabeg, that of tutor-guardian to a young prince unable as yet fully to exercise rule personally, was at this time developing into its classic form within the Great Seljuq sultanate and its associated amīrates, above all, in western Persia, Iraq, Syria and Anatolia; but it was totally unknown amongst the Ghaznavids and later the Ghūrids, and never really spread to these fringes of the Iranian and Indian worlds. It is unlikely that the author Fakhr-i Mudabbir, or any other Indo-Afghan source of the time, would use this more western technical term 'Atabeg' except in a fairly strict sense of the expression as known amongst the Seljuqs. Could therefore this Mihtar Jauhar be Sanjar's commander Jauhar, mentioned by Ibn al-Athīr as the confidant (*muqarrab*) of the sultan and holder of the *iqṭāʿ* of Ray, and Sanjar's envoy to Bahrām Shāh in 530/1135–6, during the abortive assertion of independence by the Ghaznavid sultan, to be described just below? If this identification is a possibility, we have the alternative explanations that Mihtar Jauhar was either the representative of the Seljuq presence at the court of Ghazna (in a rôle somewhat akin to that of the *shiḥna* or military governor, which the Great Seljuqs had installed in Baghdad at the side of the Abbasid caliphs) previous to this date, or else he was left as a watchdog in Ghazna to make sure of Bahrām Shāh's allegiance after the events of 529–30/1135–6.[57]

The drain on Ghaznavid finances caused by the tribute payable to the Seljuqs must have been serious, despite the inflow of treasure as a result of Bahrām Shāh's Indian campaigns, to be described below. In 529/1135 the sultan renounced his allegiance to Sanjar and stopped paying tribute. The latter accordingly prepared to take action, a further impelling motive being, according to the Seljuq historical sources, reports that Bahrām Shāh was oppressing his subjects and despoiling them of their wealth (could these accusations be connected with such complaints as those expressed by Sanāʾī in the verses describing acts of oppression by the Turkish soldiery of the Ghaznavids, cited above in Ch. 2, pp. 57–8?). The Seljuq army marched eastwards via Sīstān to Bust and Zamīn-Dāwar during an exceptionally cold winter, that of 530/1135–6, and suffered badly from lack of food and fodder; in the words of Ḥusainī and Bundārī, 'straw (*tibn*) was dearer than gold (*tibr*)'. Nevertheless, the army pushed on towards Ghazna, instilling fear into Bahrām Shāh's heart. He sent an envoy to meet Sanjar's representative, the amīr Jauhar mentioned above, described as governor of Ray, and offered submission, but panicked when he saw the full panoply and might of Sanjar's army, and fled towards his Indian provinces and finally to Lahore. Sanjar occupied Ghazna and his troops plundered the city for a second time. He communicated with Bahrām Shāh, and assured him that he had no intention of permanently annexing his kingdom; he then evacuated Ghazna and marched with his army back to Balkh, reaching there in Shawwāl 530/July 1136. Bahrām Shāh was thus able to return to Ghazna and resume his throne, but presumably as a tributary of the Seljuqs once more; precise information is lacking here.[58] The only other slight reference to Ghaznavid-Seljuq relations that we possess for the period before the Ghaznavid-Ghūrid fighting began, is a bare mention that the rulers of Sīstān, Ghūr, Ghazna and Māzandarān fought at Sanjar's side in his battle with the Qara Khitai at the Qaṭwān Steppe in Transoxania in 536/1141, but no further details are known of this.[59]

It is regrettable that, from the whole of Bahrām Shāh's long reign, we know virtually nothing of the raids that the sultan must surely have undertaken against the infidel Hindu princes of northern India, as indeed the *Ṭabaqāt-i Nāṣirī* affirms, though with absolutely no details.[60] Nor are the Indian sources, as opposed to the Islamic ones, any more explicit. This was an age when such great dynasties of northern and central India as the Paramāras of Mālwa, the Kalachuris of modern Madhya Pradesh, the Gāhaḍavalas of Kanauj, and others, formed a puissant barrier against Islamic expansion. One of the very few items of information that we have from this Indian dimension of the problem and coinciding with Bahrām Shāh's sultanate is that the Chāhamāna ruler of Śākambharī Arṇorāja (reigned from before 1133 till before 1153) repelled an incursion of Turushkas or Muslims who had attacked the Sapādalaksha country of eastern Rajputana by way of the great Thar Desert, killing a large number of them.[61]

What information we do possess concerning Bahrām Shāh and India relates wholly to his assertion of authority within Ghaznavid

India over Malik Arslan's commander-in-chief there, Muḥammad b. ʿAlī of the Bū Ḥalīm Shaibānī family (whence the name for him of 'Bāhalīm' which appears in some sources), who had aided Malik Arslan in his final attempt of 510/1117 to regain Ghazna. As noted above, during the civil strife over the succession, Muḥammad b. ʿAlī gave his loyalty and support to Malik Arslan, and he refused to recognise the ultimate triumph in Ghazna of Bahrām Shāh. The story of what subsequently happened between Muḥammad b. ʿAlī and Bahrām Shāh is known to us in fair detail from a long anecdote in the *Ādāb al-ḥarb*, with briefer mentions in the *Ṭabaqāt-i Nāṣirī* and later sources like Mīrkhwānd and Firishta.

There appear to have been two consecutive but distinct rebellions by Muḥammad b. ʿAlī against Bahrām Shāh's attempts to extend his authority over the Ghaznavid territories in northern India. He refused outright to recognize the new sultan's succession in Ghazna, so the latter marched into India with a substantial army, defeated Muḥammad b. ʿAlī in battle and captured him at Lahore on 27 Ramaḍān 512/11 January 1119. Acknowledging, however, Muḥammad b. ʿAlī's pre-eminence as a military commander and his unrivalled experience of conditions in India, the sultan pardoned him and reinstated him as governor.[62]

Yet once Bahrām Shāh had returned to Ghazna, Muḥammad b. ʿAlī, his son Muʿtaṣim (who is described as a mighty warrior, able to wield an iron mace of 40 *mans*' weight) and their followers rose once more against the central government. The rebel leader built a fortress at Nāgōr, in the neighbourhood of Bhīra in the Siwālik Hills region. He gathered there what Firishta enumerates as an army of Arabs, Persians, Afghans and Khalaj, and also enlisted the military support of what Fakhr-i Mudabbir describes as various dependent Indian potentates, 'Rānas, Thakkurs and leading princes of Hindustan', until he had an army of 70,000 men, Muslims and Hindus. In 513/1119 Bahrām Shāh again marched down to the Indus valley with 10,000 men, and proceeded towards Multān for an engagement with the rebel army. Muḥammad and his son Muʿtaṣim chose the terrain for this, a marshy district near a village called Kīkyūr (?), which they then partly flooded in order to create a morass and thus place the sultan's army at a tactical disadvantage. Gulam Mustafa Khan quotes Maulānā Abū Ẓafar Nadwī that this swamp must have been created near Multān, at the confluence of the Sutlej and Jhelum (read Chenab?) rivers, or near Ucch at Ghaghar, and also cites a divergent view of Miss Iqbal Shafi; but these can only be guesses, in the absence of more specific topographical information from Fakhr-i Mudabbir. Bahrām Shāh summoned Muḥammad b. ʿAlī to obedience once again, recounting the past services which his father and other members of the Shaibānī family had rendered to the Ghaznavid cause in India, and offering him a robe of honour and the fresh grant of the governorship and command in India, if only he would renounce his rebellious posture.

Yet this démarche elicited no response. From an ode by Sayyid Ḥasan, it appears that Bahrām Shāh and his army crossed the Indus in long boats, and the two armies clashed in some marshy terrain of the western Panjab. Muḥammad b. ʿAlī's attack on the sultan's centre was halted, and he himself killed; a violent storm arose, aiding the sultan's forces by whipping up the waters in the faces of the rebel army, so that much of it was swallowed up in the morass. As well as Muḥammad b. ʿAlī himself, varying numbers of his sons are reported to have been killed (seventeen according to Fakhr-i Mudabbir, ten according to Jūzjānī; but Sanā'ī, in a passage of the *Ḥadīqat al-ḥaqīqa* praising Bahrām Shāh's victory here, alludes to the death of only one son, presumably Muʿtaṣim). One of Muḥammad b. ʿAlī's sons is said to have gone over to the sultan's side, thus saving himself, and Fakhr-i Mudabbir notes that the S.y.w.r.riyān (Shaibāniyān?) of his own time were the descendants of this son Ibrāhīm. He further observes that whenever anyone digs out an irrigation canal or well in this spot, he finds the decayed remains of armour and weapons, and skeletons of men and horses. Sayyid Ḥasan accompanied Bahrām Shāh's army for the expedition, and in various poems refers to incidents connected with it; one poem, actually written in India, mentions the season of autumn, thus placing these events in the autumn of the year, some eight or nine months after Bahrām Shāh's first Indian expedition.[63]

According to Firishta, the sultan then appointed Sālār Ḥusain b. Ibrāhīm ʿAlawī as governor in India, and returned to Ghazna.[64] It seems that the son of this Sālār Ḥusain, [Abū Sahl?] ʿAlī, also held high command in India subsequently under Bahrām Shāh, for Sayyid Ḥasan has a eulogy addressed to 'the Sipahsālār ʿAlī-yi al-Ḥusain Māhūrī',[65] and he commanded the Indian troops of the Ghaznavid army during Bahrām Shāh's battle with the Ghūrid Saif ad-Dīn Sūrī in 544/1149, since Sayyid Ḥasan again states in an ode celebrating the sultan's victory,

Around the Shah, contingent upon contingent of the armies of Hindustan, so that you would say that golden particles of dust had clustered round the disc of the sun from the place of sunrise.

The commander of the *ghāzīs* from amongst them was ʿAlī-yi Bū Sahl [read thus, with Gulam Mustafa Khan's manuscript, for the *bud pīl* of Riḍawī's text], to whom the Sultan's power and fortune had given the body of Rustam and the brave heart of Ḥaidar [sc. ʿAlī b. Abī Ṭālib].[66]

Ibn al-Athīr's account of this phase of the Ghaznavid-Ghūrid hostilities (see below, Ch. 4, p. 114) names the Sālār al-Ḥasan b. Ibrāhīm ʿAlawī as the Ghaznavid commander in India whose troops Bahrām Shāh summoned to his aid against the Ghūrids. In this confusion over personages, the exactly contemporary source of Sayyid Ḥasan is obviously to be preferred. If we restore the complete name of the Ghaznavid commander in India at this time as '[Abū Sahl] ʿAlī b. Ḥasan b. Ibrāhīm ʿAlawī', it becomes easy to see how Ibn al-Athīr's source could have confused the son with the father.

At a later point in Bahrām Shāh's sultanate, we find as his governor in India Abū Muḥammad Ḥasan b. Abī Naṣr Manṣūr Qā'inī, at the side of the monarch's eldest son Jalāl ad-Daula Daulat Shāh, who held command of the Indian troops there; the evidence for this comes from one of Sayyid Ḥasan's poems addressed to prince Daulat Shāh and mentioning 'Muḥammad-i Manṣūr' as his right-hand man. Despite the difference in *nisbas*, 'Qā'inī' and 'Maimandī' (relating to two widely-separated places, Qā'in in Qūhistān and Maimand in Zābulistān), Gulam Mustafa Khan has collected a number of references to Abū Muḥammad Ḥasan Qā'inī in the verses of Masʿūd-i Saʿd-i Salmān, demonstrating clearly that this official and his father Abū Naṣr Manṣūr b. Saʿīd were from the stock of the great vizier Aḥmad b. Ḥasan Maimandī, including such lines as

Khwāja Manṣūr b. Saʿīd, who brought to life once more the traditions of Aḥmad b. Ḥasan.

and

I implore you, deliver the message which I entrust to you, from this sorrowing, heart-constricted slave,

To the crown of all nobles of the royal presence, Khwāja-yi ʿAmīd Ṣāḥib Maimandī

Manṣūr b. Saʿīd, who is a sovereign lord, whose charisma gives a freshness of sovereignty itself.[67]

The father ʿImād ad-Dīn Abū Naṣr Manṣūr b. Saʿīd was an exalted personage in the Ghaznavid administration, having served as ʿ*Āriḍ* or War Minister under Ibrāhīm b. Masʿūd and possibly under Masʿūd III, in whose reign he died, see above, Ch. 2, p. 73.

Concerning Bahrām Shāh's viziers, the sultan inherited at the outset of his reign the wise and long-experienced ʿAbd al-Ḥamīd b. Aḥmad b. ʿAbd aṣ-Ṣamad, but the latter, doubtless too closely identified with the preceding régimes, was speedily killed off by the sultan (see above, Ch. 2, p. 72). The new incumbent of the vizierate was one Aḥmad b. Ḥusain, known from some lines of Masʿūd-i Saʿd-i Salmān,

> Since in every project, Aḥmad has displayed the verve and efficiency of Bahrām, the sultan has chosen him for the high office of the vizierate.
>
> In his able hands, from that pen whose movement is like the decisive actions of Bahrām, the good and the evil of friends and foes have become apparent.
>
> As for this office of vizier, the nature of whose sword is like that of Mars (*Bahrāmī*), its sphere of life has become joyful through taking up the brisk activity of your service.

He probably did not hold the office for long, since no eulogies of him by such poets as Sayyid Ḥasan or Sanā'ī seem to have survived.[68]

There is much uncertainty about the holders of the vizierate for the rest of Bahrām Shāh's reign; we have no mentions of them in the biographical works nor in the histories, and depend upon odd scraps of information in the works of contemporary poets and the inferences to be drawn from these scraps. Gulam Mustafa Khan gives as the successors of Aḥmad b. Ḥusain, firstly Muntakhab al-Mulk Qiwām ad-Dīn Majd al-Mulk Abū ʿAlī Ḥasan b. Aḥmad, to whom Sayyid Ḥasan addressed fulsome eulogies, one of which places the following words in Qiwām ad-Dīn Ḥasan's mouth,

> Praise be to God, that for the interests of this kingdom, I am a remembrance and inheritor of two viziers!

Secondly, he gives his son Najīb al-Mulk Ḥusain b. Ḥasan as vizier during Bahrām Shāh's last years, after his return from India to the throne in Ghazna following the sacking of the capital by ʿAlā' ad-Dīn Ḥusain Jahān-Sūz.[69]

These two were certainly highly-placed dignitaries of the Ghaznavid administration, close in the sultan's confidence and employed by him for the highest civil and military duties. A poem of Sayyid

Ḥasan's refers to the events of 543–4/1148–9, when the Ghūrid Saif ad-Dīn Sūrī temporarily occupied Ghazna, and records the return of both Bahrām Shāh and 'the sun of the kingdom Ḥasan-i Aḥmad'. Najīb al-Mulk Ḥusain was the commander of some military expedition of the sultan's closing years, since a *tarjīʿ-band* of the same poet refers to his victorious return from 'the western land' (*zi bākhtar*), conceivably a counter-raid into Ghūr or northern Afghanistan made whilst ʿAlāʾ ad-Dīn Ḥusain was being held captive by Sanjar.[70]

However, there is nothing specific in these citations from Sayyid Ḥasan showing categorically that these two men were actually viziers, even if Qiwām ad-Dīn Ḥasan could be described as the descendant of earlier viziers and despite the fact that the poet addressed to both of them a considerable number of *qaṣīda*s and *tarjīʿ-band*s. Sayyid Ḥasan equally eulogised Qiwām ad-Dīn Ḥasan's father Qiwām al-Mulk Aḥmad b. ʿUmar (not Aḥmad b. Ḥusain, the shadowy vizier of the early part of Bahrām Shāh's reign, mentioned above), described as *khāzin* or treasurer to the sultan; one of the poems dedicated to him was written specifically to congratulate him on being granted this office.[71] This gives a clue to the office that members of the family held in succession during these decades, that of treasurer and overseers of the royal properties and palaces (the privy treasury, *khazīna-yi khāṣṣ*). In these numerous poems by Sayyid Ḥasan, the son and grandson are described not as viziers, but are frequently accorded the designation of *khāṣṣ* 'courtier, intimate companion of the ruler', as in the refrain of one *tarjīʿ-band*,

> Master Ḥasan b. Aḥmad-i Khāṣṣ,
> That quintessence of the alchemy of sincere friendship.[72]

The persons to whom Sayyid Ḥasan does distinctly refer as being viziers are, rather, the Khwāja ʿAmīd Jamāl ad-Dīn Rashīd ad-Din Abū Ṭāhir Muḥammad (four poems) and Qiwām ad-Dīn Abū Muḥammad Ṭāhir (one poem). It looks at first sight as if a confusion of names and patronymics is involved here, and that possibly only one person is intended; yet internal evidence of the poems shows plainly that it is a question of two distinct people. Thus in one *tarjīʿ-band* we have the refrain,

> The one who is as clearly distinguishable as the moon from the stars,
> His patronymic is Bū Ṭāhir, and he is the pure one [*ṭāhir*].

and in an ode we have

> The mainstay of the state and of the faith [*qiwām-i daulat u dīn*] Bū Muḥammad-i Ṭāhir, from whom both religion and government have acquired adornment and splendour.[73]

Whatever the relative chronology of the periods of office concerned, it appears that Abū Ṭāhir Muḥammad at least was vizier at the time of the first Ghūrid occupation of Ghazna, for Sayyid Ḥasan's lengthy and sonorous ode celebrating Bahrām Shāh's re-occupation of his capital, after retailing the exploits of the sultan's three sons Samā' ad-Daula Masʿūd, Muʿizz ad-Daula Khusrau Shāh and Muʿīn ad-Daula Shāhanshāh, and before going on to record the heroic rôle of the commander-in-chief of the Indian troops, Sālār ʿAlī b. Ḥusain (see above, p. 103 and below, Ch. 4, p. 114), says

> The learned and just vizier, the perfect and auspicious mediator, as can be seen from both of these designations and names of the Prophet [sc. *Ṭāhir* 'the Pure One' and *Muḥammad*].[74]

Although his sultanate was latterly clouded by the menace of the Ghūrids, and although he bequeathed to his two successors what was only a simulacrum of the once-mighty Ghaznavid empire, Bahrām Shāh's reign was notable for a florescence within it of Persian literature, comparable to that of the first Ghaznavid period with its outpouring of lyric poetry and epic, and the sultan's court formed the natural focus of this blossoming. The poets of a slightly older generation, ʿUthmān Mukhtārī, Masʿūd-i Saʿd-i Salmān and Sanā'ī, were active in the early part of the reign only. The date of ʿUthmān Mukhtārī's death is unknown, but he only addressed two major *qaṣīda*s to Bahrām Shāh, compared with a large number written for his predecessor Malik Arslan, so that the inference is that he died early in the new reign, or chose to remain silent, or migrated from Ghaznavid territory soon after the death of his patron Malik Arslan. Masʿūd-i Saʿd died in 515/1121–2, and after a life full of vicissitudes, enjoyed the favour and largesse of Bahrām Shāh for the last three or four years of his life, to the point that he could address the new sultan soon after the latter's accession,

> No-one has such rank or position or degree or such flourishing affairs as I, your servant, enjoy today.
>
> At every court session, your servant receives from your thoughtfulness some fresh act of favour; not a week passes without a gift from you of 100,000 [dirhams]![75]

Abū l-Majd Majdūd b. Ādam Sanā'ī, the first of the three great writers of mystical *mathnawī* poems in mediaeval Persia (his later compeers being Farīd ad-Dīn ʿAṭṭār and Jalāl ad-Dīn Rūmī), probably died in 525/1131 or a decade later in 535/1141,[76] after having undergone, so the literary biographers state, a spiritual conversion to Ṣūfī mysticism from the worldly rôle of court poet. It was in his old age that he completed his lengthy and discursive *mathnawī* on morality and ethics, the *Ḥadīqat al-ḥaqīqa*, dedicating it to Bahrām Shāh in 525/1131. Whatever the literary merits of the poem—and E. G. Browne's condemnatory opinion was that it was as inferior to Rūmī's *Mathnawī* as Robert Montgomery's *Satan* was to Milton's *Paradise Lost*—it became widely read and had a great influence on the subsequent development of Persian mystical poetry. Sanā'ī was perhaps more effective as a panegyric poet in the mould of the early Ghaznavid masters and of Masʿūd-i Saʿd-i Salmān, as may be seen in the numerous odes that, despite his turning towards the Ṣūfī path, he nevertheless addressed to the sultan.[77]

The great period of poetic activity by Ashraf ad-Dīn Abū Muḥammad Sayyid Ḥasan b. Muḥammad Ghaznavī falls within Bahrām Shāh's reign, and it was under his patronage that his poetic genius flowered in both the fields of *qaṣīda* and of *ghazal*, in the development of which latter genre his *Dīwān* is especially important. The later Indo-Persian *tadhkira*s relate how, towards the end of his life, in *ca.* 545/1150, the intrigues of the poet's enviers brought down on him the sultan's displeasure and he had to leave Ghazna. The real reason seems to have been that Sayyid Ḥasan had stayed in Ghazna during the Ghūrid chief Saif ad-Dīn Sūrī's occupation of the city, and may well have been ready to accommodate himself to the new régime there, which could have appeared as a permanency. When, however, Bahrām Shāh regained his throne, Sayyid Ḥasan deemed it prudent to depart in 544/1149–50 for Nīshāpūr, and it was from there that he addressed to the sultan poems of apology and also the long ode celebrating Bahrām Shāh's ultimate victory over and killing of Sūrī. From Nīshāpūr he made the Pilgrimage to Mecca and Medina, and then spent the rest of his days in Baghdad, western Persia and Khurasan, at the courts of various Seljuq rulers like sultans Masʿūd b. Muḥammad, Sanjar and Sulaimān Shāh b. Muḥammad, of the Khwārazm-Shāh Atsïz and of the Qarakhanid ruler in Khurasan, Maḥmūd Khan b. Muḥammad. He died in the district of Juwain in northern Khurasan, probably at some point between 555/1160 and 557/1162.[78]

After these poets, the most notable literary figure of Bahrām

Shāh's court was undoubtedly Abū l-Ma'ālī Naṣrallāh or Naṣr b. Muḥammad b. 'Abd al-Ḥamīd, son of the vizier of Ibrāhīm and Mas'ūd III (see above, p. 72) and *mamdūḥ* of 'Uthmān Mukhtārī and Sayyid Ḥasan. Abū l-Ma'ālī Naṣrallāh's great service to Persian letters consists in his elegant Persian prose version of the collection of animal fables, *The fables of Bidpai*, which had been translated into Arabic as *Kalīla wa-Dimna* by Ibn al-Muqaffa' from a Middle Persian version of the Indian original. It was dedicated to Bahrām Shāh and completed in *ca.* 538–9/1143–5; the popularity of this version led to numerous remodellings of the text over the years, so that it is difficult to discern Abū l-Ma'ālī Naṣrallāh's own hand in it, but it was not until the 10th/16th century that a need was felt for a new, more florid version, leading to Ḥusain Wā'iẓ Kāshifī's *Anwār-i Suhailī*. Abū l-Ma'ālī Naṣrallāh was as much statesman as littérateur, as befitted the representative of a line of viziers and secretaries, and under Khusrau Shāh himself served as vizier (see below, Ch. 4, p. 127).[79]

A lengthy list of other competent poets who thronged Bahrām Shāh's court could be compiled, most of whose verses are known only from citations in the biographical notices of the *tadhkirat ash-shu'arā'* literature. They include the Sayyid ash-Shu'arā' 'Leader of the poets' Abū Bakr b. Muḥammad Rūḥānī of Ghazna, called by 'Aufī 'the second planet Mercury', author of a long *Saugand-nāma* of eighty-three verses, written in the last years of Bahrām Shāh's reign and fortunately preserved; it is of historical value from its many references to other contemporary writers and important figures of state.[80] Jamāl ad-Dīn Muḥammad and Ḥasan were sons of Nāṣir-i 'Alawī, and like their father, poets. Ḥasan died young, and Mas'ūd-i Sa'd Salmān wrote an elegy on his death,[81] but Muḥammad, from being the panegyrist of Mas'ūd III, lived on to become a prolific eulogist of Bahrām Shāh; 'Aufī accords the two brothers Muḥammad and Ḥasan the grandiloquent titles of Akmal ash-Shu'arā' 'Most consummate of poets' and Fakhr as-Sāda 'Splendour of the leaders' respectively.[82] Shihāb ad-Dīn Abū r-Rajā' (Abū r-Riḍā?) Shāh 'Alī Ghaznavī wrote several poems in praise of Bahrām Shāh, but lived on till the very end of the Ghaznavids and the heyday of the Ghūrids.[83] Fakhr al-Milla wa-d-Dīn Muḥammad b. Maḥmūd Nīshāpūrī was an interesting and versatile figure at the sultan's court, the author of several works known only by their titles, including a commentary, the *Baṣā'ir-i Yamīnī* (thus called either because of its dedication to Yamīn ad-Daula Bahrām Shāh, or because it was a commentary on ʿUtbī's *Yamīnī?*); a *Ra'y-ārāy*, the Persian translation of the *Ghurar-i siyar* (presumably Thaʿālibī's history, the *Ta'rīkh Ghurar as-siyar*); and a *Ṣaḥīfat al-iqbāl*, described as a literary contest (*muʿāraḍa*) between the sword and the pen. He played a diplomatic rôle on Bahrām Shāh's behalf in 530/1136, when the sultan made his unsuccessful bid to throw off his vassal relationship to Sanjar (above, pp. 100–1); Bahrām Shāh sent him to Sanjar's camp at Tigīnābād in order to convey his submission to the Seljuq sultan, which he achieved by reciting a well-turned poetic quatrain to Sanjar.[84] Muḥammad b. ʿUthmān ʿUtbī Yamīnī the secretary and Saʿd ad-Dīn Mukhtār ash-Shuʿarā' 'Chosen one of the poets' Masʿūd Nā'ukī were also eulogists of Bahrām Shāh, and ʿAufī quotes a fair amount of their poetry, without, however, giving any biographical details.[85] Finally, this same author enumerates various other contemporary poets from the fringes of the Indo-Persian world, with brief specimens of their verses, including authors stemming from Lahore, Bust or Tigīnābād, Sakāwand and Ghazna, whose connection with Bahrām Shāh's court circle is unfortunately not made explicit by him.[86]

FOUR

The Struggle with the Ghūrids and the last Ghaznavid Sultans

1.

The Ghūrid onslaught and Bahrām Shāh's last years

The decline and fall of the once-mighty Ghaznavid empire is poorly documented. Thrown back by Bahram Shāh's reign essentially upon what is now eastern Afghanistan, the Panjab and probably Sind and Baluchistan, its affairs ceased much to interest the general and dynastic historians writing in the central Islamic lands; these last were more concerned with such pressing questions as the break-up of the Great Seljuq empire, the formation of the Atabeg principalities and the menaces from Central Asia of the Qara Khitai and the Khwārazm-Shāhs. Accordingly, we depend basically on the accounts of Ibn al-Athīr, representing the historiography of the central Islamic lands, and of Minhāj ad-Dīn b. Sirāj ad-Dīn Jūzjānī, representing that of Afghanistan and northern India.

As noted above in Ch. 2, pp. 61–2, Ibn al-Athīr had difficulty in acquiring reliable information on events which took place on the far eastern fringes of the Iranian world and in India. For events in Khurasan in the 6th/12th century, such as the rise of the Khwārazm-Shāhs of the line of Anūshtigin Gharcha'ī, Sanjar's misadventures with the Oghuz, and the imperialist operations in Khurasan and towards the Caspian Sea of the Ghūrid sultans, he depended *inter alia* upon a work by the local historian of Baihaq in Khurasan, Abū l-Ḥasan ʿAlī b. Zaid Baihaqī, called, after his grandfather, Ibn Funduq (d. 565/1169–70). Ibn Funduq was a careful and accurate historian who enjoyed considerable contemporary fame and whose work was quoted by Yāqūt, Ibn Khallikān, Juwainī and Ḥamdallāh Mustaufī, as well as by Ibn al-Athīr.[1] The latter quotes Ibn Funduq's *Mashārib at-tajārib wa-ghāwārib al-gharā'ib* explicitly *sub anno* 568/1172–3 for the internecine disputes of members of the Khwārazm-

Shāh family in Khurasan, which may mean, as Barthold observed, that for events in the years immediately before 568/1172–3, Ibn al-Athīr possibly had a continuation of the *Mashārib at-tajārib* to hand. Ibn Funduq's own history—which is no longer extant but which apparently covered the history of the Iranian world from the time when ʿUtbī's *Yamīnī* left off, sc. from *ca.* 411/1020 onwards—could clearly have provided Ibn al-Athīr with information about such decisive steps in the decline of Ghaznavid authority as the Ghūrid ʿAlāʾ ad-Dīn Ḥusain's sack of Ghazna in 545/1150 and the seizure of Ghazna by the Oghuz some years later; and Ibn Funduq's putative continuator could equally have provided material on the deposition of Khusrau Malik by Shihāb ad-Dīn Muḥammad Ghūrī and the ending of the dynasty in 582/1186.[2]

Ibn al-Athīr himself was fully aware of the handicaps under which he laboured here. His chronology of events in the Ghūrid-Ghaznavid warfare is uncertain and his accounts are repetitious, and he confesses after his account of ʿAlāʾ ad-Dīn Ḥusain's sacking (recounted under the year 547/1152–3, after an account has already been given under 544/1149–50) that 'The history of the Ghūrids has already been given under the year 543 [read 544], and there is concerning that disagreement over certain matters with the account now given here; but we have heard all this by word of mouth or have read it in their books [*wa-kullan samiʿnāhu wa-raʾaināhu fī muṣannafātihim*—but in whose books?], and because of it, we have set down both versions'. He goes on to complete this entry by recounting Shihāb ad-Dīn Muḥammad's final capture of Khusrau Malik, on the authority of 'a certain worthy scholar [or 'certain worthy scholars'] of Khurasan', *baʿḍ fuḍalāʾ Khurāsān*, possibly the putative continuator of Ibn Funduq, whilst noting divergent pieces of information on these events.[3]

Jūzjānī was a local historian from northern Afghanistan—as his *nisba* implies, his family hailed from Gūzgān, the mountainous region lying between the upper Heri Rud and Balkh—and he had actually been born in the royal palace of the Ghūrids in their capital of Fīrūzkūh in Ghūr. He migrated in 624/1227 to Ucch in India and then to Delhi, writing there his *Ṭabaqāt-i Nāṣirī* in 658–9/1259–60 and thus constituting himself the dynastic historian of the Ghūrids and their Turkish slave commander successors in India.[4] Hence, when he was dealing with the decline of the Ghaznavids, he was writing about events at approximately a century's remove, and although he claimed descent from the Ghaznavid royal house through the marriage of a daughter of sultan Ibrāhīm b. Mas'ūd to one of his ancestors, he inevitably wrote from the standpoint of the Ghūrid victors. To cite one or two instances, Jūzjānī glosses over the treacherous behaviour of Ghiyāth ad-Dīn Muḥammad Ghūrī towards Khusrau Malik, and he suggests a certain justification for the Ghūrid supersession of the Ghaznavid remnants in the Panjab in that Khusrau Malik is said to have been addicted to pleasure and merrymaking, thus allowing both the Turkish soldiery and the indigenous Perso-Indian official classes to seize the substance of power.[5]

The Ghaznavid-Ghūrid hostility stemmed from the expansion of the Shansabānī line of minor chieftains in Ghūr to a position of primacy within that region. There then followed their dynamic outpouring into the lands of higher culture and of superior economic resources to the west of Ghūr, where they clashed first with the Seljuqs and then with the Khwārazm-Shāhs, and also their expansion southeastwards, where they came up against the Ghaznavids (for the relations of the Ghaznavids and Ghūrids during Ibrāhīm b. Mas'ūd's reign, see above, Ch. 2, pp. 68–9). Both Ghūr and Ghazna itself had in the first decades of the 6th / 12th century come more and more within the Seljuq sultan Sanjar's sphere of influence, but Bahrām Shāh of Ghazna nevertheless endeavoured to strengthen his house's traditional suzerainty over the Ghūr hill country. He allegedly had the Ghūrid chief Quṭb ad-Dīn Muḥammad b. Ḥusain of Warshād, the self-styled Malik al-Jabal 'King of the mountains', poisoned at the court of Ghazna, even though he was the sultan's own son-in-law; however, Ibn al-Athīr, and authors following him like Firishta, say that it was believed that Quṭb ad-Dīn Muḥammad and his brother Saif ad-Dīn Sūrī of Istiya had only come to Ghazna in order to reconnoitre the position for a future attack on the city.[6]

Be this as it may, the Ghūrid family naturally thirsted for vengeance against Bahrām Shāh, and Saif ad-Dīn Sūrī, who had escaped back to Ghūr, collected an army of cavalry and infantry (since the Ghūrī mountaineers were themselves predominantly foot-soldiers, this may imply that the Shansabānīs were already beginning to recruit or purchase free mercenary cavalrymen or Turkish *mamlūks* in order to further their expansionist aims). With his younger brothers Bahā' ad-Dīn Sām of Sanga and 'Alā' ad-Dīn Ḥusain of Wajīristān, he then marched on Ghazna. The town fell to them in Jumādā I 543/September-October 1148, the first major success of

Ghūrid arms. Bahrām Shāh had meanwhile fled to the Indo-Afghan borderlands, to a place named by Ibn al-Athīr as a spot between Ghazna and India, inhabited by Afghans (i.e. Pathans) and called K.r.mān (read Kurramān = Kurram, in the North-Western Frontier region of modern Pakistan?).[7]

We have a detailed account of the subsequent events in Jūzjānī, which can be supplemented by a briefer notice in Ibn al-Athīr and, more important, by details gleaned from the long *qaṣīda*, amounting to ninety-four verses, which Sayyid Ḥasan addressed to Bahrām Shāh in congratulation for his victory over the Ghūrids; these details have been adduced and elucidated by Gulam Mustafa Khan in his monograph *A history of Bahrām Shāh of Ghaznīn*. Saif ad-Dīn Sūrī assumed power in Ghazna, assuming the title of Sultan and appointing his brother Bahā' ad-Dīn Sām as ruler back in Ghūr. Other younger Ghūrid brothers were sent back home, as were most of the Ghūrī troops as the winter of 543/1148–9 approached, and Saif ad-Dīn Sūrī kept at his side only a small body of personal retainers, depending substantially on the local officials and garrison troops left behind in Ghazna when Bahrām Shāh had ignominiously fled. A local *sayyid*, one Majd ad-Dīn Mūsāwī (Ibn al-Athīr, 'al-Māhiyānī') seems to have led the collaborationist elements and to have acted as Sūrī's vizier, an honour for which he was later to pay dearly. However, Sūrī had misjudged the temper of the official and military classes in Ghazna, just as the usurper Toghrïl had done a century before (see above, Ch. 1, pp. 45–6). Bahrām Shāh had been gathering an army from the Panjab, under the command of the governor of Ghaznavid India, the Sālār ʿAlī b. Ḥusain b. Ibrāhīm ʿAlawī (according to Ibn al-Athīr, 'the Sālār al-Ḥasan b. Ibrāhīm al-ʿAlawī').[8] Bahrām Shāh received intelligence of Sūrī's uncertain support, and taking advantage of the deep snows which cut off the possibility of reinforcements for Sūrī from Ghūr, he marched back to Ghazna via Kabul. Sūrī and his small band of retainers fled towards Ghūr, but were overtaken by the Ghaznavid force at a place called Sang-i Sūrākh ('The perforated stone') on the upper reaches of the Helmand, and both Sūrī and Majd ad-Dīn Mūsawī were captured after a battle. According to Sayyid Ḥasan's poem, vv. 70–3, Bahrām Shāh was in the centre of the Ghaznavid army and his sons Samā' ad-Daula Masʿūd,[9] Muʿizz ad-Daula Khusrau Shāh, and Muʿīn ad-Daula Shāhanshāh each commanded contingents; the poet also fixes the date of the battle exactly as 2 Muḥarram 544/12

May 1149 (chronogram in v. 68). Sūrī and Mūsawī were brought back to Ghazna, paraded through the streets on cows or asses, dishonoured in various other ways and then crucified at the Pul-i Yak Ṭāq that is 'the One-arched bridge'; according to the second of Ibn al-Athīr's accounts of these events, it was the Alids of Ghazna who took charge of the humiliation of Sūrī. Sūrī's head was subsequently sent by Bahrām Shāh to sultan Sanjar at Ray, an event celebrated in a quatrain by Sanjar's poet Fakhr ad-Dīn Khālid Harātī.[10]

It was this episode of Saif ad-Dīn Sūrī's dishonouring and death that directly provoked the punitive expedition against Ghazna of 'Alā' ad-Dīn Ḥusain, the campaign that dealt Ghazna a mortal blow as an imperial capital and as a seat of culture for the eastern Islamic world.

There is considerable confusion in the sources over the date of 'Alā' ad-Dīn Ḥusain's expedition, and even the name of the Ghaznavid sovereign with whom he fought. Jūzjānī states clearly, and must be correct here, that the fighting was between 'Alā' ad-Dīn Ḥusain and Bahrām Shāh, and some verses placed by him in the mouth of the victorious Ghūrid explicitly boast that

> ﷺ When, out of hatred for me, Bahrām Shāh bent his bow, I plucked with my lance the quiver from his belt.

Unfortunately, Jūzjānī is vague over dates here. Ibn al-Athīr gives his account in the ensemble of Ghūrid-Ghaznavid relations under the year 547/1152–3, and places 'Alā' ad-Dīn's expedition in 550/1155, in the opening years of Khusrau Shāh's reign. As will be seen later, this may relate to a subsequent raid against Ghazna by this same Ghūrid ruler in the time of Khusrau Shāh (sc. between 547/1152 and 555/1160), confused by Ibn al-Athīr or his source with the catastrophe which had earlier befallen Ghazna. The variant accounts of later sources, with their many confusions, are set forth by Raverty in his notes, observing that 'Of all the persons mentioned in Oriental history, greater discrepancy occurs with respect to 'Alā-ud-Dīn, Jahān-soz's name and proceedings, probably, than regarding any other man'. Raverty's conclusion, after considering five separate and differing accounts, was that 'Alā' ad-Dīn's expedition must be placed at the end of 544/1150 or the beginning of 545/1150, if only on the grounds that the Ghūrid ruler would be unlikely to have waited several years before avenging his brothers, and that the Ghazna expedition fits in with his subsequent attack on the Seljuq position at Herat, when he was defeated by Sanjar and imprisoned for the next two years.[11] Raverty's reasoning was good, except that he placed this last event too early in time, sc. in the year 545/1150–1. Gulam Mustafa Khan follows this analysis on the whole, placing the attack on Ghazna in 545/1150, but pointing out that we have a firm date for 'Alā' ad-Dīn Ḥusain's attack on Herat and defeat at Nāb, 547/1152, the date given by Niẓāmī 'Arūḍī Samarqandī, who was himself with the Ghūrid forces at that battle.[12]

The actual course of events in the fighting between 'Alā' ad-Dīn Ḥusain and Bahrām Shāh is given in great detail by Jūzjānī, concerned as he was to magnify the exploits of the dynasty in whose milieu he had been nurtured. The Ghūrid leader took over the command of an expedition prepared in Ghūr by his brother Bahā' ad-Dīn Sām, who died at this juncture, and marched southwards into Zamīn-Dāwar, presumably intending to march thence up the Tarnak valley (the route of the modern Kabul-Ghazni-Kandahar highway) to Ghazna. Bahrām Shāh marched southwards also to intercept 'Alā' ad-Dīn Ḥusain with an army which included numerous cavalrymen and a force of elephants (numbered at 200 by Daulat Shāh), and on the evidence of a line of verse said to have been uttered by the Ghūrid leader, with contingents from the Indian vassal princes of the Ghaznavids:

> ❧ The support of my enemy, even though they were all Rā'īs and Rānās, I smashed to atoms with my mace the heads of those Rā'īs and Rānās.[13]

The armies met near Tigīnābād.[14] Against the Ghaznavid elephants and cavalrymen, 'Alā' ad-Dīn Ḥusain's Ghūrī infantrymen employed the tactic of the *kāṛwah*, a framework of bullock-hide stuffed with cotton which could be massed into a wall-like battle line, affording protection against an enemy charge or enemy arrows.[15] The two champions (*pahlavānān*) of the Ghūrid army, the Kharmīl Sām-i Ḥusain and the Kharmīl Sām-i Banjī,[16] led the attack on the Ghaznavid elephants, getting beneath them and ripping open the soft underbellies, unprotected by their armour. Bahrām Shāh's son Jalāl ad-Daula Abu l-Fatḥ Daulat Shāh—who is also known as the *mamdūḥ* of Sayyid Ḥasan[17]—was inveigled, with his detachment of cavalry and an elephant, into a Cannae-like envelopment position and the whole force wiped out. Bahrām Shāh's army crumbled after this. It rallied to fight at a hot spring, Jūsh-i Āb-i Garm, near Tigīnābād, but was defeated, and withdrew in disorder to Ghazna. Bahrām Shāh halted to fight outside Ghazna itself, having collected reinforcements from the town's garrison and a body on infantry, but was defeated a third time, and fled in despair towards India.[18]

The frightful seven days' plundering of Ghazna, which gave to 'Alā' ad-Dīn Ḥusain his sobriquet of 'the World-Incendiary', *Jahān-sūz*, now followed. The exact scale of the accompanying massacres of the menfolk, with enslavement of women and children, cannot easily be ascertained from the hyperbole of the sources, but Jūzjānī, who had no cause to over-paint the frightfulness of the Ghūrid ruler, states that 'In these seven days, there was rapine, plundering, killing and overbearing behaviour', and an anecdote given by Fakhr-i Mudabbir concerning the event gives the number of slain at over 60,000. All the tombs of the Ghaznavid sultans, with the exceptions of those of Maḥmūd, Mas'ūd and Ibrāhīm, were broken into and the remains exhumed and burnt. The corpses of the two martyred Ghūrids, Quṭb ad-Dīn Muḥammad and Saif ad-Dīn Sūrī, were on the other hand taken out of their mausolea, the whole Ghūrid army observed seven days and nights of mourning, and the two corpses were carried back on biers to Ghūr for a ceremonial funeral in the ancestral graveyard of the Shansabānī family.[19] Many of the splendid buildings, mosques, madrasas and palaces erected by successive generations of the Ghaznavids and adorned with the spoils of India must have been destroyed now, as did certainly some of the contents of the rich libraries of Ghazna built up in the times of Maḥmūd and Mas'ūd, when collections from Khurasan, Khwārazm and Jibāl were brought to the capital, sometimes accompanied by the scholars who had amassed them. Thus it was in the course of these vandalistic orgies that the library of the philosopher and physician Ibn Sīnā, brought from Isfahān in 425/1034 when that town had been captured from the Kākūyid 'Alā' ad-Daula Muḥammad b. Dushmanziyār, perished.[20]

Those in Ghazna who had been in any way concerned with the deaths of the two Ghūrid princes were especially singled out for revenge. The singing girls who had composed satirical verses at the time of Saif ad-Dīn Sūrī's public humiliation were shut up in a *ḥammām* or bath and suffocated. The Alids who had taken the lead in killing Sūrī and his vizier Mūsawī were, according to Ibn al-Athīr's account, thrown down from mountain tops, and the place where Sūrī and Mūsawī had been gibbeted was razed to the ground. Large numbers of the citizens of Ghazna (according to Jūzjānī, however, just the guilty Alids) were deported to Fīrūzkūh and used as forced labour to build the citadel there; Jūzjānī states that these unfortunates were compelled to carry sacks of earth from Ghazna on their backs and then were slaughtered at Fīrūzkūh and the earth mixed with their blood as mortar for towers. The same author also quotes several triumphant, gloating verses allegedly improvised by 'Alā' ad-Dīn Ḥusain on his victory, but doubtless in reality composed by one of his eulogists, if contemporary with these events at all.[21]

'Alā' ad-Dīn Ḥusain's prestige was now high, and he felt that his exploits had lifted him above the level of a petty chieftain, a mere 'king of the mountains', from one of the obscurest regions of the Islamic east, and following Seljuq example, he now assumed the title of *as-Sulṭān al-Mu'aẓẓam* and such insignia of sovereignty as the *chatr* or ceremonial parasol.[22] It is uncertain what plans there were now in the Ghūrid leader's mind at this point. He did not apparently appoint as ruler in Ghazna a member of the Shansabānī family, although the pattern of decentralised authority in the Ghūrid dominions, with the capital remaining at Fīrūzkūh but with subordinate branches ruling in Bāmiyān and Ghazna, later became the norm for the dynasty.[23] According to an anecdote of Fakhr-i Mudabbir's, 'Alā' ad-Dīn Ḥusain left behind in Ghazna an oppressive military governor called Amīr Khān (presumably a Turkish commander in the Ghūrid service), from whose tyranny the surviving populace was delivered by the spiritual intervention of a local saint, the Khwāja Imām Qudwat al-Auliyā' Shams al-'Ārifīn Abū l-Mu'ayyad.[24] 'Alā' ad-Dīn Ḥusain may have feared a sudden revanche by Bahrām Shāh, such as the latter had made against his brother Saif ad-Dīn Sūrī, or possibly, the fear of an attack from the west by the Seljuq Sanjar, Bahrām Shāh's original protector and suzerain, hence his return to the heartland of Ghūr.

This march back was accomplished via Zamīn-Dāwar and Bust, and these regions were also devastated. In particular, the Ghūrid sultan destroyed the palaces and public buildings of the Ghaznavids at Bust; it may be that these ravages marked the final abandonment of the complex of Ghaznavid palaces at Lashkar-i Bāzār near Bust.[25] Nevertheless, Bust was not subjected to such savagery as had occurred at Ghazna; it obviously flourished during the succeeding century, on the evidence of carefully carved tombstones surviving in a *ziyāra* or mausoleum there, which date from 55x/1155–66 onwards and relate to such important Sunnī dignitaries as those bearing the titles of Ṣadr, Ṣadr ad-Dīn and Muftī ash-Sharq wa-l-Gharb, and a Ḥusainid sayyid, the Naqīb an-Nuqabā' or head of the Alids in Bust.[26]

Bahrām Shāh remained in India for at least a year after his flight in wretched circumstances from Ghazna, not daring to return.[27] 'Alā' ad-Dīn Ḥusain, meanwhile, had resolved to strike an immediate blow at Sanjar, his nominal overlord but, as we have just seen, the recipient from Bahrām Shāh of 'Alā' ad-Din Ḥusain's brother Saif ad-Dīn Sūrī's head. He stopped payment of tribute to Sanjar, and taking advantage of the treachery of a former Seljuq official, 'Alī Chatrī, he advanced against Herat. He was, however, decisively defeated at Nāb in the Heri Rud valley and held prisoner by the Seljuq sultan for two years until the large ransom demanded was paid over. This defeat of the Ghūrid took place, as noted above from the information of Niẓāmī 'Arūḍī, in 547/1152. Presumably it was only in this year, when he had heard of 'Alā' ad-Dīn Ḥusain's discomfiture and captivity, that Bahrām Shāh ventured to return from India; possibly he had to expel a governor or representative of the Ghūrids from Ghazna, though we have no information about this. A *ghazal* of Sayyid Ḥasan's seems to refer to his patron's return after an absence of at least a year and also to the latter's freedom now from the fear and anxiety that had oppressed him.[28]

The date of Bahrām Shāh's death is unclear. We can dismiss those later sources, such as Ḥamdallāh Mustaufī,[29] which place it as early as 544/1149–50, for we have just seen that he did not return to his capital until 547/1152. Ibn al-Athīr places his death in Rajab 548/September–October 1153 after a reign of thirty-six lunar years.[30] Some sources place it in 547/1152–3, presumably towards the end of that year. Jūzjānī's information is of an indirect nature. He does not provide a categorical date, but states that he died after a reign of forty-one lunar years.[31] Since the date of Bahrām Shāh's defeat of his brother and predecessor Arslan Shāh b. Mas'ūd b. Ibrāhīm is fairly definitely fixed as the winter of 511/1117–18, with Arslan Shāh's execution after imprisonment in Jumādā II 512/September–October 1118,[32] this would mean that Bahrām Shāh died in 552/1157. This is indeed the date finally adopted in his monograph on Bahrām Shāh by Gulam Mustafa Khan, who places the point of his death more precisely in the early months of that year, since we know that it was in the summer months, that is the middle of 552/1157, that ʿAlāʾ ad-Daula Ḥusain again attacked Ghazna and the newly succeeded sultan Khusrau Shāh.[33] Whatever the exact date of Bahrām Shāh's death, his reign was clearly the second longest one of any member of the Ghaznavid dynasty.

Bahrām Shāh had several sons, according to the manuscripts of Jūzjānī used by Raverty (and according to marginal notes in one of the manuscripts used by Ḥabībī), amounting to nine in number, of whom Khusrau Shāh was presumably the eldest survivor after the death in battle of Jalāl ad-Daula Daulat Shāh; the subsequent fate of the other brothers after Khusrau Shāh's accession is unknown.[34] In noting Bahrām Shāh's death, the sources often dwell, in conventional fashion, upon his love of learning, his cultivation of the ulema and his liberality to poets and literary men, and it is true, as we have seen in the previous chapter, that a dazzling array of scholars and writers thronged his court. Yet taking a broader view, and placing Bahrām Shāh's reign in the historical perspective of the decline and fall of the Ghaznavid empire, it is hard not to concur with the severe judgment of Spuler: 'There is no doubt that by his treacherous murders and the personal cowardice with which he deserted his subjects in a moment of crisis Bahrām Shāh contributed, in a completely personal way, to the disintegration of his ancestors' empire, which now could no longer be checked'.[35]

2.

Khusrau Shāh and the retreat to India

As Raverty notes, great discrepancies exist in the sources, not only in regard to the date of Bahrām Shāh's death, but also in regard to the reigns of his two successors Khusrau Shāh and Khusrau Malik; the varying accounts of the post-Jūzjānī Persian and Indo-Muslim historians are resumed by him in the notes to his *Ṭabaqāt-i Nāṣirī* translation.[36] Certain of these authorities (e.g. Yāfiʿī in his *Mirʾat al-jinān*, Baiḍāwī in his *Niẓām at-tawārīkh*, Ḥamdallāh Mustaufī in his *Taʾrīkh-i guzīda*, Faṣīḥ ad-Dīn Khwāfī in his *Mujmal-i Faṣīḥī* and Fakhr ad-Dīn Banākatī in his *Rauḍat ūlī l-albāb*) bring the Ghaznavid dynasty to an end with Khusrau Shāh, either confusing the two Khusraus and conflating them into one person or else perhaps considering Khusrau Malik as a local Indian ruler in the Panjab not worthy to be included with those preceding sultans who had reigned over a still-extensive empire in Afghanistan as well as India. The better-informed of later historians, such as Mīrkhwānd in his *Rauḍat aṣ-ṣafā'*, do, however, bring the story of the Ghaznavids down to the deposition of Khusrau Malik.[37] What would be much firmer evidence for the chronology of these reigns, namely numismatic evidence, is unfortunately sparse and, when existent, often defective and cryptic; none of the extant coins of either Khusrau Shāh or Khusrau Malik known to the present writer appear to bear dates or places of minting.

Khusrau Shāh probably succeeded his father Bahrām Shāh, accordingly, early in 552/1157, at the age of thirty-seven lunar years, if the date for his birth of 515/1121 given in the *Mujmal-i Faṣīḥī* and the 12th/18th century author Mīrzā Muḥammad's *Jannat al-firdaus* is correct; Jūzjānī explicitly gives 552/1157 as his accession date.[38] The *laqab* by which he is most frequently known in the chronicles, on coins and in the panegyrics addressed to him by Sayyid Ḥasan, is Muʿizz ad-Daula, though on the evidence of a hemistich by this latter poet, referring to Khusrau Shāh as *Khusrau Bahā'-i Daulat u Dīn Shāh ibn-i Ḥasan*, he may also have had the honorific of Bahā' ad-Daula.[39] Muʿizz ad-Daula, together with the standard dynastic designation of *as-Sulṭān al-Aʿẓam*, is, however, the sole *laqab* attributed to Khusrau Shāh on his few extant coins; certain of his *dirhams* acknowledge Sanjar as the Ghaznavid ruler's suzerain, but others omit this (Sanjar died in Rabīʿ I 552/May 1157, but the news of his death in Khurasan probably took some time to reach Ghazna).[40] The attribution to Khusrau Shāh in Ḥabībī's text of the *Ṭabaqāt-i Nāṣirī* of the title Yamīn ad-Daula wa-d-Dīn (actually that of his father Bahrām Shāh) and, in the manuscripts used by Raverty for his translation, those of Muʿīn ad-Daula wa-d-Dīn (read, rather, Muʿizz ad-Daula wa-d-Dīn, since in the list of names of Bahrām Shāh's sons, this *laqab* of Muʿīn ad-Daula is given to another son, Shāhanshāh) and Tāj ad-Daula (the *laqab* of Khusrau Shāh's own son Khusrau Malik) are unconfirmed in other sources and are obviously the result of a confusion of persons by Jūzjānī or perhaps by later copyists.

In endeavouring to elucidate the course of events in Khusrau Shāh's and Khusrau Malik's reigns, we enter a realm of deep confusion. It seems fairly well established that Khusrau Shāh had to face a fresh attack on Ghazna by ʿAlā' ad-Dīn Ḥusain, now released from captivity amongst the Seljuqs, in the summer of the very year of his accession, sc. 552/1157. It was doubtless this recurrence of Ghūrid attacks which created uncertainty in the minds of later chroniclers as to whether Ghazna had been sacked during the reign of Bahrām

Shāh or that of Khusrau Shāh. Two separate sources point to the historicity of this fresh attack. Jūzjānī implies that 'Alā' ad-Dīn Ḥusain sent an ultimatum to Khusrau Shāh demanding the cession of Zamīn-Dāwar, Bust and the whole of the Jurūm (sc. the *garmsīr* of southeastern Afghanistan, so-called in contrast to the more northerly *sardsīr* or cold region of Zābulistān, Ghazna and Kabul) to his nephew Shams ad-Dīn, later Ghiyāth ad-Dīn, Muḥammad b. Bahā' ad-Dīn Sām. When Khusrau Shāh naturally refused this impudent demand, 'Alā' ad-Dīn Ḥusain allegedly improvised a poetic quatrain in which he referred to the earlier warfare with Bahrām Shāh over possession of Tigīnābād. One of Fakhr-i Mudabbir's anecdotes refers to a battle near Tigīnābād between 'Alā' ad-Dīn Ḥusain and Khusrau Shāh, in which the Ghaznavid army was defeated, although the Ghūrid ruler subsequently returned personally to Ghūr; this battle is described as taking place during the summer months.[41]

'Alā' ad-Dīn Ḥusain may have returned himself to Ghūr, but the region of Zamīn-Dāwar and Bust must have passed permanently under Ghūrid control, further isolating Khusrau Shāh in Ghazna and depriving him of the financial and economic resources of the fertile and populous *garmsīr*; with the capture of Sanjar by the Oghuz and the Seljuq sultan's death soon afterwards, the Ghaznavids had of course lost their only possibility of help or relief in the shape of a Seljuq diversionary attack on the Ghūrid dominions from the west. 'Alā' ad-Dīn Ḥusain died in Rabī' II 556/April 1161, and was succeeded at Fīrūzkūh by his son Saif ad-Dīn Muḥammad; according to Jūzjānī, the recently-conquered *garmsīr* came under the governorship of Shihāb ad-Dīn, later Mu'izz ad-Dīn, Muḥammad b. Bahā' ad-Dīn Sām.[42]

Whether Khusrau Shāh retreated to his Indian possessions in the Panjab when his position in Ghazna was threatened by 'Alā' ad-Dīn Ḥusain's appearance in Zamīn-Dāwar is unclear, though some sources imply this. There would have been no pressing, immediate reason for precipitate flight unless Ghazna itself were threatened, but thoughts of retreat to India, in face of a worsening situation in eastern Afghanistan, must have come naturally to a Ghaznavid sultan. Lahore and the Panjab promised refuge in times of stress— Mas'ūd b. Maḥmūd, depressed by his defeat at the hands of the Seljuqs, had been on his way thither in 432/1040 when his troops had mutinied and proclaimed his brother Muḥammad as sultan (see above, ch. 1, pp. 14ff.), and Bahrām Shāh had fled to the Panjab from 'Alā' ad-Dīn Ḥusain. Conversely, the rich resources of India, in both manpower and treasure, had often made it the springboard for revanches to re-establish control over Ghazna and eastern Afghanistan, for example at the time of Toghrïl's usurpation in 443/1051–2 (see above, Ch. 1, pp. 45–6).

The consensus of authorities places Khusrau Shāh's death in /555 1160, with Ibn al-Athīr giving the month, Rajab 555/July 1160; Jūzjānī gives no date for his death, but states that he ruled for seven years after his accession in 552/1157, that is he would not on this count have died till 559/1164. Ibn al-Athīr passes the conventional judgment on Khusrau Shāh, that he was just and fair towards his subjects, cultivating the ulema and listening to their advice; Jūzjānī on the other hand comments that he was weak and powerless and thus unable to retain his grip over his territories, and states that he left behind three sons, Maḥmūd, Khusrau Malik and Kai Khusrau.[43]

3.

Khusrau Malik's reign and the end of the dynasty

We thus arrive at the reign of the last of the Ghaznavid sultans, Khusrau Malik b. Khusrau Shāh (555–82/1160–86). According to Jūzjānī again, he had the honorific of Tāj ad-Daula [wa-d-Dīn], which is confirmed by the hemistich of an ode addressed to him by the poet ar-Ra'īs Muḥammad b. Rashīd, which speak of 'The pre-eminent one amongst the roster of monarchs, Tāj-i Dīn Khusrau Malik'. He possessed secondly the honorific of Sirāj ad-Daula wa-d-Dīn, and this was used in addressing him by more than one poet of the Lahore court circle in verses which have come down to us, for example in a verse of Fakhr ash-Shu'arā' Muḥammad b. 'Alī, called Sirājī, who presumably derived this *takhalluṣ* from his close relationship to the sultan. Thirdly, a coin described by Raverty but otherwise apparently unknown, struck in Lahore and dating from the first year of his reign 555/1160, attributes to him, according to Raverty, the *laqab* of Ẓahīr ad-Daula wa-d-Dīn. Finally, Jūzjānī further applies to him the title of *Sulṭān-i Ḥalīm*, 'the Wise and forebearing sultan', by which he was probably known in ordinary parlance, just as his great-great-grandfather Ibrāhīm had been known as the *Sulṭān-i Raḍī*.[44] It is the two honorifics mentioned here first, sc. those of Tāj ad-Daula and Sirāj ad-Daula, which appear on coins of Khusrau Malik in the collections of the British Museum and Lahore, together with the regnal designation of *as-Sulṭān al-Aʿẓam*; one of the coins also provides us with the *kunya* of Abū l-Muẓaffar.[45]

Jūzjānī records that Khusrau Malik succeeded to the Ghaznavid throne in Lahore, implying that control of Ghazna had by that time passed out of Ghaznavid hands. In view of the gradual encroachment of the Ghūrids on the region of Zābulistān and its eventual near-encirclement, it is not hard to discern how the Ghaznavid position could have become untenable under Ghūrid pressure. Nevertheless, our two oldest sources here, Ibn al-Athīr and Jūzjānī, concur that the transfer of power from the Ghaznavids in Ghazna was not directly due to the Ghūrids but to a band of Oghuz military adventurers from Khurasan who were sufficiently strong enough to maintain themselves in Ghazna for some twelve or fifteen years. According to Ibn al-Athīr, Khusrau Malik (whom he erroneously calls Malik Shāh) withdrew to Lahore, unable to withstand the attacks of the Oghuz under their leader the amīr Zanjī b. ʿAlī b. Khalīfa ash-Shaibānī, and he places this event under the year 559/1164. He further mentions a brief re-occupation of Ghazna by Khusrau Malik in Jumādā II 559/May 1164, but this is otherwise unconfirmed and can only have been temporary. Jūzjānī places the Oghuz occupation of Ghazna as having taken place during Khusrau Shāh's reign, which on the basis of his implicit statement that Khusrau Shāh died in 559/1164 and his explicit one that the Oghuz occupation lasted for twelve years, would fit chronologically; but it does not fit with the more precise and credible date in Ibn al-Athīr for Khusrau Shāh's death of Rajab 555/July 1160. Whichever set of dates and figures one adopts, there are difficulties and contradictions involved (see further, below). As a provisional, working basis, the assumption is made here that it was early in Khusrau Malik's reign that the Oghuz seized Ghazna; but it is really impossible to make a categorical judgment.[46]

The appearance of the Oghuz injected a new element into the affairs of eastern Afghanistan for several years to come. The Great Seljuq sultanate in the east had in effect collapsed with the Oghuz rebellion in Khurasan and the ensuing capture of Sanjar by them during the years 548–51/1153–6. A forceful, former Turkish ghulām of Sanjar's, Mu'ayyid ad-Dīn Ai Aba (d. 569/1174), succeeded to real power in Khurasan and drove the Oghuz tribesmen out of the main towns there.[47] It was this dispersal of the Türkmens that sent certain bands of the Oghuz eastwards and led to their establishment in Ghazna, rather as Alptigin had migrated eastwards two centuries before and halted at Ghazna on the periphery of the Islamic world. The Oghuz in Ghazna are said to have behaved there tyranically, 'as was the case in every land where they gained control', and from Ghazna they raided as far as Tigīnābād.[48]

The duration of their occupation of Ghazna is fixed by Ibn al-Athīr at fifteen years and by Jūzjānī at twelve.[49] The Oghuz control of Ghazna placed a considerable obstacle in the way of Ghūrid expansion towards the plains of India, but it was not until 569/1173–4 that the Ghūrids succeeded in capturing it from them. In that year (the date being given by Jūzjānī), sultan Ghiyāth ad-Dīn Muḥammad and his brother Muʿizz ad-Dīn Muḥammad came with a strong force of Ghūrīs, Khalaj and Khurāsānīs and attacked the town. They were initially repulsed by the protective earthworks which the Oghuz had caused to be thrown up, but managed in the end to break through, to capture the Oghuz standard and to slaughter large numbers of the Türkmens. From Ghazna, the Ghūrid troops went on to seize two places which Ibn al-Athīr gives as K.r.mān (Kurram again?) and Sh.n.w.rān (a name which is very reminiscent of the present-day Shinwari tribe of Afghans, whose tribal territories lie to the south-west of the Khyber Pass in the direction of the Kurram river valley),[50] and in the next year of 570/1174–5, Muʿizz ad-Dīn Muḥammad captured Gardīz. Ghiyāth ad-Dīn Muḥammad then appointed his brother to be sultan in Ghazna under his own supreme overlordship.[51] Calculating backwards from 569/1173–4, and adopting Jūzjānī's figure of a twelve years' occupation by the Oghuz, we arrive at the date of 557/1162 for the beginning of Oghuz rule in Ghazna, that is two years after the beginning of Khusrau Malik's reign; but if we adopt Ibn al-Athīr's figure of a fifteen years' occupation, then the date of 554/1159 places us in the last year or so of Khusrau Shāh's reign.

The greater part, if not all, of Khusrau Malik's reign was accordingly spent as sultan in the Panjab, and we would like to have information about his rule in Lahore, the structure of administration there, the extent of Islamisation amongst the population of the Panjab, and so on, questions on which the sources are silent. Jūzjānī's condemnatory remarks that, although beneficent, Khusrau Malik was addicted to pleasure, so that both the Turkish soldiery and the Perso-Indian official classes in the outlying districts were able to enjoy almost unfettered power, can hardly be true of a monarch who managed to retain his throne, amidst a threatening and gradually-deteriorating situation for the Ghaznavids, for some twenty-six years, a respectable reign by contemporary standards.[52] Moreover, the Ghaznavid position in the Panjab could not have been maintained by a purely quiescent leadership, for there was still fierce Hindu resistance in northern India to the Muslim armies in the later 6th/12th century. It was only as a result of the victories of the Ghūrid Muʿizz ad-Dīn Muḥammad, and especially, the second battle of Tarā'īn or Tarāorī near Karnal in 588/1192, the killing of the Chauhān or Chāhamāna monarch Pṛithvīrāja and the occupation of Delhi, that there was a general collapse of Hindu resistance leading to the opening-up of the Ganges plain for the Muslims to raid as far eastwards as Bengal.[53]

Fakhr-i Mudabbir notes the prowess of both Khusrau Shāh and Khusrau Malik as warriors, and refers in particular to Khusrau Malik's outstanding skill as an archer and as a wielder of the battle-axe. He mentions warfare carried on by him with the Hindus, and his capture in battle of a Hindu potentate named Sukarwāl (? Śukrapāla).[54] The poets of Khusrau Malik's court circle (for which, see below) refer in their eulogies of the sultan to his conquests;[55] even allowing for the usual poetic hyperbole, this cannot have been based on a complete absence of warfare or *ghāzī* activity during his reign. An inscription found near Benares of the Gāhaḍavāla ruler Jayachandra (whose dynasty ruled in the Ganges-Jumna plain after the Kalachuris from the end of the 11th century onwards) refers to the repulse of an attack by the Muslims on that Rājā's father Vijayachandra; Jayachandra succeeded Vijayachandra at some time before June 1170, and the Muslim aggressor was probably Khusrau Malik, since this must antedate Muʿizz ad-Dīn Muḥammad Ghūrī's raids into the Ganges-Jumna region by at least two decades.[56] We know also from one of the chroniclers' accounts of the struggles between Muʿizz ad-Dīn Muḥammad and Khusrau Malik in the latter years of the Ghaznavid sultan's reign that Khusrau Malik had during the course of his rule extended his authority into the hill region of northern Panjab, the fringes of Kashmir, allying with the Hindu tribe there of the Khokhars against their suzerain, the Rājā of Jammū (see further, below, pp. 129–30). It is therefore clear that until his dynasty's end, Khusrau Malik carried on as keenly as he could the ancestral Ghaznavid traditions of *ghazw* against the unbelievers; that we do not know more about this activity probably arises from the overshadowing effect of the massive victories of Muʿizz ad-Dīn Muḥammad and his commanders, to which Jūzjānī, for instance, naturally devotes much space in his history.

Khusrau Shāh and Khusrau Malik also emulated the examples of their illustrious predecessors by their rôles as patrons of a distinguished array of poets and scholars, briefly in Ghazna and then more extensively at the Lahore court. It is likely that Lahore already possessed some cultural traditions as a centre for Islamic scholarship and literary activity, though we are ill-informed about this, apart from our knowledge of those parts of the career of Masʿūd-i Saʿd-i Salmān spent in his native Panjab with patrons who were governors or commanders in India for the Ghaznavids, and the fact that Abū l-Faraj Rūnī was almost certainly a native of the Lahore region.[57]

The translator of *Kalīla wa-Dimna*, Abū l-Maʿālī Naṣrallāh or Naṣr b. Muḥammad b. ʿAbd al-Ḥamīd, scion of a distinguished family of viziers and officials for the Ghaznavids (see above, Ch. 3, p. 109), served Khusrau Shāh as head of his *Dīwān* for a brief period before he fell victim to the slanders of his enemies and was put to death by the sultan. ʿAufī quotes from a Persian ode of his dedicated to Khusrau Shāh, and he also gives a quatrain which Naṣrallāh addressed to him from prison in a vain attempt to save his life.[58]

It is, indeed, ʿAufī who provides us with valuable information about what was obviously a numerous and talented circle of poets at Khusrau Malik's court and who quotes numerous examples of their verse, which in all cases seems to have survived only here in the *tadhkirat ash-shuʿarā'* literature and not as independent *dīwān*s of the individual authors. ʿAufī himself travelled from Khurasan and Sīstān shortly after 615/1218 and stayed at Lahore before proceeding to the court in Sind of Nāṣir ad-Dīn Qabācha. Whilst in Lahore, he had the opportunity to gather information about local literary men and scholars of the preceding generation or so, and he states explicitly that he heard some of the verses of the poets of Khusrau Malik's former circle through the intermediacy of the *Shaikh al-Islām* in Lahore, Ẓahīr al-Milla wa-d-Dīn.[59]

The poets include Jamāl ad-Dīn[60] Abū l-Maḥāsin Yūsuf b. Naṣr the secretary, author of two *dīwān*s in Arabic and Persian respectively, who had such a high opinion of his poetic talent that he would only dedicate his poems to rulers, such as Khusrau Malik himself; and the Ra'īs Shihāb ad-Daula wa-d-Dīn Muḥammad b. Rashīd (d. 598/1201–2), whom Qazwīnī surmised was a son (more probably a grandson) of Ibrāhīm b. Masʿūd's courtier and the *mamdūḥ* of Masʿūd-i Saʿd-i Salmān, Abū Rashīd ar-Rushd b. Muḥtāj, see above, Ch. 2, p. 53f. From his title of *al-Amīr al-ʿAmīd*, Thiqat ad-Dīn Muḥammad b. Yūsuf Darbandī, called Jamāl al-Falāsifa 'Adornment of the philosophers', may have acted as vizier or chief secretary to Khusrau Malik, until the time came when he realised that 'the rose of governmental power in this terrestial life is not free from the pricking of the thorn, and the satiety of its pleasures is not free from the painfulness of the resultant hangover'. He had written fine *qaṣīdas* in his youth, but now left office and renounced all worldly ambition for a life of contemplation; ʿAufī noted that his tomb was in one of the Lahore cemeteries and was still much visited by those seeking intercession.[61]

Jamāl ad-Dīn Muḥammad b. ʿAlī Sirājī, called Fakhr ash-Shuʿarā' 'Pride of the poets', derived his *takhalluṣ* of 'Sirājī' from his close companionship to the sultan, one of whose titles was, as we have seen above, Sirāj ad-Daula; and Sadīd ad-Dīn ʿAlī b. ʿUmar Muʿizzī Ghaznavī obtained his name of Sharaf an-Nudamā' 'Exaltedness of the boon-companions' from his membership of the circle of boon-companions or commensals, and his *nom-de-plume* of Muʿizzī presumably from his association with Muʿizz ad-Daula Khusrau Shāh.[62] The overthrow of the Ghaznavids in Lahore did not entail a violent break with the past from the cultural point of view and, so far as we know, the city itself did not suffer materially when Muʿizz ad-Dīn Muḥammad Ghūrī captured it and installed his own governor. At least two of Khusrau Malik's poets were welcomed into the Ghūrid fold. The poet and physician Ḍiyā' ad-Dīn ʿAbd ar-Rāfiʿ b. Abī l-Fatḥ Harawī, author of a well-known *Risāla jalāliyya* describing a New Year's gift offering (*naurūziyya*), passed from a highly-honoured status under Khusrau Malik into the service of Muʿizz ad-Dīn Muḥammad; and the *ʿAmid* Jamāl ad-Dīn Abū Bakr b. al-Musāʿid Khusrawī, called Iftikhār ash-Shuʿarā' 'Pride of the poets', whose *takhalluṣ* of 'Khusrawī' indicates a particularly close relationship to Khusrau Malik, subsequently became a member of the Ghūrid sultan's circle of panegyrists. A further poet of Lahore, of unspecified date but apparently contemporary with the poets just mentioned, was Ḥamīd ad-Dīn Masʿūd b. Saʿd Shālī-kūb, described by ʿAufī as the equal of Rūdakī and ʿUnṣurī.[63] It is not improbable that a perusal of further ones of the Indo-Muslim *tadhkiras*[64] would reveal the names of other authors from this final Ghaznavid period.

The dynamic of the powerful Ghūrid sultans, expanding westwards into Khurasan against the Khwārazm-Shāhs and the Qara Khitai, and eastwards towards the plains of India, was bound to find the surviving Ghaznavid state in the Panjab an obstacle that had ultimately to be removed. Eastern Afghanistan was secured for the Ghūrids by the ejection of the Oghuz from Ghazna in 569/1173–4. The new ruler there, Muʿizz ad-Dīn Muḥammad, was now able to utilise the town in its historic rôle as a spring-board for raids down to the Indus valley and beyond. But the continued Ghaznavid possession of the Panjab, including Peshawar and the lower reaches of the Kabul river valley, led the Ghūrid sultan to direct his first expeditions across the Gomal Pass and through what was in later times to be the country of the Mahsud Pathans to the Indus at Dera Ismail Khan. In 574/1178, Muʿizz ad-Dīn Muḥammad took an army via Multān and Ucch—which he had wrested from their local Qarmaṭī, sc. Ismāʿīlī Shīʿī, rulers in 571/1175–6[65]—but was unwise enough then to cross the Thar Desert southwards to Mārwār and towards Gujarāt; at Kāsahrada, at the foot of Mount Ābū in the southern Aravalli range, his exhausted and starving army was soundly beaten by Mūlarājā II, the Chaulakya ruler of Nahrawāla in Gujarāt.[66]

The disastrous outcome of this expedition for the Muslims now concentrated Muʿizz ad-Dīn Muḥammad's attention on the Ghaznavid Panjab. He seems to have made at least two attacks against Lahore before finally succeeding in ending Ghaznavid rule there. According to Ibn al-Athīr's account, the Ghūrid forces had attempted to push through the Indo-Afghan hill country down to the Indus immediately after their capture of Ghazna from the Oghuz, but had been deterred by Khusrau Malik's bringing up an army to the Indus crossings.[67] In 575/1179–80, however, Muʿizz ad-Dīn Muḥammad captured Peshawar, and two years later, in 577/1181–2, made his first strike towards Lahore. Khusrau Malik sent an embassy of conciliation, led by one of his sons and with the present of a fine elephant, and Muʿizz ad-Dīn Muḥammad was persuaded to withdraw. In the following year, the Ghūrid was occupied by an expedition against Daibul in Sind, in the course of which the Sūmra chief of Lower Sind was forced to acknowledge Ghūrid suzerainty.[68]

In 581/1185–6 the Ghūrid leader secured a chance to intervene in the Panjab at the instigation of Chakradeva, king of Jammū. Khusrau Malik had during the earlier part of his reign extended Ghaznavid authority northwards towards the southern fringes of

Kashmir, in alliance with the Khokhar hill tribesmen there, who had with Ghaznavid support renounced their former allegiance to Chakradeva. Chakradeva therefore sent a delegation to Muʿizz ad-Dīn Muḥammad, inciting him to attack Khusrau Malik. The Ghūrid sultan devastated the region around Lahore, but could not capture it. He retired northwards, and at Chakradeva's suggestion repaired the fortress of Sialkot as a bastion against the Khokhars, leaving there as governor his commander Ḥusain b. Kharmīl. Khusrau Malik and the Khokhars subsequently besieged Sialkot in vain, and in 582/1186 Muʿizz ad-Dīn Muḥammad returned, and with help from Vijayadeva, Chakradeva's son and successor, at last captured Lahore; he then appointed ʿAlī Karmākh, formerly governor of Multān, as his deputy in Lahore.[69]

The above account of the three-cornered struggle between Khusrau Malik and his Khokhar allies, the Hindu kings of Jammū, and Muʿizz ad-Dīn Muḥammad, is largely taken from a Hindi chronicle of the kings of Jammū, which Raverty resumes in his notes to the *Ṭabaqāt-i Nāṣirī* translation but which he does not actually name. Jūzjānī's account here is bold and laconic, but there is much more detail on the final capture and treacherous treatment of Khusrau Malik, much of it of a somewhat anecdotal nature, in the extended account of Ibn al-Athīr. According to this, Muʿizz ad-Dīn Muḥammad besieged Lahore, and promised Khusrau Malik *amān* or a guarantee for himself and his family, the preservation of his wealth, the marriage of Khusrau Malik's son with one of his own daughters and a grant of *iqṭā*ʿs, if only he would yield and recognise the Ghūrid supreme sultan Ghiyāth ad-Din Muḥammad in the *khuṭba*. Khusrau Malik refused, but as the city's position grew parlous, he feared lest the populace betray him; he therefore sent the *qāḍī* and the *khaṭīb* of Lahore to negotiate peace terms. After his surrender, Khusrau Malik spent two months in honoured status, until Ghiyāth ad-Dīn Muḥammad sent an envoy requiring Muʿizz ad-Dīn Muḥammad to send Khusrau Malik to him. Whereas Khusrau Malik had the bond of *amān* with Muʿizz ad-Dīn Muḥammad, he knew that he would have no protection against the latter's brother. He was reluctant to go, a reluctance strengthened by the warnings of the local people as he passed through Peshawar, where pro-Ghaznavid sentiment was still strong. Khusrau Malik quoted to the son of the *khaṭīb* of Peshawar, a faithful old servant of the Ghaznavid dynasty, this pathetic line of Arabic verse,

> For it is not now like the old times in the encampments, but chains have been placed around our necks.[70]

When Khusrau Malik and his son reached Ghūr, they were never brought face-to-face with Ghiyāth ad-Dīn Muḥammad, but were immured in one of the castles there and never seen again.[71]

As noted above, Jūzjānī's account here is more sketchy, but has some additional details about the actual deaths of the last Ghaznavids. He says that Khusrau Malik and his son Bahrām Shāh (probably the son who had been sent as a hostage to Muʿizz ad-Dīn Muḥammad in 577/1181–2) were conveyed from Lahore to Ghazna and thence to Ghiyāth ad-Dīn Muḥammad's capital at Fīrūzkūh; Khusrau Malik was then imprisoned in the fortress of Balarwān in Gharchistān, and Bahrām Shāh in that of Saifrūd in Ghūr. Five years later, in 587/1191, they were both put to death; in the previous year, Ghiyāth ad-Dīn and Muʿizz ad-Dīn had both been involved in warfare in Khurasan with Sulṭān Shāh, brother of the Khwārazm-Shāh Tekish, and they may have feared some attempt to rescue the two surviving Ghaznavids and use them as pawns in warfare or negotiations.[72]

ʿAufī in his *Jawāmiʿ al-ḥikāyāt* has an anecdote about Khusrau Malik's delivery of Lahore to Muʿizz ad-Dīn Muḥammad as the result of a stratagem employed by the latter; the only detail which rings historically true, however, is mention of Khusrau Malik's son (Bahrām Shāh ?) being kept at Ghazna during the last years of his father's independent reign, presumably as a hostage.[73]

Thus the rivalry, which had extended over some half-century, between the Ghaznavids and Ghūrids, ended in the victory of the latter and the destruction of the ancient sultanate of Ghazna; the town was never again to enjoy the status of capital of a mighty empire, and Bābur, visiting Ghazna in 910/1504–5, was to wonder how such an insignificant place could once have been so celebrated and flourishing.[74] As for the Ghūrids, they were not destined to enjoy for long their position as heirs to the Ghaznavids in the eastern Islamic world, and their period of florescence and fame proved to be much briefer than that of the preceding dynasty; only twenty-four years after Khusrau Malik had been executed, the Ghūrid dominions came under the control of the Khwārazm-Shāhs.

APPENDIX A

Ibn Bābā al-Qashānī on the History of the Ghaznavids

I.

Introduction

The *Kitāb Ra's māl an-nadīm* of Abū l-ʿAbbās Aḥmad b. ʿAlī al-Qāshānī or al-Qāshī is, as its name 'The boon-companion's stock-in-trade' implies, an *adab* work, containing information considered of practical value to the class of commensals, story tellers and professional entertainers. The author himself is a most obscure character. We find scattered mentions of him in later authors, for example Damīrī and Yāqūt, but none of the compilers of biographical dictionaries, such as Yāqūt or Ṣafadī, have specific entries on him, with the exception of Samʿānī, who mentions him *s.v.* 'al-Qāshī' and describes him as an *adīb*, very knowledgeable about history and *adab*, and the author of many fine books.[1] The Aḥmad b. ʿAlī al-Qāshānī al-Lughawī ('the grammarian'), called L.w.h. or Ibn L.w.h. (*luwwa*, 'aloes wood', the sort of euphuistic name one would give to a slave?), to whom Yāqūt actually does devote a biography in his *Irshād al-arīb*, cannot be our Ibn Bābā; the Qāshānī of the *Irshād* entry was clearly a frequenter of the grammarians' circles of Iraq some two centuries before Ibn Bābā's time, since such well-known scholars as Ibn Duraid, Nifṭawaih and Ibn Fāris are mentioned as being in contact with him.[2] However, in his geographical dictionary, the *Muʿjam al-buldān*, *s.v.* 'Qāshān', Yāqūt really does mention our Ibn Bābā as Abū l-ʿAbbās Aḥmad b. ʿAlī b. Bāba al-Qāshī, describing him as a littérateur who wrote a book on the sub-sects of the Shīʿa (*kitāb allafahu fī firaq ash-Shīʿa*), which Yāqūt had read.[3] Ibn Bābā at one stage in his career travelled to Khurasan—Yāqūt says that having arrived at Merv, he stayed there till his death some time after the year 500/1106–7—where he deplored the dire straits into which the honourable profession of *nadīm* and *sāmir* had fallen, and it was this which impelled him to write his *Kitāb Ra's māl an-nadīm*.

This work has now been for the first time edited by Dr Muḥammad Ṣāliḥ Badawī of Mecca as his Ph.D. thesis, *A critical edition of Ibn Bābā's Kitāb Ra's māl an-nadīm, with an introduction and summary* (Manchester 1975), and it is to be hoped that this will eventually be published. Meanwhile, a brief account of the work is accessible in the present author's article 'Early sources for the history of the first four Ghaznavid sultans (977–1041)', *IQ*, VII (1963), 17–18, and there is an article on the author by *idem* in *EI²* *s.v.* 'al-Ḳās͟hānī, al-Ḳās͟hī, Abu 'l-ʿAbbās Aḥmad b. ʿAlī'. Only three manuscripts of the *Kitāb Ra's māl an-nadīm* are so far known, two in Istanbul and one in India. The Istanbul ones were sketchily described by Viqar Ahmad Hamdani,[4] and have now been fully analysed by Dr Badawī in op. cit., I, 18 ff. One of these manuscripts, Turhan Valide = Yeni Cami 234 (now in the Süleymaniye Library) is ostensibly an autograph, but is more probably a later copy transcribed from the autograph. In its colophon the author states that he compiled his book in Ramaḍān 501/April–May 1108 for a so-far unidentified patron called al-Amīr ar-Ra'īs Saʿd al-Mulk Abū l-Fatḥ Muḥammad b. Bahrām b. ʿAlī (perhaps a member of the Seljuq prince Sanjar b. Malik Shāh's court circle in Merv) and completed it in the following month, 10 Shawwāl 501/25 May 1108. On this basis, Ibn Bābā wrote during the caliphate of al-Mustaẓhir (487–512/1094–1118), yet there is mention in the book of the caliph al-Muqtafī, who ruled half-a-century later (530–55/1136–60); the whole question of this apparent anachronism is discussed by Dr Badawī in op. cit., I, 28–30. The third manuscript, that of Patna, was not available to Dr Badawī, but a description of it may be read in that library's catalogue; it apparently gives the history of the Abbasid caliphs up to al-Muqtafī's reign, and is a late 19th-century manuscript.[5]

The seventh and final chapter of the *Kitāb Ra's māl an-nadīm* is an historical one, in which the author deals with the Orthodox caliphs, the Umayyads, the Abbasids (down to al-Muqtadī, succeeded in 467/1075); the twelve Imāms of the mainstream Twelver Shīʿa; the Imāms of the Bāṭiniyya or Seveners, including the Fāṭimids down to al-Mustaʿlī (succeeded in 487/1094); the Ṭāhirids; the Sāmānids; the Dailamīs or Būyids; and finally, the Ghaznavids, down to Masʿūd b. Ibrāhīm (succeeded in 492/1099). The Seljuqs he left aside for treatment in a later work, so he says; if this book was ever composed, we have no record of it. The selection of dynasties treated certainly shows that Ibn Bābā had the interests of a patron in the eastern Iranian world in mind, for there is no mention of events in the Muslim west in his book.

2.

Translation of the passage on the Ghaznavids[6]

[f.203a] The amīrs and sulṭāns in Ghazna of the house of Nāṣir ad-Dīn Sebüktigin

§1.[f.203b] [These were] nine in number, sc. Sebüktigin, Maḥmūd, Muḥammad, Mas'ūd, Maudūd, 'Abd ar-Rashīd, Farrukh-Zād, Ibrāhīm and Mas'ūd.

§2. As for Sebüktigin, he was a slave of the Ḥājib Alptigin and had been brought from Barskhān. Alptigin himself was a slave of Ismā'īl b. Aḥmad; he served Ismā'īl, then his son Aḥmad b. Ismā'īl, then his grandson Naṣr b. Aḥmad, then his great-grandson Nūḥ b. Naṣr, and finally the latter's son 'Abd al-Malik. When 'Abd al-Malik fell from his horse and was killed, they set up on the throne in his place his brother Manṣūr b. Nūḥ. 'Abd al-Malik, however, had enjoined Alptigin that if he were to suffer any fatal accident, Alptigin should set up in his place his son. Alptigin accordingly reacted strongly to Manṣūr's elevation to the throne; Manṣūr in turn became apprehensive and attempted to arrest Alptigin. Alptigin was at this time commander-in-chief of the army of Khurasan, and when he became apprised of the amīr Manṣūr's fears and suspicions, he left Khurasan and made for India. There he became occupied with warfare and raiding, dying at Ghazna in the year 352[/963].

§3. Power passed to his son Isḥāq, once he had made a journey to the court of Bukhārā and sought pardon for his father's untoward actions; he then returned to Ghazna with assent to his succession there and with a patent of investiture from the amīr of Khurasan. Isḥāq died in Dhū l-Qa'da of the year 355 [/October–November 966]. In his place there succeeded his commander-in-chief, who was called Bilgetigin. Bilgetigin was hit by a stray arrow [f.204a] at the gates of Gardīz, and died in the year [3]62 [/972–3]. They set up in his stead the other commander of the army, called Böri, but he was a confirmed drunkard; affairs got out of control and disorder grew. Among the ghulāms of Alptigin and his son Isḥāq, Sebüktigin was vigilant, firm, energetic, accustomed to enforcing discipline and to exacting obedience. Without waiting for a specific commission from the amīr Böri (since the latter spent his time drinking and was deeply addicted to unworthy pleasures), Sebüktigin set about restoring the position and bringing order out of chaos. Hence the army agreed to appoint him as their leader. He assumed command and acted as their commander on the basis of certain conditions which he imposed on them, this being in Shaʿbān of the year 366 [/March–April 977]. He then inaugurated a policy of making expeditions into India, where he achieved mighty victories, made many conquests and took a great amount of plunder. His followers grew rich and benefited from his auspicious leadership, until his prestige became high, his renown became everywhere recognised and his fame spread far and wide.

§4.Now the Sīmjūrīs, who were accustomed to hold command of the army of Khurasan, rebelled against the amīr Nūḥ b. Manṣūr b. Nūḥ. b. Naṣr. So Nūḥ called upon Sebüktigin for help, summoning him to Bukhara for this purpose. The latter came along and collected together an army. Amīr Nūḥ crossed over [the Oxus river], with Sebüktigin preceding him, and he fought a battle with the Sīmjūrīs at the gates of Herat, putting them to flight. Amīr Nūḥ returned to Bukhara; he appointed Maḥmūd b. Sebüktigin to be commander of the army of Khurasan, and sent Sebüktigin back to Ghazna. After that, warfare broke out between Maḥmūd and the Sīmjūrīs [f. 204b] on two further occasions, and Maḥmud routed Abū ʿAlī b. Sīmjūr at the gates of Ṭūs. With this, no-one remained to raise a banner for Abū ʿAlī or his partisans again, and Maḥmūd remained as commander in Khurasan.

§5.Then, after this, Sebüktigin became ill at Balkh, and wished to return to Ghazna. He was carried back, a sick man, on a litter, but when he reached the staging-post known as Madr u Mūy, the decree of God, which cannot be turned back, overtook him and he died. This was in Shaʿbān of the year 387 [/August–September 997]. The funeral bier was transported back to Ghazna. Sebüktigin's period of governorship and military command there was from Shaʿbān in the year [3]66 [/March–April 977] to Shaʿbān in the year [3]87 [/August–September 997]. When he had left Ghazna, he had entrusted to his son Ismāʿīl all his affairs and the government of those territories, and had said to him, 'Your brother Maḥmūd will be satisfied with command of the army of Khurasan'. However, when Sebüktigin died, Maḥmūd had no thought for anything else but getting control of power in Ghazna. He hurried thither; Ismāʿīl submitted and handed over power to him, becoming one of Maḥmūd's military commanders, both of them achieving exalted positions after then. Sebüktigin's period of rule amounted therefore to twenty-one years.

§6.His son Abū l-Qāsim Maḥmūd b. Sebüktigin ruled after him, as inheritor of Ghazna from his father and as commander of the army in Khurasan on the authority of the Sāmānids. According to what the historian of the Ghaznavids Abū l-Faḍl al-Baihaqī relates, Maḥmūd was born on the night before ʿĀshūrā day in the year 361 [= night of 9–10 Muḥarram / 1–2 November 971]. He continued to recognise the authority of the Sāmānid [f. 205a] family and to place their name in the *khuṭba* from the pulpits of Ghazna and Khurasan down to the year [3]89 [/999], two years after his father's death.

§7.Manṣūr b. Nūḥ crossed [the Oxus river] to Merv and Sarakhs, and warfare broke out between him and his commander-in-chief (*Ḥājib al-Bāb*) Begtuzun. The latter sought the help of Fā'iq; they made an agreement together, blinded Manṣūr b. Nūḥ and set up in his place his brother ʿAbd al-Malik b. Nūḥ. Maḥmūd was outraged by these events, and he and his brother marched on Merv with a numerous and heavily-equipped army and many elephants. He attacked the enemy and put them to flight, killing large numbers of their forces. Some of the fleeing troops perished in the desert around Merv, the rest managed to escape across the river with ʿAbd al-Malik to Bukhārā. Maḥmūd now made the *khuṭba* in the first place for al-Qādir billāh, and in the second place for himself; now the Sāmānids had never made the *khuṭba* for al-Qādir, but had said, 'We gave our allegiance originally to aṭ-Ṭā'iʿ, and whilst he is still alive, it would be morally wrong for us to renounce our allegiance to him'. This victory was on the 27th day of Jumādā I in the year 389 [/16 May 999]. When the news of all this reached al-Qādir billāh in Baghdad, he rejoiced greatly, and sent to Maḥmūd an envoy with robes of honour and an investiture charter for Khurasan; the envoy reached Maḥmūd at Balkh. He was now firmly established in power, and retained this authority during a long reign. His practice was to lead an expedition into India one year and then return the next; he would keep a watch on affairs in India, and at the same time keep a wary eye on the Qarakhanids of Transoxania. The stories of Maḥmūd's exploits are very numerous and his victories were extremely extensive; unfortunately, there is [f. 205b] insufficient room here to go into them. He died in Ghazna on Thursday, 23

Rabīʿ II in the year 421 [/30 April 1030], having entrusted his kingdom to his son the amīr Muḥammad b. Maḥmūd.

§8.The amīr Muḥammad b. Maḥmūd b. Sebüktigin. Despite his son the amīr Masʿūd's noble virtues, his solidity of character, his sagacity and his courage, Maḥmūd was on bad terms with him; it was said that he used to envy men of outstanding force of character. Instead, he showed favour to his other son Muḥammad, although he did not regard Muḥammad very highly in his estimation; moreover, he used continually to find fault with Masʿūd, whilst continuing to assign to him offices and commands. When Maḥmūd led his expedition to ʿIrāq [ʿAjamī], he took Masʿūd with him, entrusting Ghazna and Khurasan to Muḥammad's care, intending thereby to facilitate Muḥammad's accession to power and to strengthen his authority; but in the event, all that was of no benefit to Muḥammad. Maḥmūd fell ill at Ray. He ordered Masʿūd to stay in ʿIrāq [ʿAjamī] and to subdue the whole of that region, and then he himself turned back. By giving these instructions, Maḥmūd aimed at getting Masʿūd away from the capital, the treasuries and the strongholds, should death come upon him, so that the path to power would be left clear for Muḥammad. When he felt the approach of death, he told his companions, 'I am fully aware that Masʿūd will not stay in ʿIrāq one moment when he hears of my death. He will ride swiftly against Muḥammad, and will cause all sorts of troubles for him. However, I am determined to carry out my decision and my desire concerning Muḥammad; perhaps God will protect him from harm and deliver him safely from Masʿūd's threats'. He wrote letters explaining his intentions to the seat of the caliphate.

§9.When Maḥmūd was on the point of death, Muḥammad was away in Gūzgān. So Maḥmūd sent an envoy [f. 206a] to fetch him back quickly to the capital, in order that he might give his last charge to Muḥammad; but Muḥammad failed to reach his father in time. Instead, Maḥmūd gave his last instructions to ʿAlī al-Qarīb, the Ḥājib al-Kabīr and commander of the army, and to his vizier Ḥasanak an-Nīshāpūrī, telling them to get the army and other members of the official classes to give their allegiance to Muḥammad. After doing this, he died. Amīr Muḥammad reached Ghazna forty days after his father's death and assumed power there. The people gave their allegiance to him. Muḥammad plunged himself into drinking, pleasure and vain amusements, and began to lavish largesse and to dissipate his treasuries, until his prestige dropped, his authority weakened and other people's respect for him declined. The Ḥājib ʿAlī and the vizier Ḥasanak had been close friends, but because of Muḥammad's decline in popular favour, there arose an estrangement and contention between them, and without either the amīr's knowledge or permission, the Ḥājib arrested the vizier.

§10. Just as Maḥmūd had foretold, amīr Masʿūd did not remain in ʿIrāq [ʿAjamī] one single day once he had heard the news of his father's death. He left Iṣfahān, on the pretext that all the people desired him as their ruler, and without being deflected from his purpose by anything, reached Nīshāpūr. A part of Muḥammad's army inclined towards his cause because they knew of his reputation for noble virtues, strength in battle and bravery. Muḥammad marched out from Ghazna with the intention of repelling his brother Masʿūd from his treasured possessions and of combatting him. They brought the vizier along in fetters, taking no notice of Muḥammad's instructions regarding him. When the forces approached a place near Bust called Tigīnābād, the Ḥājib ʿAlī sent his brother Il-Direk to Masʿūd, bearing messages of conciliation and seeking to ingratiate himself with him. Masʿūd received him, heaped gifts on him and assured him of all sorts of future acts of generosity.

§11. [f. 206b] Meanwhile, the Ḥājib ʿAlī and the amīr Yūsuf, amīr Masʿūd's paternal uncle, conspired together to seize and confine Muḥammad in a nearby castle and then join Masʿūd, who was at that time in Herat. They successfully accomplished this and then came to Masʿūd, feeling sure that they would be treated with great respect and that they would be given exalted positions in the amīr's retinue. But when they entered his presence, Masʿūd ordered them to be carried off to one of the cells and imprisoned there in company with a group of other prominent former supporters of Muḥammad, and he exclaimed that 'All these men hold that it is lawful to transfer power from one brother to another'. He then sent someone to act as custodian over his brother Muḥammad, and in this fashion, amīr Muḥammad's period of rule came to an end. That was in Shawwāl of the year 422/[September–October 1031], after twenty months only in power; amīr Masʿūd was now in unchallenged control.

§12. The Amīr Abū Saʿīd Masʿūd b. Maḥmūd b. Sebüktigin now ruled over the various provinces of his father's empire in quite a praiseworthy manner, except that Khurasan was now very disturbed and in turmoil because of the Türkmens. Masʿūd kept sending army after army against them, but all the troops would come back beaten and discomfited. In the end, he was compelled in Ramaḍān 431 [/May–June 1040] to march against them in person. He reached Sarakhs, and the Türkmens fled before him in disarray towards Merv. En route, they blocked up the wells used by travellers across the Merv desert. Unaware of this, Masʿūd hurried after their tracks. Both beasts and men suffered terribly from thirst, and the horses and mules perished. After enduring dreadful hardships, the soldiers managed to escape on camel back, and [f. 207a] they sought refuge at a village called Dandānqān, the first of the villages of the Merv oasis. But the people of Dandānqān shut the gates in Masʿūd's face. Hence the army was forced to move onwards for two farsakhs, until they saw the Türkmens drawn up in groups of fighting men on the sandhills, not with the express intention of giving battle, but because of their habitual practice of deploying themselves openly; then if they saw an opportunity of giving battle, they would seize it, but if not, they would take refuge in flight. When the enfeebled condition of the Ghaznavid troops, their disordered state and the treacherous behaviour of one group within the army to another became fully apparent, the Türkmens were emboldened to attack. The chiefs of Masʿūd's army contemplated surrendering him to the enemy, telling him, 'You are now in a position of total ruin; your troops have betrayed you, and there is no way out except in flight and saving your own skin, so that you may have an opportunity of making a fresh start on this problem'. So Masʿūd rode off on an elephant and escaped in a most ignominious fashion, finally reaching Ghazna. He stayed there some months resting and recuperating and recovering his spirits. Then he set about confronting that group of commanders who had let him down on the day of battle, such as the Ḥājib Sübashï, Begtoghdï, the Ḥājib ʿAlī b. Dāya, and others; he confiscated their goods and exterminated the lot of them by executing, crucifying and skinning them alive.

§13. Masʿūd now sent his son Maudūd and his vizier Aḥmad b. ʿAbd aṣ-Ṣamad with the cream of the royal ghulāms to Balkh, in order to repel the Türkmens if they invaded those regions. He himself decided to proceed to India and collect together armies of the Hindus, because of the qualities which he discerned in them of usefulness, fortitude in fighting round their standard, trustworthiness and loyalty. When he reached Waihind, he crossed the Indus with his family and children. The eunuch commander Nūshtigin al-Balkhī saw [f. 207b] his opportunity, and came to an agreement with the rest of the army which had not yet crossed the Indus. They plundered the remainder of Masʿūd's baggage and openly raised the flag of rebellion against him. They brought out once more Masʿūd's brother Muḥammad, who had been blinded, but was at that time with them and in good health, and they set him up as amīr. They then crossed the river after Masʿūd. When Masʿūd became aware of their evil machinations, he sought protection from them by shutting himself up, together with his children and his harem, in the ribāṭ of Mārīkala. Nūshtigin, in company with all those who had rallied to his side and also the amīr Muḥammad, besieged the ribāṭ until they managed to get hold of Masʿūd. They brought him to the fortress of Gīrī; then soon afterwards they burst in and killed him, chopping off his head. They then marched off towards Peshawar.

§14. Amīr Maudūd and Aḥmad b. ʿAbd aṣ-Ṣamad were meanwhile still in the region of Ghazna, waiting for the end of winter so that they might go down to Balkh. They got news of what had happened, so they returned to the town of Ghazna itself. They gathered together all the troops they could possibly collect, and flew after the rebel forces just like a hawk swooping down on its prey. Eventually they caught up with that bunch of treacherous and faithless scoundrels on the 13th of Rajab [4] 32 [/19 March 1041], and fought with them for a whole day, from the beginning of the day's light to its end. All the rebels fell into the hands of the troops from Ghazna, including the amīr Muḥammad and his son Aḥmad, who had been flying with his father's wings, and the whole of the evil-doers. Amīr Maudūd showed extensive generosity and forgiveness, but he put into effect the decree of God Most High in the cases of the son of [his father's] paternal uncle Yūsuf, the son of amīr Muḥammad, Nūshtigin al-Balkhī and three others of the leading [f. 208a] commanders, by execution, crucifixion and stoning. Amīr Masʿūd's death was in Ṣafar of the year [4] 33 [/October 1041], and the period of his rule was ten years and some odd months.

§15. After him, the amīr Abū l-Fatḥ Maudūd b. Masʿūd succeeded to power in Shaʿbān [4] 33 [/March–April 1042]. He governed well and kept firm order in the state, except for the continued presence of the Türkmens in Khurasan. If destiny had prolonged the days of Maudūd (may God have mercy on him) and if fate had assisted him, he would have dealt with them once and for all; but the decree of God Most High, which cannot be staved off by any possible means, came down upon him. He was afflicted with an intestinal disorder (*qūlanj*) whilst he was encamped at the gates of Ghazna. When he despaired of ever recovering, he despatched his vizier to Sīstān, with cavalry and infantrymen, and he himself went into the town of Ghazna. But when the vizier reached the fortress of Mandīsh, which is a fortress on the road to Bust, the news of amīr Maudūd's death came to him.

§16. Now when Maudūd had neared the point of death, he had appointed as his successor one of his sons, who was only five years old. The latter ruled for five days only, and then the army transferred its allegiance to Maudūd's brother ʿAlī b. Masʿūd; but he in turn only remained in power for forty-five days. The story behind this is that when Maudūd returned to Ghazna after seizing and wreaking his vengeance on his father's murderers, he also arrested his uncle ʿAbd ar-Rashīd b. Maḥmūd and shut him up in the aforementioned fortress of Mandīsh. He remained there all the subsequent days of his life. The vizier ʿAbd ar-Razzāq b. Aḥmad b. al-Ḥasan [f. 208b] al-Maimandī received the news of Maudūd's death when he was actually encamped just below this fortress; he fetched out ʿAbd ar-Rashīd, brought the latter back with him to Ghazna, and set him up as amīr. The date of amīr Maudūd's death was Wednesday, 21 Rajab in the year 441 [/19 December 1049], and he was twenty-nine years old at the time.

§17. The amīr ʿAbd ar-Rashīd b. Maḥmūd acceded to power on 27 Shaʿbān in the year [4]41 [/24 January 1050]. Amīr Maudūd had a Turkish ghulām called Ṭoghrïl, an energetic and courageous warrior. Maudūd had singled him out for special consideration and had promoted him; and he had elevated his status by giving him the hand of his own sister in marriage. When ʿAbd ar-Rashīd came to the throne, he continued to treat Ṭoghrïl with equal generosity. Ṭoghrïl, for his part, used to behave in an easy and familiar way with ʿAbd ar-Rashīd, and he kept requesting the amīr to provide him with an army and resources so that he might march against the Türkmens and recover Khurasan from them. He had managed to secure a victory over the amīr Alp Arslan b. Chaghrï Beg at Hupyān during the campaign of Chaghrï Beg, when the latter had been repulsed by the Ghaznavid forces and put to flight. The latter victory was accounted to Ṭoghrïl's credit also. ʿAbd ar-Rashīd wanted to be free of Ṭoghrïl's presence, so he authorised him to march to Sīstān with a force of his followers fairly small in numbers. He set off with them, defeated Bīghū, the paternal uncle of Chaghrī Beg, hurled him out of Sīstān, and took possession of the province.

§18. All the rest of the slave troops who were in the capital Ghazna now rallied to Ṭoghrïl's side and joined his forces. [f. 209a] Ṭoghrïl became excited by the idea of seizing the throne for himself. His partisans did homage to him, and the whole body of them marched swiftly back from Sīstān and attacked ʿAbd ar-Rashīd in Ghazna. The unfortunate amīr had no resource left except to seek immediate refuge in the citadel of Ghazna, whilst Ṭoghrïl took over the royal palace and centre of government and assumed the throne, with the army rallying to his side. Then he stormed the citadel and forced ʿAbd ar-Rashīd to come forth, after which he killed him.

§19. The leading people in the state now criticised Ṭoghrïl's action and began to conspire together. The Ḥājib Khirkhīz, who was at that time in India, disapproved violently of what they had done, and blamed them for their complicity. He wrote menacing letters to them so that everyone, great or small, now refused to serve Ṭoghrïl and started to execrate and vilify him totally. It happened that one of the palace ghulāms, who was not particularly prominent or well known, used to frequent the wine shops and drink wine there in the company of dissolute persons. He was reprimanded for this behaviour while he was drunk, so he resolved secretly to assassinate Ṭoghrïl, making no-one privy to his intention. One day when Ṭoghrïl was seated on his throne, with all the courtiers and troops drawn up in ranks before him, this slave attacked him with a spear which he was concealing, transfixing and killing him with it. All the people standing by assumed that he had done that with the complicity of the whole assembly, so that none of them moved from his place. This ghulām was called Nūshtigin and was noted for his fine singing voice; he now became famed for his deed.

§20. The general body of leading men in the state agreed to appoint as ruler over themselves a suitable member of the traditional ruling house of the Ghaznavids. The amīr Farrukh-Zād b. [f. 209b] Masʿūd had been incarcerated in one of the strongholds. Khirkhīz arrived back from India three days after Ṭoghrïl's assassination. They decided to send for Farrukh-Zād and make him amīr; this was accordingly done. All these events took place in the year [4]43 and part of [4]44 [/1051–2].

§21. The amīr Abū Shujāʿ Farrukh-Zād b. Masʿūd b. Maḥmud succeeded to power in the state. He was a noble-minded and just ruler, who reigned equitably and had a praiseworthy nature; through his coming to the throne, the flow of water which had dwindled away and the splendour which had departed came back once more. He died on 17 Ṣafar in the year 451 [/4 April 1059].

§22. The just sulṭān Ibrāhīm b. Masʿūd. Sulṭān Abū l-Muẓaffar Ibrāhīm was imprisoned in a certain fortress in some region or other. He was offered the supreme power; he responded favourably and ascended the throne. He exercised power for an extremely long reign. He behaved with justice towards his subjects; he was noble-minded, restrained in his behaviour, firm in judgment and successful in the affairs which he undertook. He had all these virtues to such a pitch that he excelled all the other members of his dynasty in praiseworthy characteristics, with the exception that Maḥmūd was superior in martial vigour and strength. His presence inspired awe and respect; he was always victorious in a struggle; he was always in perfect control of himself; and his armies were always triumphant in battle. He was always able to put his commands into execution and to enforce his prohibitions. No-one was able to find fault with any of his actions, nor could any of his personal qualities be criticised unless for his undue interest in the various sects and religious faiths; people used to speak critically because of this. Nevertheless, Ibrāhīm [f. 210a] remained the cynosure of all eyes from the remote corners of the world; his munificence was much sought-after and suppliants came from afar seeking his liberality. He lavished his riches on all sorts of good causes, until the ineluctable decree of God came down upon him in Dhū l-Qaʿda of the year 492 [/September–October 1099]. He had several sons by various mothers, and these sons contested among themselves the succession to the throne.

§23. The just amīr Masʿūd b. Ibrāhīm. Then the Amīr Abū Saʿīd Masʿūd b. Ibrāhīm b. Masʿūd got the upper hand over his rivals, and his authority was established in all the provinces of the empire. He forged a powerful military machine, and he acted with such justice and mildness towards his subjects that these good qualities quite overshadowed the praiseworthy conduct of his father and put it out of people's minds. His just rule became renowned throughout the world; every fearful person sought refuge in his territories and every seeker after beneficence and goodness made his way towards him. God aids whom He wills with His conquering power!

§24. With regard to the sultans of our own epoch and the governors of our own time from the house of Seljuq, we have decided to devote a special work to them. This will deal with their beginnings exactly as they took place, the unfolding of their distinctive features, the conquests by their supporters in Khurasan, Iraq, Rūm, Syria, the lands of Fārs and the Ḥijāz, and the point to which their dominion has spread, stage by stage and year by year. For this reason, we have not mentioned them here.

3.

Commentary

§1. It will be noted that the ephemeral rulers Masʿūd II b. Maudūd and ʿAlī b. Masʿūd are omitted from Ibn Bābā's list of the Ghaznavid sovereigns.

§2. *Sebüktigin's slave origin from Barskhān.* This origin from Barskhān, a district on the shores of the Ïsïq-Köl in Semirechye (in the modern Kirghiz SSR), is confirmed only in the alleged *Pand-nāma* of Sebüktigin, a collection of counsels supposedly written for the seven-year-old prince Maḥmūd when Sebüktigin marched to occupy the region of Bust in *ca.* 367/977–8 and left Maḥmūd behind in Ghazna as his nominal deputy. See Nāẓim 'The Pand-Nāmah of Subuktigin' *JRAS* (1933) text 610, tr. 621, and Erdoğan Merçil 'Sebüktegin'in Pend-nâmesi (Farsça metin ve türkce tercumesi)' *Islâm Tetkikleri Enstitüsü Dergisi* VI/1–2 (Istanbul 1975) text 213, tr. 227; the original Persian text is contained within the 8th/14th century author Shabānkāra'ī's *Majmaʿ al-ansāb fī t-tawārīkh*, on which see below. There is no solid basis for the categorical assertion recently made by M. A. Shaban in his *Islamic history, a new interpretation. 2. A.D. 750–1055 (A.H. 132–448)* (Cambridge 1976) 180–1, that Sebüktigin was not a slave at all, but 'a native leader of the region of Ghaznīn'; it is unlikely that Ibn Bābā, writing only one hundred years after Sebüktigin's death, could have been mistaken over the questions of servile status and Central Asian origins, whatever the reliability or otherwise of the *Pand-nāma*.

ʿAbd al-Malik b. Nūḥ's son. This was Naṣr b. ʿAbd al-Malik, a child, whose rule in Bukhārā lasted for only one day before Manṣūr b. Nūḥ was raised to the throne by Fā'iq and the party at court opposed to Alptigin; see Barthold *Turkestan down to the Mongol invasion*[3], 251, and R. N. Frye in *The Cambridge history of Iran. IV. From the Arab invasion to the Saljuqs*, ed. Frye (Cambridge 1975) 152.

§3. *Alptigin's son.* The name of this son appears more usually in the sources as Abū Isḥāq Ibrāhīm b. Alptigin.

The chronology of the predecessors of Sebüktigin in the governorship of Ghazna. See on this Nāẓim, *The life and times of Sulṭān Maḥmūd of Ghazna*, 175–6, who did not however know of Ibn Bābā's work and had at his disposal a manuscript of Shabānkāra'ī's *Majma' al-ansāb*, which is defective for this particular period; for this last source, see Bosworth, 'Early sources for the history of the first four Ghaznavid Sultans (977–1041)', 18–20. Reference should now be made, pending the appearance at some future time of a critical edition, to the Istanbul manuscript Yeni Cami 909, used by the present author in his various works on the Ghaznavids and by Merçil in the article cited above; the relevant section on the predecessors of Sebüktigin is at ff. 164a–165b. A discussion of several difficult points in the history and chronology of these Turkish commanders may further be found in Bosworth, 'Notes on the pre-Ghaznavid history of Eastern Afghanistan', 12–24, see also idem, in *The Cambridge history of Iran*, IV, 164–5. The dates given here by Ibn Bābā for the deaths of Alptigin's son and of Bilgetigin provide additional information, and in the case of the latter's death, correct Nāẓim's data.

The siege of Gardīz by Bilgetigin. The necessity for military operations here indicates that the family of the indigenous rulers of Zābulistān at this time, the mysterious Lawīks or Lowīks, whilst displaced from Ghazna by Alptigin and the Turkish slave former troops of the Sāmānids, still held on in the adjacent town for a decade or so longer; for more information on the Lawīks, see Bosworth, art. cit. A more circumstantial account of Bilgetigin's death in battle is given by Fakhr-i Mudabbir, *Ādāb al-ḥarb*, India Office ms. f. 76a, ed. Khwānsārī, 246–7; Fakhr-i Mudabbir claimed descent on his mother's side from Bilgetigin, cf. Shafi, 'Fresh light on the Ghaznavids', 191, so that some family tradition may be enshrined here. The anecdote here states that the besieging Turkish army fell back from Gardīz when its commander was killed; hence the town probably did not come under permanent Turkish control until Sebüktigin's rule was firmly established in Ghazna. See in general for this dark period of the region's history, Bosworth, art. cit.

The date of Bilgetigin's death. Jūzjānī, *Ṭabaqāt-i Nāṣirī*, I, 227, tr. I, 73, states that he was amīr in Ghazna for ten years, but this must be an over-estimate, even on the assumption that Bilgetigin was killed in 364/974–5, as certain later sources assert, see Nāẓim, op. cit., 27.

The Amīr Böri. For the noun *böri* (= 'wolf' in all Turkish languages except the southwestern group, which has *kurt*, see Sir Gerard

Clauson *An etymological dictionary of pre-thirteenth century Turkish* [Oxford 1972], 356); the text writes Bīrī, as against Kāshgharī's usual orthography of *burī*. It seems nevertheless impossible to read this name of Ibn Bābā's as Pīrēy, as does Raverty in his translation of Jūzjānī, loc. cit., or as Pīrī, as does Nāẓim, in loc. cit.

The date of Sebüktigin's assumption of leadership. This is given more exactly in Jūzjānī, loc. cit., as Friday, 27 Shaʿbān 366/20 April 977; Ibn al-Athīr, ed. Tornberg, VIII, 503, ed. Beirut, VIII, 683–4, gives only the year.

§4. *The rebellion of the Sīmjūrīs.* Detailed accounts of the historical background to these events, including the fall of the Sāmānids and the rise of Maḥmūd of Ghazna, are given in Barthold, op. cit., 250 ff., in Nāẓim, op. cit., 24 ff., 36 ff., and by Frye and Bosworth in *The Cambridge history of Iran*, IV, 155–60, 168–9.

§5. *The date and place of Sebüktigin's death.* According to the *Ḥudūd al-ʿālam*, tr. Minorsky, 109, cf. 342, Madr u Mūy were 'two small towns within the limits of Andarāb'; they lay in fact on the route from Baghlān to Bāmiyān and Parwān, in the basin of the Surkhāb river. Ibn Bābā's information here is further to be found in Jūzjānī, see Nāẓim, op. cit., 32. The exact day of Sebüktigin's death does not seem to be mentioned in any of the sources.

The succession of Ismāʿīl b. Sebüktigin. It was suggested by the present writer in his article 'A Turco-Mongol practice amongst the early Ghaznavids?' *CAJ*, VII (1962) 237–40, that the anomalous and surprising designation of Ismāʿīl as Sebüktigin's heir in Ghazna, and the designation of Muḥammad as Maḥmūd's heir there a generation later, might be connected with the ancient steppe past of the Turks and with the institution of ultimogeniture amongst the early Mongols. In the light of information communicated to me by the late Sir Gerard Clauson, that the Mongol institution of the *očigin* appears to be an indigenous Mongol one, and is in any case known only from much later times, I would not now seriously maintain this view. History provides plenty of examples of rulers making unfathomable, and even wildly impossible, choices of heirs.

Ismāʿīl as one of Maḥmūd's subsequent commanders. Ibn Bābā has here confused Ismāʿīl with Maḥmūd's other brother Abū l-Muẓaffar Naṣr, who was governor in Bust at Sebüktigin's death and who supported Maḥmūd in the struggle for the throne; he subsequently became governor of Sīstān and commander-in-chief of the army of Khurasan for Maḥmūd, see Nāẓim, op. cit., 38–9, 70, 152. After

Maḥmūd's victory over him, Ismāʿīl was in actuality imprisoned or exiled amongst the tributary petty dynasty of Farīghūnids in Gūzgān, see ibid., 41.

§6. *The date of Maḥmūd's birth.* This is also the date given by Jūzjānī, I, 228, tr. I, 76, and also, according to Nāẓim, op. cit., 34, in ʿAufī's *Jawāmiʿ al-ḥikāyāt*, where Baihaqī is also quoted as an authority; the part of the *Mujalladāt* mentioning this information must be lost.

§7. *The Ḥājib Begtuzun.* The second element in this name must be the old Turkish title *tōḏun* (the vowel *ō* being indicated from Chinese transcriptions), a title found in the Tiu-kiu empire for an office-holder coming after the *élteber* in the hierarchy. By Kāshgharī's time the title had lost most of its importance, for he defines it as 'the village headman who divides out irrigation water' (Clauson *An etymological dictionary of pre-thirteenth century Turkish*, 457), but it was clearly still a title of prestige in the preceding century.

The march of Maḥmūd and his brother on Merv. Ms Nuruosmaniye adds after *maʿa akhīhi* the name Ismāʿīl; again, we have a confusion with Maḥmūd's other brother Naṣr, see above s.v. §5.

The Sāmānids' khuṭba for aṭ-Ṭā'iʿ. Ibn Bābā fails to mention that Maḥmūd, like his Sāmānid overlords, had until this point always recognised aṭ-Ṭā'iʿ and not al-Qādir as caliph both on their coins and in the *khuṭba*; see Bosworth, *The Ghaznavids*, 28–9, G. Hennequin 'Grandes monnaies sāmānides et ghaznavides de l'Hindū Kush 331–421 A.H., étude numismatique et historique' *Annales islamologiques*, IX (Cairo 1970) 155–6, and M. Mitchiner *The multiple dirhems of medieval Afghanistan* (London 1973) 20–2. Hennequin also notes here that one of the coins examined by him (the coins in question are a collection of Sāmānid and early Ghaznavid dirhams from the regions of Ṭukhāristān and Badakhshān), minted by Maḥmūd in 389/999, lacks the usual formula of caliphal acknowledgement, but has in the usual place for this on the coin's reverse a formula he proposes very tentatively to read as *Allāh mumallik* 'God [is] the establisher of thrones and kingdoms'. He accordingly plausibly suggests that this coin dates from just before Maḥmūd's recognition and official investiture by al-Qādir as ruler in Khurasan, and represents an attitude of canny opportunism and temporising by Maḥmūd or one of his subordinates. The deposed caliph aṭ-Ṭā'iʿ actually died shortly after this time in 393/1003, having been imprisoned by the Būyid ruler Bahā' ad-Daula, see al-Khaṭīb al-Baghdādī *Ta'rīkh Baghdād* (Cairo 1349/1931) XI, 79.

§8. *Muḥammad b. Maḥmūd's first sultanate.* Amongst all the sources coming after Gardīzī and Baihaqī, Shabānkāra'ī, in his *Majmaʿ al-ansāb*, ff. 182a–184a, has the most detailed account of this reign, doubtless deriving ultimately from Baihaqī's *Mujalladāt*, in its additional details, from the missing part.

§9. *Maḥmūd's dying charge.* According to Shabānkāra'ī, f. 180a, Maḥmūd did manage before his death to give his *waṣāyā* or final injunctions to his sons, his brother Yūsuf and his sister Khuttalī Khātūn (the Ḥurra-yi Khuttalī of Baihaqī), the latter being made superintendent of the interests of Maḥmūd's harem, his wives and concubines.

The Ḥājib ʿAlī al-Qarīb. This name appears in similar form in Baihaqī and Jūzjānī, sc. as ʿAlī-yi Qarīb (not ʿAlī Qurbat, as in Raverty's tr. of the *Ṭabaqāt-i Nāṣirī*, I, 89), but also in certain sources in the Persian form of ʿAlī-yi Khwīshāwand. Gardīzī, ed. Nāẓim, 78, 93, ed. Ḥabībī, 185, 194, names him as ʿAlī b. Il-Arslan al-Qarīb; cf. also Baihaqī, 82, tr. 148, where we have 'the Ḥājib [ʿAlī b.] Il-Arslan, Zaʿīm al-Ḥujjāb'. What the precise degree of relationship to the Ghaznavid royal house consisted of here is unknown; it may have been a bond of foster-relationship or through marriage, or, as R. Gelpke suggested in his *Sulṭān Masʿūd I. von Ġazna. Die drei ersten Jahre seiner Herrschaft*, 48, *Qarīb/Khwīshāvand* may simply have been an honorific title bestowed by Maḥmūd as a token of esteem; cf. the form of address *ʿamm* 'paternal uncle' by which Masʿūd subsequently referred to ʿAlī Dāya, another Turkish general, see below under §12. For the celebrated Ḥasanak, scion of the prominent Nīshāpūr family of the Mīkālīs, see Bosworth, op. cit., 182–4, and EI^2 s.v. (B. Spuler).

Muḥammad's assumption of the throne in Ghazna. Shabānkāra'ī, ff. 181b–182a, states that the notables and leading men in the state (*aʿyān u arkān*) invited a reluctant Muḥammad, conscious of his inferiority to his brother in experience and popularity with the army, to assume power, because Muḥammad was comparatively near at hand, whilst Masʿūd was away in western Persia, and there was a fear lest strife, *fitna*, erupt in Ghazna if the throne were not quickly filled. This last argument was the one subsequently adduced by ʿAlī Qarīb to Masʿūd when he was negotiating with the latter to betray Muḥammad's cause (ibid., f. 182b).

§10. *Muḥammad's departure from Ghazna to encounter Masʿūd's forces.* According to Shabānkāra'ī again, f. 183b, Muḥammad marched out of the capital with 20,000 men, but after ʿAlī Qarīb had suborned the men away from their allegiance, he was in the end left with only 60 of the royal ghulāms.

Tigīnābād. This place in the early Islamic region of ar-Rukhkhaj or Zamīn-Dāwar has never been identified, but must have lain very near to Qandahār; it is mentioned as late as Juwainī (sc. in the 7th/13th century), and an 18th-century European traveller's map of the area records a 'Tecniabad' (this map is reproduced by K. Fischer in his 'Zur Lage von Kandahar an Landverbindungen zwischen Iran und Indien' *Bonner Jahrbücher des Rheinischen Landmuseums in Bonn CLXVII* (1967) 191–2). The origin of this curious Turco-Persian hybrid name is equally obscure, and there is nothing definitely to identify the *tégin* 'prince', or the Turkish soldier whose name included this widespread component. J. Marquart, in his 'Das Reich Zābul und der Gott Žūn vom 6.–9. Jahrhundert' *Festschrift Eduard Sachau*, ed. G. Weil (Berlin 1915) 269, building on his theory of an early settlement of ethnic Turks in the southern Hephthalite kingdom of Zābul, interpreted Tigīnābād as being a shortened version of Ai-tigin-ābād, from the name Ai-tigin-shāh. He omitted to say who this mysterious personage was, although the inference is that he was a local ruler after whom or after whose capital the place was named. In fact, it is now dubious that the Turkish title of *tégin*, certainly known amongst the Orkhon Turks, was ever known in pre-Islamic eastern Afghanistan, the evidence from coin legends having been rejected by Ghirshman, and the evidence from Chinese transcriptions of names, evidence made much of by Marquart and his co-worker the sinologist de Groot, being notoriously vague and unreliable.

There seems to be no unambiguous attestation of this place name before the early Ghaznavid period. Geographers like Maqdisī link with Panjwāy, the main town of ar-Rukhkhaj, a place called Bakrāwādh; this writer states, *Aḥsan at-taqāsīm*, ed. M. J. de Goeje (Leiden 1906), 305, that 'Bakrāwādh is a big town; its Friday mosque is situated in the bazaar, and the people get their water from a perennial stream'. Much depends on whether we correct this name to Tigīnābād (as did Marquart, in his *Ērānšahr nach der Geographie des Ps. Moses Xorenacʿi*, in *AGGW*, N.F. III/2 [Berlin 1901] 272 n. 6), or alternatively, correct the spelling Tigīnābād to the place name Bakrāwādh (as suggested by G. Le Strange *The Lands of the Eastern Caliphate* [Cambridge 1905] 347). But it is strange that the *Ḥudūd al-ʿālam*, which records several places in Zābulistān and Zamīn-Dāwar, including Panjwāy, does not mention Tigīnābād. Minorsky, in his commentary to the *Ḥudūd al-ʿālam*, 345, opined that Tigīnābād might possibly lie on the site of Qandahār, and this hypothesis is worth serious consideration, as we shall see below.

For Qandahār itself, whilst mentioned in the 3rd–4th/9th–10th century geographers, unaccountably drops out of mention during the Ghaznavid and Ghūrid periods. Could it therefore be that Tigīnābād was a re-naming of Qandahār during the middle years or the second half of the 4th/10th century, a naming of its conqueror from amongst the Turkish ghulām commanders of the Sāmānids who established themselves firstly at Bust and then at Ghazna? From the Bust group, we know of a Qaratigin, and from the Ghazna one, an Alptigin, a Bilgetigin and a Sebüktigin, all with this component *tigin* in their names. Or if Tigīnābād were not identical with Qandahār, could it be that Qandahār drops out of mention temporarily because it was overshadowed by the newly-constructed, nearby settlement of Tigīnābād? Maqdisī, 304, speaks of the settlement called al-ʿAskar, half-a-farsakh from Bust on the Ghazna road, and described as 'something like a town' and as the residence of the ruler or seat of local authority (*as-sulṭān*). This site is obviously that on the Helmand river banks which we now know as Lashkar-i Bāzār, where the early Ghaznavids had a great complex of palaces and other buildings. It seems equally possible that such a military and administrative settlement should have been made not far from Lashkar-i Bāzār and in the heart of ar-Rukhkhaj, in order to secure and dominate a region not long brought within the Islamic orbit, but that it should then have been abandoned in the later Ghaznavid period.

The fertile Qandahār plain provides several potential sites where rocky outcrops exist and where the *qalʿa* of Kūhtīz in Tigīnābād, where the deposed Muḥammad was imprisoned (see below), could have been built; of course, Old Qandahār, with its impressive rock-perched citadel ruins, is a fine example of these outcrops. Dr David Whitehouse, who made a preliminary archaeological survey of the site of Old Qandahār in spring 1974, has mentioned to the present author the existence of these possible sites in the area, such as that of the modern site of Sang-ḥiṣār.

On the above analysis, when Gardīzī, ed. Nāẓim, 11, ed. Ḥabībī, 139, speaks of Yaʿqūb b. Laith's marching from Sīstān to Bust and from there to Panjwāy and Tigīnābād to fight the Zunbīl or local ruler of Zamīn-Dāwar, he would be using the name in familiar, contemporary usage for the place, and not necessarily the one used in the early Ṣaffārid period.

Il-Direk. Ibn Bābā's text has *y.l.d.r.k*, which yields perfectly good sense from *él* 'realm, land ruled by an independent ruler' + *tirēk/ dirēk* 'support, column' (cf. Clauson *An etymological dictionary*, 121–2, 543). In a Uighur Turkish Manichaean text of the early 9th century, *tirek* is a title, presumably 'support [of the realm]'; cf. Arabic honorifics like ʿImād ad-Daula and Rukn ad-Daula, and also the Alp-Direk, a Qïpchaq chief who came to the Khwārazm-Shāh Tekish b. Il-Arslan at Jand in 591/1195 (Barthold *Turkestan down to the Mongol invasion*,[3] 343). However, in Baihaqī, 1, 4, 50, 56–9, tr. 72, 74, 117–18, 123–7 and *passim*, the name of ʿAlī Qarīb's brother, undoubtedly identical with Ibn Bābā's Il-Direk, is invariably written *m.n.g.y.t.rāk* (as also in Gardīzī, ed. Nāẓim, 96, ed. Ḥabībī, 196). This could be interpreted as *Mengü-Direk 'everlasting support' (*beñgü/meñgü* 'eternal, everlasting', Clauson, op. cit., 350–1), the first element being quite a common one in Turkish onomastic, cf. Mengü-tigin, Mengü-bars, Mengü-temür, Mengü-verish (J. Sauvaget 'Noms et surnoms de Mamelouks' *JA* CCXXXVIII (1950) 56). The gap between the consonant ducti of the two names in Ibn Bābā and Baihaqī-Gardīzī seems, however, unbridgeable.

The Ḥājib ʿAlī al-Qarīb's attempt to ingratiate himself with Masʿūd. According to Shabānkāra'ī, *Majmaʿ al-ansāb*, f. 184a, the somewhat apprehensive ʿAlī eventually came to Masʿūd at Herat and brought with him presents, including a pearl necklace and 1,000 dinars, but as Ibn Bābā goes on to relate in §11, this did not in the long run benefit ʿAlī and the others responsible for the betrayal of Muḥammad.

§11. *The amīr Yūsuf b. Sebüktigin.* Yūsuf, a younger brother of Maḥmūd's and more of the age-group of Masʿūd and Muḥammad (the three children had been educated together, see Bosworth *The Ghaznavids*, 129), had been made commander-in-chief of the army by Muḥammad on his accession (Gardīzī, ed. Nāẓim, 93, ed. Ḥabībī, 194). In spite of, or perhaps because of, his defection to Masʿūd's side, Masʿūd never trusted him, and although he was not involved in the almost immediate destitution of ʿAlī al-Qarīb and his brother, the sultan did in 422/1031 have him arrested on suspicion of disloyalty, see Bosworth, op. cit., 96, 232. He was imprisoned in the stronghold of Sakāwand, in the Lōgar valley near Kabul, where he died in the following year 423/1032 (Baihaqī, 252, tr. 339–40). A lasting feeling of hatred against Masʿūd was now engendered amongst Yūsuf's kindred and former ghulāms. Hence there were to be found in the Seljuq camp in Khurasan just before the decisive battle of Dandānqān deserters who were former troops of amīr Yūsuf and of the other fallen Turkish generals, and Yūsuf's son Sulaimān was one of the ringleaders, with ʿAlī Qarīb's son, in the *putsch* of 432/1040–1, which raised Muḥammad to the throne for a second time at the head of the mutineers from Masʿūd's army (see above, Ch. 1, pp. 19–20).

The seizure and confinement of Sultan Muḥammad. According to Baihaqī, 1, 70, tr. 71, 137, ʿAlī Qarīb and his brother initially confined Muḥammad in the stronghold of Kūhtīz at Tigīnābād before he was moved by Masʿūd to more permanent quarters in the fortress of Mandīsh in Ghūr (for this last, see below, commentary on §15). The correct name of this fortress at Tigīnābād is uncertain. Kūhtīz is the form of the Tehran 1307/1890 lithograph of Baihaqī and that adopted by Ghanī and Fayyāḍ and by Saʿīd Nafīsī in their editions, whereas Morley in his Calcutta 1862 Bibliotheca Indica edition read Kūhshīr. What is interesting is the apparent appearance of this name as the fortress of Kūhizh in the *Ta'rīkh-i Sīstān*, 207, where it is mentioned as the seat of Ṣāliḥ b. al-Ḥujr's revolt in ar-Rukhkhaj against Yaʿqūb b. Laith in 253/867.

The seizure of ʿAlī Qarīb and his accomplices. In Masʿūd's letter to his brother Muḥammad, which reached the latter just after his transference to captivity at Mandīsh, the sultan sardonically remarks that ʿAlī, the one who set up and deposed rulers, has now himself been cast down, *ʿAlī-yi Ḥājib, ki amīr-rā nishānda būd, farmūdīm tā bi-nishānand* (Baihaqī, 76, tr. 142); ʿAlī had previously referred to himself in conversation with the Chief Secretary Abū Naṣr Mishkān as a 'king-maker', *amīr-nishān* (ibid., 54, tr. 121).

The period of Muḥammad's rule. The extent of Muḥammad's first sultanate is given here wrongly; we should read 421 for 422 (i.e. Shawwāl 421/October 1030), giving him a reign of six months, as is confirmed by Baihaqī, Gardīzī and Jūzjānī, see Bosworth *The Ghaznavids*, 228.

§12. *The Dandānqān campaign.* Baihaqī gives a highly-detailed, eyewitness account of this last campaign of Masʿūd's against the Seljuqs in Khurasan, which has been made the subject of a special article by B.N. Zakhoder, see Bosworth, op. cit., 251–2. Ibn Bābā's brief account agrees substantially with this, with the additional and improbable detail of the Ghaznavid generals' contemplated surrender of their sultan to the Türkmens in order to save their own skins.

The Türkmens' tactics before joining battle. Ibn Bābā's mention of the Türkmens as drawn up in groups on the sandhills accords with the information in Gardīzī, ed. Nāẓim, 107, ed. Ḥabībī, 203, that the Türkmen cavalrymen were drawn up, according to their custom, in compact groups awaiting the enemy: *bar rasm-i khwīsh bi-ārastand ki īshān ḥarb ba-kardūs kunand hama kardūs kardūs shudand.*

The army chiefs' words 'you are now in a position of total ruin'. The translation here follows the reading of ms. Nuruosmaniye 3296, *innaka bi-maḍīʿatin*; ms. Turhan Valide writes here a slightly different consonant ductus for the second word, which might be interpretable as *innaka la-muḍīʿuhu* 'you will bring about the total destruction of the army'.

Masʿūd's 'confronting that group of commanders'. Ms. Nuruosmaniye has the slightly weaker *facilior lectio* of *muqātala* 'attacking' for *muqābala* 'confronting'.

The Ḥājib ʿAlī b. Dāya. The name of this commander is given in full by Gardīzī, ed. Nāẓim, 93, ed. Ḥabībī, 194, as 'Abū l-Ḥasan ʿAlī b. ʿAbdallāh, known as ʿAlī-yi Dāya'. In Ottoman Turkish, *dāy* meant 'maternal uncle' and *dāya* 'foster-mother, wet-nurse' (Radloff *Versuch eines Wörterbuch der Türk-dialecte* III, 815, 1605–6). If we can project this southwestern Turkish word back to the Ghaznavid period (and many of the Ghaznavids' military slaves must have been recruited from southwestern Turkish speaking peoples like the Oghuz and Qïpchaq), it may be that we have a term of endearment or affiliation to the Ghaznavid ruling family similar to that tentatively ascribed to ʿAlī Qarīb, see above, commentary on §9. Despite this possibility, ʿAlī b. Dāya shared the fate of those other generals upon whom Masʿūd vented all the spleen resulting from his defeat.

The extermination of the generals. According to Gardīzī, ed. Nāẓim, 108, ed. Ḥabībī, 203, the three generals named here were imprisoned in a fortress in India, where they died.

§13. *Masʿūd's despatch of Maudūd and Aḥmad b. ʿAbd aṣ-Ṣamad to Balkh, and the rebellion of the army at the Indus crossing.* For an exposition of all these events, see above, Ch. 1, pp. 11ff.; for the career of the vizier Aḥmad [b. Muḥammad] b. ʿAbd aṣ-Ṣamad, see above, Ch. 1, p. 34.

The general Nūshtigin al-Balkhī. This name, very frequently found as a name of Turkish military slaves, is a not unusual compound of Iranian and Turkish elements (whatever the ultimate origin of *tégin*, which Clauson thought belonged to a non-Turkish substratum of the language, see *An etymological dictionary of pre-thirteenth century Turkish*, 483). The *nūsh/anūsh* element is Iranian *anōš* 'undying', 'born of an undying parent', hence Nūshtigin/Anūshtigin, something like 'immortally-born prince'. F. Justi *Iranisches Namenbuch* (Marburg 1895) 18, lists a considerable number of people bearing this name.

The mutineers' marching-off towards Peshawar. The manuscripts of Ibn Bābā have B.r.shūr for something like P.shāwur, to which the meaningless *ba-Dīnawar* of Baihaqī, 331, 690, where the killing of Masʿūd is being mentioned, should be corrected.

§14. *The battle between Maudūd and the rebels*. For this, see above, Ch. 1, pp. 22–4.

'*The decree of God Most High* [*concerning traitors*]'. Ibn Bābā, or his source, is doubtless thinking of such Qur'ānic passages on *qiṣāṣ* as *S. al-Baqara* = ii. 173/178, 'O you who have believed, retaliation in the matter of the slain is prescribed for you . . .', or *S. al-Mā'ida* = v. 37/33, 'The recompense of those who make war on God and His messenger and exert themselves to cause corruption in the land is that they should be killed or crucified . . .'.

§15. *The fortress of Mandīsh*. Mandīsh appears not infrequently in the sources for Ghaznavid and Ghūrid history as an important fortress in the eastern part of Ghūr, and originally as the seat of the local Ghūrī chief Muḥammad b. Sūrī upon whom Sebüktigin and Maḥmūd imposed their suzerainty, see Nāẓim, *The life and times of Sulṭān Maḥmūd of Ghazna*, 70–2; consequently, Jūzjānī mentions it several times in his account of the origins and early history of the Shansabānī rulers of Ghūr, the later dynasty of Ghūrid sultans (see above, Ch. 2, pp. 68–9). As noted above, in the commentary on § 11, it was to Mandīsh that the deposed Muḥammad was in 421/1030 transferred from Tigīnābād; and Mandīsh was one of the fortresses from which Masʿūd collected his treasuries before proceeding to India (see above, Ch. 1, pp. 15–16). If Ibn Bābā is correct here in describing Mandīsh as being 'on the road to Bust', it must have lain in the eastern mountains of Ghūr to the northwest of Zamīn-Dāwar and not far from the course of the upper Helmand.

§16. *The two ephemeral reigns of Masʿūd II b. Maudūd and ʿAlī b. Masʿūd*. See for these events, above, Ch. 1, pp. 37–8, and for the vizier ʿAbd ar-Razzāq b. Aḥmad b. Ḥasan Maimandī, see pp. 34–5.

§§17–19. *The reign of ʿAbd ar-Rashīd and the usurpation of Toghril*. See for these events, above, Ch. 1, pp. 39–47.

§§20–1. *The accession and reign of Farrukh-Zād.* See for these events, above, Ch. 1, pp.46–9.

§22. *The reign of Ibrāhīm.* For this, see above, Ch. 2, pp.50–81.

§23. *The reign of Mas'ūd III b. Ibrāhīm.* For this, see above, Ch. 3, pp.82–9.

APPENDIX B

A List of the Ghaznavid Rulers in Ghazna and India

366–582 / 977–1186

NOTE. This list amplifies and, in the light of further research, in one or two places corrects the Appendix *A list of the rulers in Ghazna 963–1099* in *The Ghaznavids, their empire in Afghanistan and eastern Iran 994–1040*, 307, and the list in *The Islamic dynasties, a chronological and genealogical handbook*, 181.

Abū Manṣūr Sebüktigin b. Qara Bechkem, governor in Ghazna and India on behalf of the Sāmānids, 27 Shaʿbān 366 / 20 April 977.
Ismāʿīl, governor in Ghazna and India, Shaʿbān 387 / August 997.
Abū l-Qāsim Maḥmūd, governor and then independent sultan in Ghazna and India, Rabīʿ I 388 / March 998.
Abū Aḥmad Muḥammad (first reign), sultan in Ghazna and India, end of Rabīʿ II 421 / beginning of May 1030.
Abū Saʿīd Masʿūd I, sultan in Ghazna and India, Shaʿbān 421 / August 1030.
Abū Aḥmad Muḥammad (second reign), sultan in India, 13 Rabīʿ II 432 / 20–21 December 1040.
Abū l-Fatḥ Maudūd, sultan in Ghazna and India, 23 Shaʿbān 432 / 28 April 1041.
Masʿūd II, sultan in Ghazna and India, third quarter of 440 / winter 1048–9?
Abū l-Ḥasan ʿAlī, sultan in Ghazna and India, third quarter of 440 / winter 1048–9?
Abū Manṣūr ʿAbd ar-Rashīd, sultan in Ghazna and India end of 440 / spring 1049?
[Usurpation in Ghazna of Toghrïl, end of Shaʿbān 443 / beginning of January 1052?]
Abū Shujāʿ Farrukh-Zād, sultan in Ghazna and India, 9 Dhū l-Qaʿda 443 / 13 March 1052.

Abū l-Muẓaffar Ibrāhīm, sultan in Ghazna and India, 19 Ṣafar 451/6 April 1059.
Abū Saʿd Masʿūd III, sultan in Ghazna and India, Shawwāl 492/August 1099 or shortly afterwards.
Shīr-Zād, sultan in Ghazna and India, Shawwāl 508/March 1115.
Abū l-Mulūk Malik Arslan, sultan in Ghazna and India, 6 Shawwāl 509/22 February 1116.
Abū l-Muẓaffar Bahrām Shāh, sultan in Ghazna and India acknowledging Seljuq suzerainty, early summer 511/summer 1117.
Khusrau Shāh, sultan in Ghazna and India and then in India only, early 522/spring 1157?
Abū l-Muẓaffar Khusrau Malik, sultan in India, Rajab 555/July 1160.
[Ghūrid conquest 582/1186]

Abbreviations

AGGW	*Abhandlungen der Königlichen Gesellschaft der Wissenschaften zu Göttingen*, Phil. Hist. Kl. (Berlin)
AO	*Acta Orientalia* (Leiden, Copenhagen)
BEtO	*Bulletin des Etudes Orientales* (Damascus)
CAJ	*Central Asiatic Journal* (The Hague-Wiesbaden)
EI[1]	*Encyclopaedia of Islam*, 1st edn. (Leiden–London)
EI[2]	*Encyclopaedia of Islam*, 2nd edn. (Leiden–London)
IC	*Islamic Culture* (Hyderabad)
IQ	*Islamic Quarterly* (London)
JA	*Journal Asiatique* (Paris)
JAOS	*Journal of the American Oriental Society* (New Haven, Conn.)
JASB	*Journal of the Asiatic Society of Bengal* (Calcutta)
JNES	*Journal of Near Eastern Studies* (Chicago)
JRAS	*Journal of the Royal Asiatic Society* (London)
MW	*Muslim World* (Hartford, Conn.)
SI	*Studia Islamica* (Paris)
WNZ	*Wiener Numismatische Zeitung* (Vienna)
WZKM	*Wiener Zeitschrift für die Kunde des Morgenlandes* (Vienna)
ZDMG	*Zeitschrift der Deutschen Morgenländischen Gesellschaft* (Leipzig, Berlin, Wiesbaden)

Notes and References

CHAPTER ONE

1 See now for its exact position, Minorsky's Second Series of Addenda to the *Ḥudūd al-ʿālam*,[2] ed. C. E. Bosworth (London 1970) xxxviii–xxxix.

2 Baihaqī *Ta'rīkh-i Masʿūdī*, ed. Q. Ghanī and ʿA. A. Fayyāḍ (Tehran 1324/1945) 630 ff., 639, tr. A. K. Arends *Istorya Masʿuda 1030–1041*[2] (Moscow 1969) 765 ff., 775.

3 Baihaqī, 240–1, 242–5, 291, tr. 325–6, 327–31, 385; Gardīzī *Zain al-akhbār*, ed. M. Nāẓim (Berlin 1928) 97–8, ed. ʿAbd al-Ḥayy Ḥabībī (Tehran 1347/1968) 197; cf. Bosworth *The Ghaznavids, their empire in Afghanistan and eastern Iran 994–1040* (Edinburgh 1963) 54, 127.

4 For the history of the former people at this time, see idem 'The Kūfichīs or Qufṣ in Persian history', *Iran, Journal of the British Institute of Persian Studies* XIV (1976) 9–17.

5 Read as Kızh/Kīj in Khwānsārī's edition of this work (see n. 10 below), but as Tīz by Shafi in her translation of the anecdote (see n. 10 below); the India Office manuscript is ambiguous, but resembles Tīz rather than Kīzh/Kīj.

6 Thus plausibly corrected by Shafi from the Q.r.māshīr of the text.

7 S.w.r.j in Khwānsārī's text, read by Shafi as Broach (B.rūj); the India Office manuscript has S.r.w.j.

8 Thus identified by M. Nāẓim *The life and times of Sulṭān Maḥmūd of Ghazna* (Cambridge 1931) Appx. J, 197–202.

9 Thus read by Shafi; Khwānsārī has ʿ.m.r.bīla, and the India Office manuscript virtually the same.

10 *Ādāb al-ḥarb*, India Office ms. 647, ff. 28b–29a, ed. Aḥmad Suhailī Khwānsārī (Tehran 1346/1967), 104–5, tr. I. M. Shafi 'Fresh light on the Ghaznavids', *IC*, XII (1938) 201.

11 Whereas there was quite a rich array of mints operating under the early sultans, after the loss of the western provinces (sc. from the reign of Maudūd onwards) the minting of coins appears to have been concentrated on Ghazna and Lahore, cf. D. Sourdel *Inventaire des monnaies anciennes du Musée de Caboul* (Damascus 1953) XV–XVI.

12 Baihaqī, 645–8, tr. 782–5; Gardīzī, ed. Nāẓim, 108, ed. Ḥabībī, 203; Ibn Bābā *Kitāb Ra's māl an-nadīm*, Istanbul ms. Turhan Valide 234, f. 207a; Mīrkhwānd *Rauḍat aṣ-ṣafā'*, ed. and F. tr. Wilken *Historia*

Gasnevidarum persice et latine (Berlin 1832) text 107, tr. 247; Firishta *Gulshan-i Ibrāhīmī*, Manchester ms. Lindesiana, Persian 380, f. 63a, tr. J. Briggs *History of the rise of the Mahomedan power in India till the year A.D. 1612* (Calcutta 1966) I, 66.

13 Baihaqī, 643, tr. 780, cf. Bosworth *The Ghaznavids*, 261 ff.

14 See *EI*² Suppl. art. 'Banīdjūrids' (Bosworth).

15 Ibn Funduq *Ta'rīkh-i Baihaq*, ed. Aḥmad Bahmanyār (Tehran 1317/1938) 120–1; Ḥusainī *Akhbār ad-daula as-saljūqiyya*, ed. Muḥammad Iqbāl (Lahore 1933) 27; cf. W. Barthold *Turkestan down to the Mongol invasion*,³ ed. C. E. Bosworth (London 1968) 303–4.

16 Concerning this name, see below, n. 80.

17 Ibn al-Athīr *al-Kāmil fī t-ta'rīkh*, ed. C. J. Tornberg (Leiden 1851–76) IX, 330–1, ed. Beirut 1385–7/1965–7, IX, 483–5.

18 Baihaqī, 644–5, 649–50, tr. 781–2, 787–8.

19 ibid., 624, tr. 759.

20 ibid., 652–4, tr. 790–2, cf. Bosworth *The Ghaznavids*, 62.

21 Baihaqī, 652, 657, tr. 789–90, 796; Gardīzī, ed. Nāẓim, 108–9, ed. Ḥabībī, 204; Mīrkhwānd, 107, tr. 247; Firishta, loc. cit.; Sir H. M. Elliot and J. Dowson *The history of India as told by its own historians. II. The Muhammadan period* (London 1869) 144–5.

22 The exact date of departure, Tuesday, 12 Muḥarram 432/22 September 1040, is given by Ḥusainī, 13.

23 Gardīzī, ed. Ḥabībī, 204; Baihaqī, 654, tr. 792.

24 Gardīzī, ed. Nāẓim, 110, ed. Ḥabībī, 205.

25 The *nisba* is apparently from Kurnik, a place in Sīstān according to Yāqūt *Mu'jam al-buldān* (Beirut 1374/1955–7) IV, 457, mentioned also by Ya'qūbī in his history in connection with events in the early 3rd/9th century, see the *Ta'rīkh-i Sīstān*, ed. Malik ash-Shu'arā' Bahār (Tehran 1314/1935) 180 n. 9.

26 Baihaqī, 331–2, 643, 648–9, tr. 419, 779–80, 786.

27 On the questions involved in the problem of the ethnic nature of the Khalaj and the apparent process of Afghanisation that they underwent, see Bosworth *The Ghaznavids*, 35–6, and idem *EI*² art. 'Khaladj. i. History'. Gardīzī's usage of the term 'Afghan' is an early instance of this last in Islamic sources, the earliest mention so far known being that of the *Ḥudūd al-'ālam* seventy years previously.

28 Gardīzī, ed. Nāẓim, 109, ed. Ḥabībī, 204; Baihaqī, 658, 662, tr. 797, 802. Gardīzī's information that the leader of the expedition—even if only nominally—was the prince Īzad-Yār b. Mas'ūd cannot be accurate, since we have the much more explicit and detailed information of Baihaqī that Īzad-Yār was on a mission to India at this time, see below.

29 Baihaqī, 661, tr. 800. The identifications of M.r.manāra and Gīrī are those of S. H. Hodivala *Studies in Indo-Muslim history: a critical commentary on Elliot and Dowson's 'History of India as told by its own historians'* I (Bombay 1939) 160, 169, 194–5, and Addenda, p. xiii.

30 See O. Pritsak 'Die Karachaniden' *Der Islam* XXXI (1954) 36–7, 44–6, for the exact identification of this Qarakhanid prince.

31 Baihaqī, 629, 643, 659, tr. 765, 780, 797–8.

32 Gardīzī, ed. Nāẓim, 109, ed. Ḥabībī, 204; Mīrkhwānd, 113, tr. 252; Firishta, loc. cit., tr. I, 66.

33 This fortress of Naghar or Barghund is to be equated, according to Hodivala, op. cit., 168, with the N.gh.r or N.gh.z of Yazdī's *Ẓafar-nāma* and 'Abd ar-Razzāq Samarqandī's *Maṭla' as-sa'dain*, situated near Iryāb and perhaps identical with the modern Baghzan in the Kurram Agency of the North-West Frontier Province of Pakistan.

34 For these formally-bestowed forms of address, see Bosworth 'The titulature of the early Ghaznavids' *Oriens* XV (1962) 228–9.

35 Baihaqī, 659–60, tr. 798–9; Gardīzī, ed. Nāẓim, 109, ed. Ḥabībī, 204; Ḥusainī, 13, naming an extra, fifth son of Muḥammad's, 'Abd ar-Raḥīm, who figures also in Ibn Funduq's *Ta' rīkh-i Baihaq*, 71, with the nickname of *al-Ahwaj* 'the tall one, the impetuous one'. Elliot and Dowson *The history of India* II, 147–9.

36 Baihaqī, 661–3, tr. 801–2; Elliot and Dowson, op. cit., II, 149–53.

37 Baihaqī, 639, 664, tr. 775–6, 803.

38 The consonant ductus of this particular name, clearly ending in -kōt, is reminiscent of the fortress of Sānkōt (?) somewhere in the Lōghar valley region towards which Sultan Maudūd was heading when he died, see below, p. 27.

39 Baihaqī, 664, tr. 803; Gardīzī, ed. Nāẓim, 109, ed. Ḥabībī, 204; Ḥusainī, 13. According to Ibn al-Athīr, ed. Tornberg, IX, 331, ed. Beirut, IX, 485, Mas'ūd left Ghazna seven days after the departure of the expedition to Balkh under Maudūd and Aḥmad b. 'Abd aṣ-Ṣamad, which itself departed, this historian says, in Rabī' I.

40 Gardīzī, ed. Nāẓim, 109, ed. Ḥabībī, 204; Ibn Bābā, ff. 207a–b; Ḥusainī, 13–14; Ibn al-Athīr, ed. Tornberg, IX, 331, ed. Beirut, IX, 485; Jūzjānī, I, 234, tr. I, 95; Mīrkhwānd, 107–8, tr. 247.

41 For Muḥammad's poetical interests, see Bosworth 'The poetical citations in Baihaqī's *Ta'rīkh-i Mas'ūdī*' (forthcoming).

42 On the probable situation of this fortress of Mandīsh, see the discussion below, in the Appendix, commentary to §15.

43 Baihaqī, 75–6, tr. 141–2.

44 For a discussion of the question of Muḥammad's blindness, see also A. de Biberstein Kazimirski *Menoutchehri, poète persan du 11ème siècle de notre ère (du 5ième de l'hégire)* (Paris 1886) 37, 38, 131 n. 3.

45 Ibn Bābā, f. 207a; cf. on Waihind, Nāẓim 'The Hindu Sháhiya kingdom of Ohind' *JRAS* (1927) 483.

46 *Ṭabaqāt-i Nāṣirī*, tr. Raverty, I, 95 n. 4. Bīrūnī in his *India* identifies Mārīkala with Takshaśila, i.e. Taxila, twelve miles to the northwest of Rawalpindi, see Hodivala *Studies in Indo-Muslim history* I, 193–4.

47 cf. Baihaqī, 272, 442, 661, 690, tr. 363, 544, 800, 835. Readings such as the K.srī of Gardīzī, ed. Nāẓim, 110, are accordingly to be rejected, and Tornberg chose the inferior reading of his manuscripts, K.y.kī, cf. Ibn al-Athīr, IX, 332, with the correct reading in n. 4 (= ed. Beirut, IX, 485 n. 5). The place is further mentioned by Jūzjānī, II, 126, tr. II, 1043–4, in the account of Chingiz Khan's attack on India after defeating

the Khwārazm-Shāh Jalāl ad-Dīn in 618/1221; for its location, see above,

48 Gardīzī, ed. Nāẓim, 109–10, ed. Ḥabībī, 204–5; Ibn Bābā, f. 207b; Ḥusainī, 13–14; Ibn al-Athīr, ed. Tornberg, IX, 331–2, ed. Beirut, IX, 485–6; Jūzjānī, I, 234, tr. I, 95; Mīrkhwānd, 108–9; tr. 247–9; Firishta, f. 63b, tr. I, 67.

49 See Bosworth *The Ghaznavids* 110, 231–2.

50 Baihaqī, 570, tr. 696, cf. Bosworth, op. cit., 106.

51 Gardīzī, ed. Nāẓim, 110, ed. Ḥabībī, 205; Ibn Bābā, ff. 207b–208a; Ḥusainī, 14; Ibn al-Athīr, ed. Tornberg, IX, 332, ed. Beirut, IX, 486; Mīrkhwānd, 109–10, tr. 249; Firishta, f. 63b, tr. I, 67–8.

52 Ibn al-Athīr, ed. Tornberg, IX, 333, ed. Beirut, IX, 486–7; cf. Bosworth, op. cit., 77, 101, 235.

53 Baihaqī, 432, 452, tr. 532, 555–6.

54 ibid., 503–4, 535, tr. 615–16, 654; Gardīzī, ed. Nāẓim, 103, ed. Ḥabībī, 200; Elliot and Dowson *History of India* II, 135–6.

55 Baihaqī, 559–60, tr. 683–4.

56 No Saʿīd is mentioned among the nine sons of Masʿūd enumerated by Jūzjānī, I, 234 n. 4, tr. I, 95; but this author omits to mention ʿAbd ar-Razzāq, whose existence is attested by at least three mentions in Baihaqī.

57 Baihaqī, 215 (where, at the time of the opening of the marriage negotiations with the Qarakhanids—for which see below—the sultan says that Maudūd *mihtar-i farzandān-i mā-st wa baʿd az mā walī ʿahd-i mā dar mulk way khwāhad būd*), 564–5, tr. 296, 689–90.

58 For this identification, see Pritsak 'Karachanidische Streitfragen 1–4. 2. Wer war ʿAlī-Tigin?' *Oriens* III (1950) 216–24.

59 Baihaqī, 215, 424–6, 527, tr. 296, 524–6, 644–5; cf. Barthold *Turkestan down to the Mongol invasion*,[3] 294–5, 299–300, R. Gelpke *Sulṭān Masʿūd I. von Ġazna. Die drei ersten Jahre seiner Herrschaft (421/1030–424/1033)* (Munich 1957) 74–6, and Pritsak, 'Die Karachaniden' 33–4.

60 Jūzjānī, I, 235, tr. I, 97; Ibn al-Athīr, ed. Tornberg, IX, 381, ed. Beirut, IX, 558.

61 Gardīzī, ed. Nāẓim, 110–11, ed. Ḥabībī, 205; Ibn al-Athīr, ed. Tornberg, IX, 334, ed. Beirut, IX, 488.

62 Ibn Bābā, f. 207b; Ḥusainī, 14; Ibn al-Athīr, loc. cit.

63 Ibn al-Athīr, ed. Tornberg, IX, 333, ed. Beirut, IX, 487; Mīrkhwānd, 111, tr. 250.

64 Jūzjānī, I, 234, tr. I, 96; cf. Hodivala *Studies in Indo-Muslim history* I, 195.

65 Baihaqī, 625–6, tr. 759–60.

66 Gardīzī, ed. Nāẓim, 111, ed. Ḥabībī, 206.

67 ibid., ed. Nāẓim, 111–12, ed. Ḥabībī, 206 (who speaks of executions by arrow shots and by tying the victims to the tails of enraged horses); Ibn Bābā, ff. 207b–208a; Ḥusainī, 14; Ibn al-Athīr, ed. Tornberg, IX, 334, ed. Beirut, IX, 488; Shabānkāra'ī *Majmaʿ al-ansāb fī t-tawārīkh*, Istanbul ms. Yeni Cami 909, f. 187b; Mīrkhwānd, 111–12, tr. 250–1; Firishta, ff. 64a–b, tr. I, 68–9.

68 Ḥusainī, loc. cit.; Ibn al-Athīr, loc. cit.; Jūzjānī, tr. I, 97 n. 2; Fakhr-i Mudabbir *Ādāb al-ḥarb*, ff. 93a–b, ed. Khwānsārī, 318; Mīrkhwānd,

112–13, tr. 252; Firishta, f. 64b, tr. I, 69; Masson *Narrative of various journeys in Baluchistan, Afghanistan and the Punjab* (London 1842) I, 184; Hodivala *Studies in Indo-Muslim history* I, 195.

69 Ibn al-Athīr, loc. cit.; Ibn Bābā, f. 208a.

70 Gardīzī, ed. Nāẓim, 110, ed. Ḥabībī, 205, cf. Saif ad-Dīn ʿUqailī *Āthār al-wuzarā'*, India Office ms. 1569, f. 87b (list of the Ghaznavid sultans, their reigns and titles, not in the printed edition of Urmawī); anon. *Mujmal at-tawārīkh wa-l-qiṣaṣ*, ed. Malik ash-Shuʿarā' Bahār (Tehran 1318/1939) 429; E. Thomas 'On the coins of the Kings of Ghazní' *JRAS* IX (1848) 348, no. 87; S. Lane Poole *Catalogue of oriental coins in the British Museum* II (London 1876) 163–4, nos. 536–42; idem *Additions to the Oriental Collection in the British Museum*, Part I (London 1889) 224–31, nos. 535a–542f; C. J. Rodgers *Catalogue of the coins in the Government Museum, Lahore* (Calcutta 1891) Supplement, II; idem *Catalogue of coins in the Indian Museum* (Calcutta 1896) 156; Sourdel *Inventaire des monnaies anciennes du Musée de Caboul* 63–5; Bosworth 'The titulature of the early Ghaznavids' 230.

71 Ibn Bābā, ff. 208a–b; Ibn al-Athīr, ed. Tornberg, IX, 381–2, ed. Beirut, IX, 559.

72 Ḥusainī, 26; Ibn al-Athīr, ed. Tornberg, IX, 334, 347, ed. Beirut, IX, 488, 506; see also above, p. 11. Exactly where lay the place mentioned by Ḥusainī is unknown, but it was probably in Bādghīs or Gharchistān. It is unlikely that we have a reference, at this early date, to the ruined fortress of Qara Bāgh in Bādghīs described by C. E. Yate in his *Northern Afghanistan or letters from the Afghan Boundary Commission* (Edinburgh 1888) 101, unless some aboriginal, local name has been subsequently assimilated to the Turco-Persian expression *Qara Bāgh* 'Dark garden'.

73 Ibn al-Athīr, ed. Tornberg, IX, 334, ed. Beirut, IX, 488; cf. Pritsak 'Karachanidische Streitfragen 1–4' 224, 227, idem 'Die Karachaniden' 36–7, and Barthold *Turkestan down to the Mongol invasion*[3] 304.

74 Ḥusainī, 26–7; Ibn al-Athīr, ed. Tornberg, IX, 354, ed. Beirut, IX, 518; Mīrkhwānd, 114, tr. 253.

75 cf. Bosworth 'Dailamīs in Central Iran: the Kākūyids of Jibāl and Yazd' *Iran* VIII (1970) 82–3.

76 Ḥusainī, 28; Ibn al-Athīr, ed. Tornberg, IX, 381–2, ed. Beirut, IX, 558–9; Mīrkhwānd, 116, tr. 254; Firishta, f. 76b, tr. I, 74; cf. Bosworth in *The Cambridge history of Iran. V. The Saljuq and Mongol periods*, ed. J. A. Boyle (Cambridge 1968) 52–3.

77 Anon *Ta'rīkh-i Sīstān*, ed. Bahār (Tehran 1314/1935) 362.

78 ibid., 363–4.

79 The *ʿayyārs* and similar groups, a persistent element in many sectors of eastern Islamic social history, have attracted a fair amount of attention from scholars; see Bosworth *The Ghaznavids*, 167 ff., for a summary of views, with special reference to the phenomenon in Khurasan and Sīstān, and now E. Ashtor *A social and economic history of the Near East in the Middle Ages* (London 1976) 187–90, 224–5.

80 See Baihaqī, 624, 626, tr. 759, 760.

81 The orthography B.y.ghū is invariably that of the *Ta'rīkh-i Sīstān* and its manuscript, and the rendering Bīghu is accordingly used here in the first place. One should however note that O. Pritsak in 'Der Untergang des Reiches des oğuzischen Yabğu', *Fuad Köprülü armağanı* (Istanbul 1953) 407, renders this name as Payghu, and states that he has demonstrated, in an excursus to his unpublished *Karachandische Studien*, that Payghu is a Central Asian totemistic title, referring to the falcon or sparrow-hawk; the name should accordingly be distinguished from that of another early Seljuq leader, Mūsā Yabghu.

82 *Ta'rīkh-i Sīstān* 365–6.

83 The Shangaliyān seem to have been one of the long-established factions (*ta'aṣṣubāt*) of Sīstān, being mentioned in the *Ta'rīkh-i Sīstān*, 328, as in existence as far back as 341/952–3, when civil strife arose in Ūq between the faction of Shangal and that of Zātūraq; the origin of the name is unknown.

84 Ibid., 366–8; Ibn al-Athīr, ed. Tornberg, IX, 354, ed. Beirut, IX, 518; Mīrkhwānd, 114, tr. 253.

85 This son is not named, but cannot have been 'Abd ar-Razzāq, by this time Maudūd's vizier, see below; Baihaqī, 375, tr. 469, mentions a further son, 'Alī, and another son, Manṣūr, was the *mamdūḥ* of the poet Farrukhī, see his *Dīwān*, ed. Muḥammad Dabīr-Siyāqī (Tehran 1335/1956) 165–6, 333–7

86 *Ta'rīkh-i Sīstān* 368–70.

87 ibid., 383.

88 ibid., 369.

89 Gardīzī, ed. Nāẓim, 104, 109, ed. Ḥabībī, 201, 204; Baihaqī, 272, 501, 524, tr. 363, 612–13, 641; Ibn al-Athīr, ed. Tornberg, IX, 334, ed. Beirut, IX, 488, with the date of 426 erroneously for late 427 or early 428 as the date of Majdūd's departure for India as commander-in-chief; Elliot and Dowson *History of India* II, 134. Concerning Sa'd-i Salmān, see Hodivala *Studies in Indo-Muslim history* I, 163, on Elliot and Dowson, op. cit., V, 521, 526.

90 Ibn al-Athīr, loc. cit.; Fakhr-i Mudabbir, f. 76a, ed. Khwānsārī, 252–3, tr. Shafi, 213; Mīrkhwānd, 113, tr. 252; Firishta, f. 64a, tr. I, 69–70.

91 See S. M. Stern 'Ismā'īlī propaganda and Fatimid rule in Sind' *IC* XXIII (1949), 298–307, and for descriptions of this idol-temple, Hodivala, op. cit., 29–30.

92 See Nāẓim *The life and times of Sulṭān Maḥmūd of Ghazna* 96–7, and Bosworth *The Ghaznavids* 52, 76.

93 cf. ibid., 182–3.

94 The form of the *nisba* is conjectural; Khwānsārī has K.l.mī / L.k.mī for the name, the India Office manuscript has what looks like L.k.mī also, and Shafi has Galīmī.

95 Fakhr-i Mudabbir, ff. 76a–b, ed. Khwānsārī, 252–4, tr. Shafi, 213–14.

96 For the campaigns of Sebüktigin and Maḥmūd against these Indian rulers, see Nāẓim, op. cit., 86–96, 194–6. Sandanpāl may perhaps have been the grandson of Trilochanpāl (d. 412/1021–2) and son of Bhīmpāl (d. 417/1026).

97 Fakhr-i Mudabbir, ff. 76b–77a, ed. Khwānsārī, 254–6, tr. Shafi, 214–16.

98 ibid., f. 80a, ed. Khwānsārī, 268, tr. Shafi, 216.

99 cf. Nāẓim, op. cit., 113.

100 Ibn al-Athīr, ed. Tornberg, IX, 354–5, ed. Beirut, IX, 518–19; Mīrkhwānd, 114–15, tr. 253–4; D. C. Ganguly in *The history and culture of the Indian people. V. The struggle for empire,*[2] ed. R. C. Majumdar *et alii* (Bombay 1966) 56, 67.

101 Firishta, ff. 64b–65a, tr. I, 69–71.

102 The full name, except for the *nisba*, in Gardīzī, ed. Nāẓim, 99, 110, ed. Ḥabībī, 198, 205; Baihaqī usually writes 'Aḥmad-i 'Abd aṣ-Ṣamad'.

103 Nāẓir ad-Dīn Kirmānī *Nasā'im al-asḥār min laṭā'im al-akhbār*, ed. Jalāl ad-Dīn Ḥusainī Urmawī (Tehran 1338/1959) 45; Saif ad-Dīn 'Uqailī *Āthār al-wuzarā'*, ed. Urmawī (Tehran 1338/1959) 193; Khwāndamīr *Dastūr al-wuzarā'*, ed. Sa'īd Nafīsī (Tehran 1317/1938) 144; cf. Bosworth *The Ghaznavids* 58, 61–2, 96.

104 *Dīwān*, ed. de Biberstein-Kazimirsky, 18 (= Poem No. VII), ed. Dabīr-Siyāqī (Tehran 1338/1959) 9 (= Poem No. 7).

105 Baihaqī, 331, tr. 419; Nāṣir ad-Dīn Kirmānī, Saif ad-Dīn 'Uqailī, Khwāndamīr, locc. cit.

106 Baihaqī, 367, 664, tr. 460, 803; Nāṣir ad-Dīn Kirmānī, loc. cit.; Saif ad-Dīn 'Uqailī, 193–4 (totally confused and erroneous information here); Khwāndamīr, loc. cit. Baihaqī usually calls this particular Ṭāhir 'Ṭāhir-i Mustaufī' to distinguish him from Ṭāhir-i Dabīr, a secretary who was prominent in the early part of Mas'ud's reign but who fell into disgrace and retired in 426/1035, see Baihaqī, 442, tr. 544. Ṭāhir-i Mustaufī was enough of a poet to warrant a brief mention in Bākharzī's *Dumyat al-qaṣr wa-'uṣrat ahl al-'aṣr*, ed. 'Abd al-Fattāḥ Muḥammad al-Ḥilū (Cairo 1388/1968) II, 105, no. 269, under 'al-'Amīd Ṭāhir al-Mustaufī' (missing from Muḥammad Rāghib aṭ-Ṭabbākh's edition, Aleppo 1349/1930).

107 Baihaqī, 64, 149, 624, 626, tr. 130–1, 222, 759, 760; Nāṣir ad-Dīn Kirmānī, 45–6; Saif ad-Dīn 'Uqailī, 192 (confused reference under the section ostensibly devoted to Ṭāhir-i Mustaufī); Khwāndamīr, 145.

108 See Bosworth *The Ghaznavids* 139–41.

109 Kai Kā'ūs *Qābūs-nāma*, ed. R. Levy (London 1951) 135, 137, tr. idem, *A mirror for princes* (London 1951) 230, 234; Daulat-Shāh Samarqandī *Tadhkirat ash-shu'arā'*, ed. Muḥammad 'Abbāsī (Tehran 1337/1958) 79. Kai Kā'ūs's uncle Manūchihr b. Qābūs had married a daughter of Maḥmūd of Ghazna.

110 See *EI*[2] art. 'al-Bīrūnī' (D. J. Boilot).

111 Ibn Bābā, f. 208a–b; Ibn al-Athīr, ed. Tornberg, IX, 381–2, ed. Beirut, IX, 558–9; Mīrkhwānd, 116, tr. 254–5; Firishta, f. 67b, tr. I, 74. For Sakāwand or Sajāwand, see the *Bābur-nāma*, tr. A. S. Beveridge (London 1921) 217, and Hodivala *Studies in Indo-Muslim history* I, 165–6; it was some 50 miles south of Kabul and 35 miles north-east of Ghazna.

112 Ibn Bābā, f. 208b; Ibn al-Athīr, ed. Tornberg, IX, 381, ed. Beirut, IX, 558; Ḥusainī, 14.

113 'Un trésor de dinars ġaznawides et saljūqides découvert en Afghanistan', *BEtO* XVIII (1963–4) 198–9, 205.

114 Even the anonymous *Mujmal at-tawārīkh wa-l-qiṣaṣ*, written only some 70 years after these events, does not mention Mas'ūd b. Maudūd in its tables of the Ghaznavid sultans and their titles (405, 428–9).

115 ibid., 405, 429; Ḥamdallāh Mustaufī *Ta'rīkh-i guzīda*, ed. 'Abd al-Ḥusain Navā'ī (Tehran 1339/1960) 398.

116 Ibn Bābā, f. 208a; Ibn al-Athīr, ed. Tornberg, IX, 382, ed. Beirut, IX, 559; Jūzjānī, I, 235, tr. I, 97–8; Shabānkāra'ī *Majma' al-ansāb*, f. 188a; Mīrkhwānd, 116–17, tr. 254–6.

117 See on this feature of Ghaznavid government, Bosworth *The Ghaznavids* 62–4, 96–7.

118 The consonant ductus of this name in the manuscript which I have used looks more like Aitigin ('moon-prince' in Turkish) than anything else (cf. the common Aibeg/Aibak). Briggs has in his translation 'Aluptugeen', sc. Alptigin, but frequently produces grotesque distortions of Turkish names.

119 Firishta, ff. 67b–68b, tr. I, 75–6.

120 ibid., f. 68a, tr. I, 76; both princes' names occur in the list of Sultan Mas'ūd's sons in Jūzjānī, I, 234, n. 4, tr. I, 95.

121 Ibn Bābā, ff. 208a–b; Ibn al-Athīr, ed. Tornberg, IX, 382, ed. Beirut, IX, 559; Jūzjānī, I, 235, tr. I, 98; Mīrkhwānd, 117, tr. 255–6.

122 Ḥusainī, 14; Jūzjānī, I, 235, tr. I, 98.

123 Gardīzī, ed. Nāẓim, 61, ed. Ḥabībī, 174; Ibn al-Athīr, ed. Tornberg, IX, 382, ed. Beirut, IX, 559; Jūzjānī, I, 235 (*laqab* given erroneously in Ḥabībī's text as Bahā' ad-Daula, correct in Nassau Lees' one of Calcutta 1863 as 'Izz ad-Daula); S. M. Stern 'A manuscript from the library of the Ghaznawid amīr 'Abd al-Rashīd', in *Paintings from Islamic lands*, ed. R. Pinder Wilson (Oxford 1969) 7–31; Sourdel 'Un trésor de dinars ġaznawides et salğūqides découvert en Afghanistan' 205, cf. his list of 'Abd ar-Rashīd's known coins, 204; other sources in Bosworth 'The titulature of the early Ghaznavids' 230–1, to which should be added Rodgers *Catalogue of the coins in the Government Museum, Lahore* 29–30, Supplement, 11, and idem, *Catalogue of coins in the Indian Museum* 156.

124 Ibn Funduq *Ta'rīkh-i Baihaq* 177–8; M. Niẓámu 'd-Dín *Introduction to the* Jawámi'u 'l-ḥikáyát . . *of* . . *Muḥammad al-'Awfí* (London 1929) 62–4, 228; cf. Sa'īd Nafīsī EI^2 art. 'Bayhaḳī, Abu 'l-Faḍl'.

125 Baihaqī, 685, tr. 829.

126 cf. W. Radloff *Versuch eines Wörterbuches der Türk-Dialecte* (St Petersburg 1893–1911) IV, 1683.

127 Ḥusainī, 14; Ibn Funduq, loc. cit. In connection with the form B.r'an of the *Ta'rīkh-i Baihaq*, one recalls that on p. 51 Ibn Funduq attibutes to the son of the Oghuz Yabghu of Jand, Shāh Malik b. 'Alī (see above, p.6), the *nisba* of 'al-B.rānī'.

128 Shabānkāra'ī *Majma' al-ansāb*, f. 188a; Baihaqī, 69, 250, 252–3, tr.

136, 338, 340–1; cf. Bosworth *The Ghaznavids* 63, 96, 232. Given Baihaqī's habit of moralising reflection, it is virtually impossible that he would ever have mentioned our present Toghrïl under the events of Mas'ūd's reign without comment on the maleficent rôle which he was to play in future events; one must assume that he had attained no great significance before Maudūd's accession.

129 Jūzjānī, I, 236, tr. I, 99–100; Ḥusainī, 14–15.

130 Ibn al-Athīr, ed. Tornberg, IX, 398, ed. Beirut, IX, 580 (under the year 443/1051–2), ibid., ed. Tornberg, IX, 398, ed. Beirut, IX, 582 (year 444/1052–3); Ibn Bābā, f. 208b. See further on the campaign of 443/1051–2 against Chaghrï Beg, Bosworth, in *The Cambridge history of Iran* V, 51.

131 Jūzjānī, I, 235, tr. I, 98–9.

132 ibid., I, 236, tr. I, 100, explicitly quoted by Firishta, f. 69a, tr. I, 77–8.

133 These figures seem much more circumstantial than the round figure in Ibn al-Athīr of 1,000 cavalrymen as sent by 'Abd ar-Rashīd with Toghrïl, see ed. Tornberg, IX, 398, ed. Beirut, IX, 582.

134 *Ta'rīkh-i Sīstān* 371–3; Ibn al-Athīr, ed. Tornberg, IX, 398–9, ed. Beirut, IX, 582; Mīrkhwānd, 118–19, tr. 256–7.

135 Ibn Bābā, ff. 208b–209a; Ḥusainī, 15; Ibn al-Athīr, ed. Tornberg, IX, 400, ed. Beirut, IX, 583–4; Jūzjānī, loc. cit.; Mustaufī, 399; Mīrkhwānd, 119–20, tr. 257; Firishta, f. 68b, tr. I, 77.

136 Sourdel *Inventaire des monnaies anciennes du Musée de Caboul* 67; idem 'Un trésor de dinars ġaznawides et salǧūqides découvert en Afghanistan' 199, 205.

137 *Khirkhīz* is the normal orthography of the Arabic and Persian sources for this Turkish tribal name, se e.g. Manūchihrī, *Dīwān*, ed. de Biberstein Kazimirski, 5 (= Poem No. 1), ed. Dabīr-Siyāqī, 2 (= Poem No. 2), *mishk-i khirkhīzī* 'Kirghiz musk', and Minorsky *Sharaf al-Zamān Ṭāhir Marvazī on China, the Turks and India* (London 1942) text *19, tr. 30–1, though in Kāshgharī *Dīwān lughāt at-turk*, tr. B. Atalay (Ankara 1939–41) I, 28, 458, who was more concerned with the correct phonetic rendering of names like this, we have *Qïrqïz*. According to Firishta, f. 68b, tr. I, 76, Khirkhīz (here erroneously confused with Nūshtigin, the assassin of Toghrïl) had just before this time been active in India and had recovered Nagarkot from its temporary re-possession by the infidels.

138 Ibn Bābā, ff. 209a–b; Ḥusainī, loc. cit.; Ibn al-Athīr, ed. Tornberg, IX, 400–1, ed. Beirut, IX, 584; Jūzjānī, I, 236–7, tr. I, 100–1; Mīrkhwānd, 120–2, tr. 257–9; Firishta, f. 69a, tr. I, 77.

139 Jūzjānī, I, 235–7, tr. I, 99–101; Ḥusainī, loc. cit.; Sourdel, op. cit., 199, 206–7; Hodivala *Studies in Indo-Muslim history* I, 196.

140 Ibn Bābā, f. 209b.

141 Baihaqī, 110, 114, 136, 178, 201, 242, 254, tr. 180, 185, 206, 255, 279, 327, 342, and *passim*; *Mujmal at-tawārīkh* 405, 429; Ḥamdallāh Mustaufī *Ta'rīkh-i guzīda* 400; Saif ad-Dīn 'Uqailī *Āthār al-wuzarā'*, India Office ms. f. 87b; Sourdel *Inventaire des monnaies anciennes du Musée de Caboul*, 68; idem, 'Un trésor de dinars ġaznawides et salǧūqides

découvert en Afghanistan', 206–7, cf. the list of Farrukh-Zād's extant coins at p. 204; further references in Bosworth 'The titulature of the early Ghaznavids', 231, to which should be added Rodgers *Catalogue of the coins in the Government Museum, Lahore*, Supplement, 12, and idem *Catalogue of coins in the Indian Museum* 156–7.

142 Baihaqī, 378, tr. 472; Ibn Bābā, f. 209b; Jūzjānī, I, 237, tr. I, 101–2.

143 Ibn al-Athīr, ed. Tornberg, IX, 401, ed. Beirut, IX, 584; Mīrkhwānd, 121, tr. 259.

144 Nāṣir ad-Dīn Kirmānī *Nasā' im al-asḥār*, 46; Saif ad-Dīn 'Uqailī, op. cit., ed. Urmawī, 194–5; Khwāndamīr *Dastūr al-wuzarā'* 145–6; Firishta, ff. 69b–70a, tr. I, 79. Baihaqī, 232, tr. 316, mentions once a wife of 'Ḥasan-i Mihrān', but has nothing about the man himself.

145 ibid., 144, 520, tr. 216, 636.

146 ibid., 376, 378, tr. 470–1, 472; cf. *EI*² art. 'Bayhaḳī'.

147 'Aufī *Lubāb al-albāb*, ed. Sa'īd Nafīsī (Tehran 1335/1956) 325–7. This poet is not to be confused with the poet of the Seljuqs in the 6th/12th century, Jauharī Zargar (i.e. also a goldsmith, *ṣā'igh*, *zargar*, by profession), treated at length by Daulat-Shāh Samarqandī *Tadhkirat ash-shu'arā'*, ed. Muḥammad 'Abbāsī (Tehran 1337/1958) 132–5.

148 Ibn al-Athīr, ed. Tornberg, IX, 401, ed. Beirut, IX, 584–5; Mīrkhwānd, 122, tr. 259; Firishta, ff. 69a–b, tr. I, 78.

149 *Ādāb al-ḥarb*, f. 80a, ed. Khwānsārī, 268.

150 Ḥusainī, 28–9; Ibn al-Athīr, ed. Tornberg, IX, 401, ed. Beirut, IX, 585; Mīrkhwānd, 122, tr. 259–60; Firishta, f. 69b, tr. I, 78.

151 Ibn Bābā, f. 209b; Ibn al-Athīr, ed. Tornberg, X, 3, ed. Beirut, X, 5; Jūzjānī, I, 237, tr. I, 102; Firishta, f. 69b, tr. I, 78–9.

CHAPTER TWO

1 See on this district (also called in early Islamic times, Wujūr/Wujūristān or Hujwīr, whence the *nisba* of the famous Ṣūfī biographer 'Alī b. 'Uthmān Hujwīrī) Bosworth 'Notes on the pre-Ghaznavid history of eastern Afghanistan' *IQ* IX (1965) 20.

2 Baihaqī, 378, tr. 472.

3 Jūzjānī, I, 238, tr. I, 103–4.

4 ibid., I, 239, tr. I, 103–4.

5 Ibn al-Athīr, ed. Tornberg, X, 110–11, ed. Beirut, X, 167–8.

6 See Sa'īd Nafīsī, *EI*² art. 'Bayhaḳī'.

7 Ibn al-Athīr, ed. Tornberg, X, 3–4, ed. Beirut, X, 5–6, cf. Bosworth in *Cambridge history of Iran. V. The Saljuq and Mongol periods* 53. Chaghrī Beg, now advanced in years, died at the beginning of 452/1060, but the peace arrangements were doubtless made with the concurrence of his son Alp Arslan and seem to have been honoured by the latter.

8 cf. *Ḥudūd al-'ālam*,² tr. Minorsky, 109, 338–40; the reading of İ. Kafesoğlu in his *Sultan Melikşah devrinde Büyük Selçuklu imparatorluğu* (Istanbul 1953) 20, sc. *Chigil-kent, is highly speculative; an etymological connection with the ancient Sakas, who held this region of Bactria, is more probable than with the Turkish Chigil tribe.

9 Ibn al-Athīr, ed. Tornberg, x, 53, ed. Beirut, x, 78; cf. Kafesoğlu, loc. cit., and Bosworth in *Cambridge history of Iran* v, 93. ʿUthmān must have been speedily released, since he was shortly afterwards made governor of Walwālīj in Badakhshān, cf. Ḥusainī *Akhbār ad-daula as-saljūqiyya* 59.

10 Ibn al-Athīr, ed. Tornberg, x, 110, ed. Beirut, x, 167; Ḥusainī, 16; also in Mīrkhwānd, 126–7, tr. 265–6.

11 Masʿūd-i Saʿd *Dīwān*, ed. Rashīd Yāsimī (Tehran 1319/1940) 60–1, 407–12, 588, and perhaps also 212–14, if the Jamāl al-Mulk Rashīd there addressed is identical with Abū r-Rushd Rashīd; Rūnī *Dīwān*, ed. K. I. Chaykin (Tehran 1304–5/1925–6) 68–9, ed. Maḥmūd Mahdawī Dāmghānī (Mashhad 1347/1968) 89–90.

12 i.e. Mihtar Rashīd is vaunting the multinational nature of the Ghaznavid army, with its Turks, Tājīks, Indian, Dailamīs, Arabs, etc., seen as a source of strength, cf. Bosworth, 'Ghaznevid military organisation', *Der Islam* XXXVI (1960) 51 ff., and idem *The Ghaznavids, their empire in Afghanistan and eastern Iran* 107 ff.

13 *Ādāb al-ḥarb*, ms. India Office, ff. 48a–51a, ed. Khwānsārī, 149–60, tr. Shafi, 206–13.

14 Ibn al-Athīr, ed. Tornberg, x, 28, ed. Beirut, 41; cf. Bosworth in *Cambridge history of Iran* v, 65.

15 Ibn al-Athīr, ed. Tornberg, x, 111, ed. Beirut, x, 168; Ḥusainī, 58; Jūzjānī, I, 240, 241, tr. I, 107–8; Mīrkhwānd, 127, tr. 266. None of these sources supplies a date. Kafesoğlu *Sultan Melikşah devrinde Büyük Selçuklu imparatorluğu*, 30, n. 49, gives the date of 481/1088 for Malik Shāh's movement of troops to Isfizār and Ibrāhīm's stratagem, but it is not clear what his supporting source is for this date, unless it be a manuscript (Koprülü 1079) of the comparatively late source of Dhahabī's *Ta'rīkh Duwal al-Islām*, which he cites here. For a thorough discussion of the confusion over this Seljuq-Ghaznavid marriage alliance, see Gulam Mustafa Khan 'A history of Bahrām Shāh of Ghaznīn' *IC* XXIII (1949) 64–6.

16 Daulat Shāh *Tadhkirat ash-shuʿarā'* 106; Ḥamdallāh Mustaufī *Ta'rīkh-i guzīda* 400; Ḥusainī, 91.

17 *Dīwān* 74–5, 103–4, 569–77 (*qaṣīdas* and a *ghazal* addressed to Naṣr b. Khalaf), 21–8, 420–5, 429–34 (*qaṣīdas* addressed to Arslan Shāh b. Kirmān Shāh of Kirmān, reigned 495–537/1101–42) 10–16, 192–5, 302–6, 601 (poems addressed to Arslan Shāh's vizier Mujīr ad-Daula Abū l-Muẓaffar Ḥusain b. Ḥamza).

18 *Dīwān*, ed. Mudarris Riḍawī (Tehran 1341/1962) 85–7, 467–74 (*qaṣīdas* addressed to Sanjar) 119–25, 561–4 (exchange of letters and poems, and *qaṣīda*, addressed to the vizier Darguzīnī) 474–9 (*qaṣīda* addressed to Muʿīn ad-Dīn Abū Naṣr).

19 Sourdel *Inventaire des monnaies anciennes du Musée de Caboul* XIII; idem 'Un trésor de dinars ġaznawides et salğūqides découvert en Afghanistan', 199. Likewise, the title *Malik al-Islam* seems only to have been adopted a short time before that of *Sulṭān*, see ibid., 199–200.

20 See Sourdel *Inventaire* XIII–XIV, 74 ff.

21 *Mujmal at-tawārīkh*, 429; Jūzjānī, I, 238, tr. I, 102–3, Mustaufī *Ta'rīkh-i guzīda* 400; Saif ad-Dīn ʿUqailī *Āthār al-wuzarā'*, ms. India Office, f. 88a; Thomas *JRAS* IX (1848) 358–66, nos. 108–32; Lane Poole *Catalogue of Oriental coins* II, 168–72, nos. 550–9; idem *Additions to the Oriental Collection*, Part I, 239–40, nos. 558d,e,f, 560k; E. von Zambaur 'Contributions à la numismatique orientale' *WNZ*, XXXVI (1904) 84, no. 93; S. Flury 'Le décor épigraphique des monuments de Ghazna' *Syria* VI (1925) 70–5; Sourdel *Inventaire des monnaies anciennes du Musée de Caboul* 70–80; idem 'Un trésor de dinars ġaznawides et salǧūqides', 199–200, 206–13; J.-C. Gardin *Lashkari Bazar. II. Les trouvailles. Céramiques et monnaies de Lashkari Bazar et de Bust* (Paris 1963) 180–1.

22 Rūnī *Dīwān*, ed. Chaykin, 61, ed. Dāmghānī, 81; cf. Gulam Mustafa Khan 'A history of Bahrām Shāh of Ghaznīn' *IC* XXIII (1949) 81 n. 2. An article by this same author (in Urdu?) in the journal *Maʿārif* (Aʿẓamgarh, March–April 1944) on Islamic and Ghaznavid banners has not been accessible to me.

23 See Bosworth 'Ghaznevid military organisation' 72–4, and idem *The Ghaznavids* 124–6.

24 For details of these events, see Bosworth in *Cambridge history of Iran* V, 158–9.

25 M. F. Köprülü 'Kay kabîlesi hakkında yeni notlar' *Belleten* VIII (1944) 449–52.

26 For surveys of the war machine in general, see Bosworth 'Ghaznevid military organisation' 37–77, and idem *The Ghaznavids* 98–128.

27 Ibn al-Athīr, ed. Tornberg, X, 110, ed. Beirut, X, 167; *Ādāb al-ḥarb*, f. 80a, ed. Khwānsārī, 268–9, tr. Shafi, 216.

28 For the *ʿĀriḍ*'s department, see Nāẓim *The life and times of Sulṭān Maḥmūd of Ghazna* 137–42, and Bosworth, op. cit., 122–6.

29 See below, p. 64, and Masʿūd-i Saʿd *Dīwān* 143–5, 206–8.

30 ibid., 264, cf. also 372.

31 For the palace ghulāms, see Bosworth 'Ghaznevid military organisation' 44–50, and for the Indian troops, 54–5, also in *The Ghaznavids* 98–106, 110.

32 The governors for the Ghaznavids in Khwārazm recruited local Turkish troops there as auxiliaries, and Turkish slaves were often received in presents given to Sultan Maḥmūd by his Qarakhanid allies, such as Qadïr Khan Yūsuf of Kāshghar, see ibid., 101, 109.

33 *Dīwān* 528, cf. Köprülü op. cit., 430–2; the names of the Yaghmā and Qāy have to be corrected from the misreadings in Yāsimī's text.

34 Masʿūd-i Saʿd *Dīwān* 565, 567, 567–8; these three personages were apparently not royal princes, since their names do not figure among the many sons of Ibrāhīm and Masʿūd enumerated by Jūzjānī, some of whom do bear typically Iranian heroic names.

35 See for example, ibid., 218–20; ʿUthmān Mukhtārī *Dīwān*, ed. Jalāl ad-Dīn Humā'ī (Tehran 1341/1962) 196–206, 237–48, 296–9; Sanā'ī *Dīwān*, ed. Mudarris Riḍawī (Tehran 1341/1962) 237–81, 341–4, 447–51.

36 ʿUthmān Mukhtārī *Dīwān* 434–43; Masʿūd-i Saʿd *Dīwān* 327–8; Rūnī

Dīwān, ed. Chaykin, 116–17, ed. Dāmghānī, 141–2; Juzjānī, I, 240, tr. I, 107; Firishta, f. 72a, tr. 82.

37 If the offspring of Turkish slave soldiers were in fact adopting Arab-Islamic names, this would be an exact parallel to what happened under the Mamlūks of Egypt and Syria, where the sons of Mamlūks, the *aulād an-nās*, almost always bore Arab-Islamic names, in contrast to their fathers' Turkish ones; see D. Ayalon 'Names, titles and "nisbas" of the Mamlūks' *Israel Oriental Studies* V (Tel-Aviv 1975) 193 ff. However, we know nothing from the slave institution of the Ghaznavid army suggesting any parallel to the exclusion of the second generation from military and political power, as was the case with the Mamlūk *aulād an-nās*.

38 See Bosworth *The Ghaznavids* 115–18, and idem *EI*² art. 'Fīl. As beasts of war'.

39 Mas'ūd-i Sa'd *Dīwān* 277, 604, 620; Fakhr-i Mudabbir, loc. cit.

40 Ibn al-Athīr, ed. Tornberg, X, 72 *bis*–74, ed. Beirut, X, 113–14; Firishta, ff. 706–71a, tr. 80–1.

41 e.g. by S. M. Latif, in his *History of the Panjab from the remotest antiquity to the present time* (Lahore 1891) 90. It may be noted here, however, that two recent articles by Indian authors hardly touch at all on the campaigns of Ibrāhīm and his Ghaznavid successors, despite their titles: Sri Ram Sharma 'The Ghazanvids [*sic*] in the Punjab' *Journal of Indian history* XLVI (1968) 125–46 (deals in fact with the Ghūrid conquests), and K. S. Lal 'The Ghaznavids in India' *Bengal past and present. A journal of Modern Indian and Asian history* LXXXIX (1970) 131–52 (deals with the campaigns of Maḥmūd, then jumps to those of the Ghūrids).

42 Nāẓim *Sulṭān Maḥmūd* 90–1.

43 H. C. Ray *The dynastic history of Northern India (early mediaeval period)* (Calcutta 1931–6) II, 821–32; D. C. Ganguly 'The historical value of Dīwān-i Salmān [*sic*, copied from the heading given thus in Elliot and Dowson, see below, n. 46]' *IC* XVI (1942) 426; idem 'Northern India during the 11th and 12th centuries' in *The struggle for empire*² 51, 61 ff., 66 ff.

44 See Bosworth *The Ghaznavids* 76–8.

45 art. cit., 423–8.

46 Given in Elliot and Dowson, IV, 518–27.

47 See Fakhr-i Mudabbir, f. 89a, ed. Khwānsārī, 307, tr. Shafi, 219–20.

48 *Dīwān* 170–2.

49 ibid., 371–2.

50 Ganguly, art. cit., 423, cf. also idem in *The struggle for empire*² 94.

51 D. Sharma 'Ibrāhīm of Ghazna, the Mātaṇga slayer of Durlabharāja III of Śākambharī' *Journal of the Bihar [and Orissa] Research Society* XXX (1944) 104–5, see also S. R. Sharma 'The Ghazanvids in the Punjab' 127.

52 Mas'ūd-i Sa'd *Dīwān* 332–3; Mírzá Muḥammad b. 'Abdu 'l-Wahháb of Qazwín 'Mas'úd-i-Sa'd-i-Salmán' *JRAS* (1905) 711–13; Rūnī *Dīwān*, ed. Chaykin, 8–9, ed. Dāmghānī, 8–9; Iqbal Husain *The early Persian poets of India (A.H. 421–670)* (Patna 1937) 31–4.

53 Niẓāmī 'Arūḍī Samarqandī *Chahār maqāla*, ed. Qazwīnī (London 1910) 44–5, revised tr. E. G. Browne (London 1921) 49–50; Elliot and Dowson *History of India* IV, 522; Mírzá Muḥammad Qazwíní 'Mas'úd-i-Sa'd-i-Salmán' 729–33; Husain, op. cit., 33–4, 96 ff.

54 *Dīwān* 260–4, 307–8 (the first poem partly translated by Elliot in op. cit., IV, 522–4; Husain, op. cit., 92–4; Ganguly 'The historical value of Dīwān-i Salmān' 423–6; idem in *The struggle for empire*² 94–5.

55 On the rulers of Kanauj, see Ray *The dynastic history of northern India* I, 551–5, and genealogical table at p. 566.

56 Ganguly in ibid., 51. The term *turuṣka* (< 'Turk') became a common designation amongst the Indians for the Muslim invaders of their country, together with that of *hamvīra*/*hammīra* (< *amīr*); see the discussion in Ray, op. cit., II, 681–2, on the term *hamvīra*, 'to the Indians the accepted title for a Muhammadan prince at least during the period *c.* 1000–1300 A.D.'.

57 Jūzjānī, I, 240, tr. I, 106–7.

58 These honorifics are given by 'Aufī *Lubāb al-albāb* 70.

59 Abū l-Faraj Rūnī praises him in one of his poems as *ṣāḥib-i jaish u ṣāḥib-i dīwān* (*Dīwān*, ed. Chaykin, 133, ed. Dāmghānī, 156).

60 *Dīwān* 155, 256, 571, 702; Mírzá Muḥammad 'Mas'úd-i-Sa'd-i-Salmán' 733–6, 737 ff.; Husain *The early Persian poets of India* 105–9. Rūnī also has several poems addressed to Abū Naṣr, see his *Dīwān*, ed. Chaykin, 17–19, 43, 122–3, 133, ed. Dāmghānī, 21–3, 48–9, 151–3, 156. It is not known whether Abū Naṣr-i Fārsī ever climbed back into favour, but there is a poem of Mas'ūd-i Sa'd's (*Dīwān* 76–7) addressed to Sultan Arslan Shāh in which the writer recalls the merits and beneficence of Abū Naṣr, by then apparently dead.

61 See Nāẓim *Sulṭān Maḥmūd*, 70–3; Bosworth 'The early Islamic history of Ghūr' *CAJ* VI (1961) 127–8.

62 Firishta, f. 67a, tr. 73. It is further mentioned here that Barstigin was later sent to repel Seljuq raiders from the region of Bust, and that in 439/1047–8 he was despatched to Quṣdār in Baluchistan, where he brought to heel a local ruler who had been remiss in sending the requisite tribute to Ghazna.

63 Shabānkāra'ī *Majma' al-ansāb*, f. 188a, cf. Bosworth, op. cit., 128.

64 *Dīwān* 372.

65 Jūzjānī, I, 330–2, tr. I, 329–33; cf. Gulam Mustafa Khan 'A history of Bahrām Shāh of Ghaznīn' 199. In the later historian Mīrkhwānd we have a much vaguer and more anecdotal allusion to these events, with Ḥusain b. Sām as the vassal and confidant of Ibrāhīm, see Ch. Defrémery 'Histoire des Sultans Ghourides. Extraite de l'Histoire universelle de Mirkhond, traduite et accompagnée de notes' *JA*, ser. 4, vol. II (July–December 1843) Persian text, 172, tr. 187–8.

66 For surveys of the administrative system of the early Ghaznavids, see Nāẓim *Sulṭān Maḥmūd* 126–50, and Bosworth *The Ghaznavids* 48–97.

67 *Ādāb al-ḥarb*, India Office ms., f. 42b, omitted from the text of Khwānsārī's edition.

68 ibid., ff. 28b–29a, ed. Khwānsārī, 105–6, tr. Shafi, 201–2.

69 ibid., f. 28b, ed. Khwānsārī, 105 (with varying wording here), tr. Shafi, 201.

70 This expression 'golden-belted ones' seems to have been a standard designation of the time for the most sumptuously-equipped of the royal ghulāms, since the *Ta'rīkh-i Sīstān*, 368, mentions that in 434/1042 the Ṣaffārid amīr of Sīstān, Abū l-Faḍl b. Naṣr, executed several Ghaznavid *zarrīn-kamarān* captured in battle, see above, Ch. 1, p. 29.

71 Fakhr-i Mudabbir, ff. 29a, 30a, ed. Khwānsārī, 106, 108–9, tr. Shafi, 202–3. It should, however, be noted here that the author had an interest in vaunting the degree of the sultan's favour to the Sharīf Abū l'Faraj, in that the latter was Fakhr-i Mudabbir's own great-grandfather on the paternal side, as he mentions here. That the Sharīf's role has in fact been inflated may perhaps be inferred from the curious fact that we do not appear to possess any verses addressed to him by the great contemporary poets.

72 Nāṣir ad-Dīn Kirmānī *Nasā'im al-asḥār* 46–7 (which erroneously has 37 years (*sic*) for 'Abd al-Ḥamīd's tenure of the vizierate for Mas'ūd); Saif ad-Dīn 'Uqailī *Athār al-wuzarā'*, ed. Urmawī, 195–6 (with the correct duration of 16 years); Khwāndamīr *Dastūr al-wuzarā'* 147; Mas'ūd-i Sa'd *Dīwān* 295; Sayyid Ḥasan Ghaznawī *Dīwān*, ed. Mudarris Riḍawī (Tehran 1328/1949) 100; Bosworth *The Ghaznavids* 58; Iqbal Husain *The early Persian poets of India* 41.

73 Rūnī *Dīwān*, ed. Chaykin, 44, ed. Dāmgānī, 59, this being the opening verse of a poem addressed to him; this same poet has a further ode dedicated to 'Abd al-Ḥamīd in ibid., ed. Chaykin, 80–1, ed. Dāmghānī, 102–3.

74 *Dīwān* 40–1, 53–6, 295–7, 627; Mírzá Muḥammad 'Mas'úd-i-Sa'd-i-Salmán', 723, 729–30.

75 Nāṣir ad-Dīn Kirmānī, 46–7, substantially repeated in 'Uqailī, 195–6, and Khwāndamīr, 146; cf. Gulam Mustafa Khan 'A history of Bahrām Shāh of Ghaznīn' 229.

76 E. Berthels *EI*[2] art. 'Naṣr Allāh b. Muḥammad'; Rypka *et alii*, *History of Iranian literature* 222–3. Unfortunately, we have no details about Naṣrallāh's official career in the biographical works of Kirmānī and 'Uqailī, who close their sections on the viziers of the Ghaznavids with 'Abd al-Ḥamid b. Aḥmad, but Naṣrallāh is known as the *mamdūḥ* of the poet Sayyid Ḥasan, see Gulam Mustafa Khan, op. cit., 218–19, and Sayyid Ḥasan *Dīwān* 157–8, as was also his father Qiwām ad-Dīn Abū Naṣr Muḥammad, see ibid., 256–61.

77 Sanā'ī *Dīwān*, Introd. pp. *qāf-ṭā'* to *gāf-yā'*, and poems at 19–23, 91–2.

78 A further element of uncertainty is introduced here by the appearance of the frequently-confused names 'Muḥammad' and 'Aḥmad'.

79 Sanā'ī *Dīwān*, Introd. pp. *ṣād-dāl* f., and poems at 582–7, 1084–5, 1094–5; 'Uthmān Mukhtārī *Dīwān* 600; Mas'ūd-i Sa'd *Dīwān* 91–2 (headed to 'the Wazīr al-Wuzarā' Bihrūz b. Aḥmad'), 397–401 (headed to 'Muḥammad-i Bihrūz'); M. Niẓámu 'd-Dín *Introduction to the* Jawámi'u 'l-hikáyát *of Muḥammad al-'Awfí*, 185; Husain *The early Persian poets of India* 41–2.

80 Rūnī *Dīwān*, ed. Chaykin, 25–7, 58–9, 63, 69–70, ed. Dāmghānī, 30–1, 77–9, 84, 91–2; Sanā'ī *Dīwān*, Introd. pp. *ṣād-wāw* f., and poem at 229–35; 'Uthmān Mukhtārī *Dīwān* 284–9, 317–19, 592; Mas'ūd-i Sa'd *Dīwān* 5–9, 42–5, 66–7, 99–1–3, 194–204, 206–8, 292–4, 333–7, 412–15, 457–9, 475–7, 513, 527–8, 552–5; Iqbal Husain *The early Persian poets of India* 34–5.

81 *Chahār maqāla* 45, revised tr. 51.

82 Rūnī *Dīwān*, ed. Chaykin, 74–6, 108–9, ed. Dāmghānī, 180–1, 191–2; Sanā'ī *Dīwān* Introd. pp. *ṣād-hā'* f. and poem at 129–33; 'Uthmān Mukhtārī *Dīwān* 628–9; Mas'ūd-i Sa'd, 57–9, 72–4, 107–9, 153–9, 282–4, 312–14, 337–8, 378–8, 427–33, 453–7, 488–90, 509–10, 588; 'Aufī *Lubāb al-albāb* 423–4 (*Thiqat al-Mulk . . . waqtī ki ṣadr-i dīwān-i wizārat ba-jamāl-i u ārasta gasht . . .*); Mírzá Muḥammad 'Mas'úd-i-Sa'd-i-Salmán' *JRAS* (1906) 12–14 and *passim*; Husain, op. cit., 36–7, 109–10.

83 Baihaqī, 161 ff., tr. 235 ff.; Niẓámu'd-Dín, op. cit., 155.

84 Ibn al-Athīr, ed. Tornberg, x, 111, ed. Beirut, 167; Mīrkhwānd, 127, tr. 266.

85 Niẓámu 'd-Dín, op. cit., 155, 156, 194, 212; the last of these anecdotes is translated in Elliot and Dowson *The history of India as told by its own historians* II, 198–9.

86 *Ādāb al-ḥarb*, ff. 28a–30a, ed. Khwānsārī, 102–9, tr. Shafi, 200–3; Niẓām al-Mulk *Siyāsat-nāma* 58, tr. 48.

87 The section in Rypka *et alii*, *History of Iranian literature*, 196–7, on the later Ghaznavid poets, deals mainly with Mas'ūd-i Sa'd-i Salmān, Abū l-Faraj Rūnī and Sayyid Ḥasan; for Sanā'ī, see ibid., 236–7.

88 Bākharzī *Dumyat al-qaṣr*, ed. al-Ḥilū, II, 257, no. 303. The possible identification with Abū Ḥanīfa-yi Iskāfī arises from the fact that Bākharzī here quotes some Arabic verses by Abū Ḥanīfa Panjdihī on a handsome youth who was a shoemaker (*iskāf*); it may therefore have been this poem which brought Abū Ḥanīfa Panjdihī fame and the sobriquet of 'Iskāfī'. Panjdih, near Marw ar-Rūdh (and the scene of a famous diplomatic incident in 1885) would have been within the Ghaznavid dominions before the Seljuqs overran Khurasan.

89 Niẓāmī 'Arūḍī *Chahār maqāla*, 28, revised tr. 30; Mas'ūd-i Sa'd *Dīwān* 533; Mírzá Muḥammad, op. cit., 37–40; Husain, op. cit., 125–7.

90 *Dīwān* 290–1; Mírzá Muḥammad, op. cit., 42.

91 Bakharzī, II, 363–4, no. 350; 'Aufī *Lubāb al-albāb* 70–4; Mas'ūd-i Sa'd *Dīwān* 367, 603–4; Mírzá Muḥammad, op. cit., 42–4.

92 See idem 'Mas'úd-i-Sa'd-i-Salmán' *JRAS* (1905) 711 ff., and Iqbal Husain *The early Persian poets of India* 88 ff. In Mas'ūd-i Sa'd's *Dīwān*, poems dedicated to Maḥmūd outnumber those written for any person apart from the reigning sultans.

93 ibid., 30–1 53, 99–103, 169–76, 246, 289–90, 356–8, 401–3, 565; 'Aufī *Lubāb al-albāb* 70; Niẓāmī 'Arūḍī *Chahār maqāla* 45, revised tr. 51; Mírzá Muḥammad *JRAS* (1905) 733, 737–9; Husain, op. cit., 37–8, 105 ff.

94 Bākharzī, II, 358–60, 365–6, nos. 347, 351. Since one of the poems by

Abū l-Muẓaffar Nāṣir quoted here is addressed to the vizier ʿAbd ar-Razzāq b. Aḥmad b. Ḥasan Maimandī, who was minister to Maudūd and ʿAbd ar-Rashīd (see above), we have the middle years of the century fixed as his period of florescence.

95 Masʿūd-i Saʿd *Dīwān* 421–3; Mírzá Muḥammad 'Masʿúd-i-Saʿd-i-Salmán' *JRAS* (1906) 34–7, 49–51.

96 Niẓámu'd-Dín *Introduction to the* Jawámiʿu 'l-hikáyát *of Muḥammad al-ʿAwfī* 67–8, 224. One recalls that a work on Ḥanafī law, the *Tafrīd al-furūʿ*, is imputed to Sultan Maḥmūd by Ḥājjī Khalīfa, but this is probably apocryphal; see Nāẓim *Sulṭān Maḥmūd* 156–7.

97 See Bosworth *The Ghaznavids* 51–4, and idem 'The imperial policy of the early Ghaznawids' 57–66 and *passim.*

98 See Bosworth *The Ghaznavids* 54, 92, and 'The imperial policy of the early Ghaznawids' 63–6.

99 *Ṣubḥ al-aʿshā* VI, 404–9.

100 See Barthold *Turkestan*[3] 275, 293, and above, p. 78.

101 *Dīwān* 443, 460; Mírzá Muḥammad 'Masʿûd-i-Saʿd-i-Salmán' *JRAS* (1905) 711 n. 1.

102 *Dīwān* 113–14.

103 See Bosworth *The Ghaznavids* 86–91, 258–66.

104 Jūzjānī, I, 240, tr. I, 105; Ḥamdallāh Mustaufī *Ta'rīkh-i guzīda* 400 (the exact date in this source only). Ibn Bābā has the following month, Dhū l-Qaʿda (= September–October 1099) as the date of his death, see below, p. 143. If Ibrāhīm was 68 lunar years at his death, he must have been born in the middle years of his father Masʿūd's sultanate, in *ca.* 424/1033.

105 Muḥammad Riḍā *Riyāḍ al-alwāḥ, mushtamil bar katībahā-yi qubūr va abniya-yi Ghazna* (Kabul 1346/1967), facsimile text 133–4. This *ziyārat* contains a stone set in its *miḥrāb* with an inscription bearing the name of Sultan Masʿūd b. Ibrāhīm, possibly from his palace; see below, Ch. 3, p. 87.

CHAPTER THREE

1 Ibn al-Athīr, ed. Tornberg, X, 111, ed. Beirut, X, 168; Lane Poole *Catalogue of oriental coins in the British Museum* II, 174–5, nos. 566–8; idem *Additions to the Oriental Collection*, Part I, 244–7, nos. 566a–570r; Rodgers *Catalogue of the coins in the Government Museum, Lahore* 31–2, Supplement, 13; idem *Catalogue of coins in the Indian Museum* 159–60; Sourdel *Inventaire des monnaies anciennes du Musée de Caboul* 80.

2 *Dīwān* 354.

3 cf. S. Flury 'Le décor épigraphique des monuments de Ghazna' 75–8 and pl. XIV, and Y. A. Godard 'L'inscription du minaret de Masʿūd III à Ghazna' *Athār-é Irān* I (1936) 367–9. See also below, p. 87.

4 For the background of these events, see M. F. Sanaullah *The decline of the Saljūqid empire* (Calcutta 1938) xxxii, 106 ff., and Bosworth in *The Cambridge history of Iran. V. The Saljuq and Mongol periods* 109–11.

5 Ibn al-Athīr, ed. Tornberg, X, 239–41, ed. Beirut, X, 347–9; Bundārī *Zubdat an-nuṣra wa-nukhbat al-ʿuṣra*, ed. M. T. Houtsma (Leiden 1889)

262; Barthold *Turkestan down to the Mongol invasion*[3] 318–19; Pritsak 'Die Karachaniden' 42, 49. Ūtān/? Ūnān may conceivably be the Urgān/Urgūn of the Ghazna region mentioned by Jūzjānī as a fief of the Ghūrid prince Ḍiyā' ad-Dīn or 'Alā' ad-Dīn Muḥammad b. Shujā' ad-Dīn 'Alī in the last years of the 6th/12th century, see *Ṭabaqāt-i Nāṣirī* I, 370, tr. I, 392. Ḥabībī's confident identification of this place with modern Uruzgān is, however, by no means assured.

6 *Dīwān* 506.

7 *Ādāb al-ḥarb*, f. 80a, ed. Khwānsārī, 269, tr. Shafi, 216. For a discussion of these weapons, see J. W. Allan *The metal-working industry in Iran in the early Islamic period*, Oxford D.Phil. thesis 1976 (unpublished) I, 435 ff., 442–3.

8 *Dīwān* 244.

9 ibid., 353–64.

10 Mas'ūd-i Sa'd *Dīwān* 246–50, epitomised translation in Elliot and Dowson *History of India* IV, 526–7; Rūnī *Dīwān*, ed. Chaykin, 2–5, 43, 45, ed. Dāmghānī, 1–3, 58, 62; Ray *The dynastic history of northern India* I, 513–15, and genealogical table of the Gāhaḍavālas at p. 548; Ganguly in *The struggle for empire*[2] 52, 95; A. Bombaci *The Kūfic inscription in Persian verses in the court of the royal palace of Mas'ūd III at Ghazni* (Rome 1966) 31–2. A further poem by Abū l-Faraj Rūnī, dedicated to Mas'ūd, mentions the march of his army against Kanauj and (?) Benares (? Bān.r.sī), see his *Dīwān*, ed. Chaykin, 56, ed. Dāmghānī, 76.

11 *Dīwān* 511.

12 Mas'ūd-i Sa'd *Dīwān* 218–20, epitomised tr. in Elliot and Dowson, op. cit., IV, 524–5; Ray, op. cit., II, 699 ff., 878–81; Ganguly in *The struggle for empire*[2] 58, 68–9, 95; idem 'The historical value of Dīwān-i Salmān' 424–5, 427. The Shaibānī family, of humble Khurasanian origin, was prominent in the Ghaznavid service in India. There are several poems by Rūnī also dedicated to Najm ad-Dīn Zarīr (*Dīwān*, ed. Chaykin, 27–8, 47–51, 99–101, ed. Dāmghānī, 32–4, 62–5, 119–22); see the discussions of the family by Yāsimī, Introd. to his text of Mas'ūd-i Sa'd's *Dīwān*, pp. *nūn-hā'* to *nūn-zāy*, and by Gulam Mustafa Khan 'A history of Bahrām Shāh of Ghaznīn' 83–4 n. 3.

13 *Dīwān* 341–4.

14 See the editor's introd. to the *Dīwān* of Sanā'ī, pages *qāf-bā'* to *qāf-dāl*, and the references there, and also 'Uthmān Mukhtārī *Dīwān* 196–7.

15 Jūzjānī, I, 240, tr. I, 106.

16 Fakhr-i Mudabbir, ff. 15b, 31a, ed. Khwānsārī, 52, 109–10, tr. Shafi, 200, 203–4.

17 'Aufī *Jawāmi' al-ḥikāyāt*, partial facsimile edn. by Muḥammad Ramaḍānī (Tehran 1335/1956) 53–4; Niẓámu 'd-Din *Introduction to the* Jawámi'u 'l-hikáyát *of Muḥammad al-'Awfi* 163, 235.

18 cf. Bombaci 'Summary report on the Italian Archaeological Mission in Afghanistan. I. Introduction to the excavations at Ghazni' *East and West*, N.S. X/1–2 (1959) 19–20.

19 *Dīwān* 51, 371.

20 Bombaci *The Kūfic inscription in Persian verses in the court of the royal palace of Mas'ūd III at Ghazni* 6 ff., 33 ff.

21 cf. his *Dīwān*, 18: 'Today you have entrusted to me the *dār al-kutub*, and this honour and privilege has become for me an exalted office'.

22 Bombaci, op. cit., 33–4.

23 Rūnī *Dīwān*, ed. Chaykin, 94, ed. Dāmghānī, 117; Mas'ūd-i Sa'd *Dīwān* 272; cf. Bombaci, op. cit., 33–42.

24 See M. Molé 'L'épopée iranienne après Firdōsī' *La Nouvelle Clio* V (1953) 384–5, and Humā'ī's edition of 'Uthmān Mukhtārī's *Dīwān*, 750–844, where an edition of the text plus a long critical introduction to the poem is given.

25 Ibn al-Athīr, ed. Tornberg, x, 353, ed. Beirut, x, 504; Jūzjānī, I, 240, tr. I, 107. The actual number of Mas'ūd's sons given by the latter author varies between fifteen in Raverty's translation and eleven in Ḥabībī's n. 5, text, I, 240.

26 Mustaufī *Ta'rīkh-i guzīda*, 400; Firishta, f. 72a, tr. I, 82; cf. Raverty's n. 7, *Jūzjānī*, tr. I, 107.

27 Ibn Isfandiyār *Ta'rīkh-i Ṭabaristān*, abridged tr. E. G. Browne (Leiden-London 1905) 58–9; cf. Gulam Mustafa Khan 'A history of Bahrām Shāh of Ghaznīn', 69.

28 *Dīwān* 611, cf. Khan, op. cit., 65–6.

29 *Dīwān* 317–18, cf. Khan, op. cit., 69–70. A further reference in the opening of a poem by 'Uthmān Mukhtārī (*Dīwān* 509) addressed to the new sultan mentions his recognition as ruler as falling on the Iranian festival of Bahmanagān, i.e. the second of the month of Bahman, which corresponds to late January–early and middle February.

30 Lane Poole *Catalogue of oriental coins in the British Museum* II, 176, nos. 571–2; idem *Additions to the Oriental Collection*, Part I, 248, nos. 572m–q.

31 Mas'ūd-i Sa'd *Dīwān* 131–2, see also 318; 'Uthmān Mukhtārī *Dīwān* 485–7.

32 Ibn al-Athīr, ed. Tornberg, x, 353, ed. Beirut, x, 504; Mīrkhwānd, 128, tr. 267; Firishta, ff. 72a–b, tr. I, 82–3.

33 *Dīwān* 85–90, 171–4, 282–4, 376–85, 475–6.

34 Jūzjānī, I, 241, tr. I, 108; Firishta, f. 73a, tr. I, 84.

35 *Dīwān* 232, 387, cf. 'Uthmān Mukhtārī *Dīwān* 296–9, eulogy of ''Imād ad-Daula Sarhang Muḥammad b. 'Alī', and Humā'ī's long note on the two brothers, ibid., 279–80 n. 1.

36 Mas'ūd-i Sa'd *Dīwān* 560; Fakhr-i Mudabbir, f. 80b, ed. Khwānsārī, 270, tr. Shafi, 217; Khan 'A history of Bahrām Shāh of Ghaznīn', 64–6.

37 *Dīwān* 127–8, 317–18; 'Uthmān Mukhtārī *Dīwān* 509; Khan, op. cit., 69–72.

38 *Jawāmi' al-ḥikāyāt*, tr. in Elliot and Dowson *History of India* II, 199.

39 Muḥammad b. Ibrāhīm *Ta'rīkh-i Seljūqiyān-i Kirmān*, ed. M.T.Houtsma (Leiden 1886) 26–7, ed. M. I. Bāstānī-Pārīzī (Tehran 1343/1964) 35, cf. Houtsma, 'Zur Geschichte der Selǵuqen von Kerman' *ZDMG* XXXIX (1885) 374; Khan, op. cit., 72, citing verses from Sanā'ī's *Ḥadīqat al-ḥaqīqa* referring to Bahrām Shāh's stay in Kirmān.

40 Fakhr-i Mudabbir, f. 80b, ed. Khwānsārī, 270–1, tr. Shafi, 217–18.

41 'Aufī *Jawāmi' al-ḥikāyāt*, partial facsimile edn., 236–7; Niẓámu 'd-Din *Introduction to the* Jawámi'u 'l-ḥikáyát *of Muḥammad al-'Awfī* 177; Jūzjānī, I, 241, tr. I, 108–9; Firishta, f. 72b, tr. I, 83. Whatever the historicity of 'Aufī's anecdote, there is no doubt about the existence of Malik Arslan's envoy named in it; Sanā'ī has two long odes addressed to this last person, named in the headings as 'Qāḍī l-Quḍāt Shaikh Abū l-Barakāt b. Mubārak Fatḥī' and 'ash-Shaikh al-Imām al-Ajall Saif al-Ḥaḍratain Abū l-Fatḥ Barakāt b. Mubārak al-Fatḥī' (*Dīwān* 313–22, 329–34).

42 Ḥusainī, 90–1 (who, in his account of the Ghaznavid-Seljuq warfare of this time, erroneously calls Malik Arslan 'Ibrāhīm); Bundārī, 262–3; Ibn al-Athīr, ed. Tornberg, x, 353, ed. Beirut, x, 504; Mīrkhwānd, 128–9, tr. 267.

43 For the tactical use of elephants in the Ghaznavid army, see Bosworth *The Ghaznavids, their empire in Afghanistan and eastern Iran* 115–18, and idem EI^2 art. 'Fīl. As beasts of war'.

44 Ibn al-Athīr, ed. Tornberg, x, 353–4, ed. Beirut, x, 504–5; Jūzjānī, I, 238, tr. I, 105; Firishta, loc. cit.

45 On this poet, the eulogist of Bahrām Shāh and Sanjar, see Bosworth in EI^2, suppl., s.v.; this eulogy of Amīr Tāj ad-Dīn is cited by Khan, op. cit., 75–6, from the *Mu'nis al-aḥrār fī daqā'iq al-ash'ār* of Muḥammad b. Badr Jājarmī. Amīr Tāj ad-Dīn was also the *mamdūḥ* of 'Uthmān Mukhtārī, who addressed to him several *ghazals*, see his *Dīwān* 569–79.

46 Quoted in Jūzjānī, I, 241, tr. I, 109, in Mīrkhwānd, 132, tr. 270, in Firishta, f. 73a, and in Khan, op. cit., 77; but as Khan notes here, the verse does not apparently figure in copies of Sayyid Ḥasan's *dīwān*, and certainly not in the printed edition of Mudarris Riḍawī. Raverty, however, states that a coin struck by Bahrām Shāh in 548/1153 at Lahore has quoted on its reverse this line of poetry (*Ṭabaqāt-i Nāṣirī*, tr. I, 110, n. 1).

47 Ḥusainī, 91; Rāwandī, 168–9; Ibn al-Athīr, ed. Tornberg, x, 353–6, ed. Beirut, x, 505–7; Jūzjānī, I, 241, 258, tr. I, 109, 148; Ḥamdallāh Mustaufī, 400–1; Mīrkhwānd, 129, tr. 268; Firishta, f. 72b, tr. I, 83.

48 Khan, loc. cit., follows the translation of an anecdote of 'Aufī's in Elliot and Dowson *History of India* II, 199, and reads 'Shakrān mountains'.

49 Ibn al-Athīr, ed. Tornberg, x, 355–6, ed. Beirut, x, 507–8; 'Aufī in Elliot and Dowson, loc. cit.; Jūzjānī, I, 241, tr. I, 109; Mustaufī, 401; Mīrkhwānd, 131, 133, tr. 269, 271; Firishta, ff. 72b–73a, tr. I, 83–4; Khan, op. cit., 77–8.

50 Khan, op. cit., 79, notes that in the sub-heading of a section in Sanā'ī's *Ḥadīqat al-ḥaqīqa* we find the further patronymic of Abū l-Ḥārith.

51 See Bosworth 'The titulature of the early Ghaznavids' 217–24, for Maḥmūd s titles.

52 Jūzjānī, loc. cit.; Sayyid Ḥasan *Dīwān* 149; 'Uthmān Mukhtārī *Dīwān* 83; Lane Poole *Catalogue of oriental coins in the British Museum* II, 177–8,

nos. 573–6; idem, *Additions to the Oriental Collection*, Part I, 248–50, nos. 574a–580b; Rodgers *Catalogue of the coins in the Government Museum, Lahore* 32–3, Supplement, 13; idem *Catalogue of the coins collected by Chas J. Rodgers and purchased by the Government of the Panjáb. Part II. Miscellaneous Muḥammadan coins* (Calcutta 1894) 43–4; idem *Catalogue of coins in the Indian Museum*, 160–1; Sourdel *Inventaire des monnaies anciennes du Musée de Caboul* 81.

53 References in Khan, op. cit., 81–3; see also above, Ch. 2, p. 56.

54 See Jūzjānī, I, 258, and tr. I, 148, and the references to the coin catalogues in n. 50 above.

55 Ibn al-Athīr, ed. Tornberg, X, 389, ed. Beirut, X, 553; cf. Bosworth in *Cambridge history of Iran* V, 119–20.

56 'A history of Bahrām Shāh of Ghaznīn', 90, n. 1. For another poem of Sanā'ī's addressed to Daulat Shāh, see *Dīwān* 106–7.

57 Fakhr-i Mudabbir, ff. 13b–14a, ed. Khwānsārī, 43–5, tr. Shafi, 197–9; Ibn al-Athīr, ed. Tornberg, XI, 18, ed. Beirut, XI, 29.

58 Ḥusainī, 92; Bundārī, 264; Ibn al-Athīr, ed. Tornberg, XI, 17-18, ed. Beirut, XI, 28–30; M. Köymen *Büyük Selçuklu imparatorluğu tarihi. II. Ikinci imparatorluk devri* (Ankara 1954) 306–10; Bosworth in op. cit., 159. According to the historian of the Mongol period Juwainī *Ta'rīkh-i Jahān-Gushāy*, tr. Boyle, *The history of the World-Conqueror* (Manchester 1958) I, 279, Sanjar's tributary the Khwārazm-Shāh Atsïz was in continual attendance on the sultan during the eleven months in which he was involved with this Ghazna expedition, though nothing about Atsïz's presence is mentioned in the earlier sources.

59 Ibn al-Athīr, ed. Tornberg, XI, 56, ed. Beirut, XI, 85; Köymen, op. cit., 327.

60 Jūzjānī, I, 241, tr. I, 110, also in Mīrkhwānd, 132, tr. 270, adding that Bahrām Shāh penetrated to many regions untouched by any of his predecessors.

61 Ganguly in *The struggle for empire*[2] 82.

62 Jūzjānī, I, 241–2, tr. I, 110 (Raverty has here the date of 28 Ramaḍān); Firishta, f. 73b, tr. 85.

63 Fakhr-i Mudabbir, ff. 106b–107b, ed. Khwānsārī, 378–81, tr. Shafi, 224–7; Jūzjānī, loc. cit.; Mīrkhwānd, 132–3, tr. 270–1; Firishta, loc. cit.; Gulam Mustafa Khan, op. cit., 84–8; Ganguly in op. cit., 95–6.

64 loc. cit.

65 *Dīwān* 182–5, cf. Khan, op. cit., 89.

66 *Dīwān* 88, cf. Khan, op. cit., 202, whose manuscript of the *Dīwān* has the variant given in the second verse above.

67 Sayyid Ḥasan *Dīwān* 59–60; Mas'ūd-i Sa'd *Dīwan* 458, 527; Khan, op. cit., 226–7.

68 *Dīwān* 289–90; Khan, op. cit., 229. In these lines, the poet is playing upon the multiple connotations of the name Bahrām: the various heroic figures of the Sāsānid period, such as Bahrām Gūr and Bahrām Chūbīn, and the Persian name for the planet Mars.

69 Sayyid Ḥasan *Dīwān* 110, 169–71; Khan, op. cit., 229–31.

70 Sayyid Ḥasan *Dīwān* 170, 233. *Zi bākhtar* is the reading of the India

Office manuscript of the *Dīwān* cited here by Khan, op. cit., 231. Riḍawī's printed text (based on three complete manuscripts of the *Dīwān* in Tehran and on selections found in other works) has the vaguer *zi tākhtan* 'from the attack', which could equally refer, for instance, to a raid into India.

71 *Dīwān* 200–4.

72 ibid., 223.

73 ibid., 96, 199, cf. a similar refrain at 221–3.

74 ibid., 88.

75 *Dīwān* 72; Qazwíní 'Mas'úd-i-Sa'd-i-Salmán' *JRAS* (1906) 26–7; I. Husain *The early Persian poets of India* 111; A. J. Arberry *Classical Persian literature* (London 1958) 81–4; Rypka *et alii*, *History of Iranian literature* 196.

76 The first date is that of Rypka, op. cit., 236, n. 47, in his discussion of the date of Sanā'ī's death, where he rejects what he describes as the commonly-cited dates of 542/1147–8 and 545/1150 as unlikely; the second date is that selected by Mudarris Riḍawī, the editor of the *Dīwān*, in his Introduction, pp. *mīm-hā'* ff., after a consideration of all the conflicting evidence.

77 Browne *A literary history of Persia* II, 317 ff.; Gulam Mustafa Khan 'A history of Bahrām Shāh of Ghaznīn, 218; Arberry, op. cit., 88–94 (whose judgment on the *Ḥadīqat al-ḥaqīqa* is less severe than Browne's); Rypka, op. cit., 236–7.

78 cf. 'Aufī *Lubāb al-albāb* 116–19; Daulat Shāh *Tadhkira* 438–41; and the detailed reconstruction of the poet's life in Riḍawī's Introduction to the *Dīwān*, pp. *yā'* to *mīm-hā'*.

79 See Browne, op. cit., II, 349 ff.; E. Berthels *EI*[1] art. 'Naṣr Allāh b. Muḥammad'; Khan, op. cit., 218–19; Arberry, op. cit., 95–7; Rypka, op. cit., 222–3.

80 'Aufī, 446–9; Khan, op. cit., 220, 231–4.

89 *Dīwān* 62–3, poem headed *dar rithā'-i Sayyid Ḥasan*; this poet is of course to be distinguished—though many of the later *tadhkira* compilers became understandably confused—from the better-known Sayyid Ḥasan, sc. Ashraf ad-Dīn Ghaznavī, discussed above.

82 'Aufī, 436–41; Khan, op. cit., 220–1.

83 'Aufī, 441–5; Khan, op. cit., 221.

84 'Aufī, 233–4; Khan, loc. cit.

85 'Aufī, 449–54.

86 ibid., 234–9, 454–6.

CHAPTER FOUR

1 For general accounts of Ibn Funduq and his compositions, see Kari Sayyid Kalimullah Husaini, 'Life and works of Zahiru 'd-Din al-Bayhaqi, the author of the Tarikh-i-Bayhaq' *IC* XXVIII (1954) 297–318, and D. M. Dunlop *EI*[2] art. 'al-Bayhaḳī, Ẓahīr al-Dīn ... b. Funduḳ'.

2 Ibn al-Athīr, ed. Tornberg, XI, 249, ed. Beirut, XI, 380; Barthold *Turkestan*[3] 31; Dunlop., art. cit.

3 Ibn al-Athīr, ed. Tornberg, XI, 112, ed. Beirut, XI, 170.
4 On the author and his work, see A. S. Bazmee Ansari *EI*[2] art. 'Djūzdjānī'.
5 Jūzjānī, I, 243, tr. I, 114; and see the sarcastic remarks of the translator Raverty, ibid., tr. I, 445–6, n. 2.
6 Ibn al-Athīr, ed. Tornberg, XI, 89, ed. Beirut, XI, 135; Gulam Mustafa Khan 'A history of Bahrām Shāh of Ghaznīn' 199–200.
7 Yāqūt *Mu'jam al-buldān* IV, 455, mentions that this K.r.mān was a dependency of Ghazna and about four days' journey from it, which fits very well with Kurram; see also Bosworth *EI*[2] art. 'Kurram'.
8 See the discussion on the exact form of this name and the confusions which seem to have arisen over it, above, Ch. 3, pp. 103–4.
9 Mas'ūd's *laqab* is correctly given in Khan's manuscript (cf. the names of Bahrām Shāh's sons listed by Jūzjānī, I, 242 n. 5, tr. I, 111), but wrongly as Shujā' ad-Daula in Mudarris Riḍawī's printed edition of Sayyid Ḥasan's *Dīwān*.
10 Jūzjānī, I, 393–5, tr. I, 439–45; Ibn al-Athīr, ed. Tornberg, XI, 89–90, 107–8, ed. Beirut, XI, 135–6, 164–5 (the second of these accounts being a variant one, in which he inserts a whole string of events covering the last forty years of Ghūrid-Ghaznavid relations under the year 547/1152–3); Muḥammad b. 'Alī Rāwandī *Rāḥat aṣ-ṣudūr wa-āyat as-surūr*, ed. M. Iqbāl (London 1921) 175; Ẓahīr ad-Dīn Nīshāpūrī *Saljūq-nāma*, ed. Ismā'īl Afshār (Tehran 1332/1953) 47; Mīrkhwānd *Rauḍat aṣ-ṣafā'* in Ch. Defrémery 'Histoire des Sultans Ghourides' *JA*, Ser. 4, vol. II (July–December 1843) Persian text, 172–4, tr. 188–92; Sayyid Ḥasan *Dīwān* 81–90; Gulam Mustafa Khan 'A history of Bahrām Shāh of Ghaznīn' 201–4. Sayyid Ḥasan had apparently remained in Ghazna during the Ghūrid occupation, and had had some contact with Saif ad-Dīn Sūrī; he then had to make his peace with the returned Bahrām Shāh through an apologetic quatrain, according to 'Aufī *Lubāb al-albāb* 441 (the quatrain is not included in the printed edition of Sayyid Ḥasan's *Dīwān*).
11 *Ṭabaqāt-i Nāṣirī*, tr. I, 347–50, n. 1.
12 Gulam Mustafa Khan 'A history of Bahrām Shāh of Ghaznīn' 211–13; Niẓāmī 'Arūḍī *Chahār maqāla* 65–6, 87, revised tr. 74, 96–7; Rāwandī *Rāḥat aṣ-ṣudūr* 175–6; Jūzjānī, I, 346–7, tr. I, 357–60.
13 Daulat Shāh *Tadhkirat ash-shu'arā'* 85; Jūzjānī, I, 346, tr. I, 357, cf. Gulam Mustafa Khan, op. cit., 204, 210.
14 For the location of Tigīnābād, see below, Appendix A, pp. 149–51.
15 Raverty *Ṭabaqāt-i Nāṣirī* I, tr. 352, n. 3, explains that *kāṛwah* is a Pashto word, and cites his *A dictionary of the Puk'hto, Pushto or language of the Afghans*[2] (London 1867) col. 1151, s.v. *karrwa'h*. Under this entry, he states that this was a bullock or buffalo hide stuffed with hay or straw and rolled along in front of troops to protect them from enemy arrows, and that it was used in the warfare of the 15th century between the Yūsufzais and the Dilazāks. However, Dr N. D. MacKenzie informs me that he knows of no other attestation of the word's use; it may be that some reading in the *Ta'rīkh-i muraṣṣa'* of Afḍal Khān

or a similar history has been explained thus by Raverty in the light of Jūzjānī's usage of the term.

16 The name, or possibly title, of *kharmīl* is curious. Ḥabībī, in the notes to his text of Jūzjānī, II, 342 n. 5, suggests that it might be a form of Arabic *qarmīl* 'two-humped camel' (thus defined by Khwārazmī *Mafātīḥ al-'ulūm*, ed. G. van Vloten (Leiden 1895) 123: *al-qarāmīl, al-ibil dhawāt as-sanamain*), since in his reply to Bahrām Shāh's challenge before the first battle at Tigīnābād, 'Alā' ad-Dīn Ḥusain contrasts his own *kharmīls* or champions with the elephants of the Ghaznavids (*agar tū pīl mī-ārī, man kharmīl mī-āram*), see Jūzjānī, I, 342, tr. I, 351. Apart from this question of the name or title *kharmīl*, the institution of the two military commanders or champions of the Ghūrid forces (possibly as hereditary holders of the posts) raises interesting questions, probably to be connected with rivalry within Ghūr of two families of local chieftains, the Shansabānīs and the Shīthānīs or Shīshānīs; see the discussion in Bosworth 'The early Islamic history of Ghūr' *CAJ* VI (1961) 126–7.

17 *Dīwān* 167–9, 244–9.

18 Jūzjānī, I, 341–3, tr. I, 347–53; Ibn al-Athīr, ed. Tornberg, XI, 108–9, ed. Beirut, XI, 165; Mīrkhwānd, in Defrémery 'Histoire des Sultans Ghourides' *JA*, Ser. 4, vol. II (July–December 1843) Persian text, 174–7, tr. 192–6 (apparently derived from Jūzjānī's account); cf. Gulam Mustafa Khan, op. cit., 204–6.

19 Jūzjānī, I, 344, tr. I, 353; Fakhr-i Mudabbir *Ādāb al-ḥarb*, ms. India Office, f. 122b, ed. Khwānsārī, 437, tr. Shafi, 227; Mīrkhwānd, op. cit., Persian text, 177–8, tr. 196–7.

20 Ibn al-Athīr, ed. Tornberg, IX, 297, ed. Beirut, IX, 436; Ibn Funduq *Tatimmat ṣiwān al-ḥikma*, ed. Muḥammad Shafī' (Lahore 1935) 45; Ḥusainī *Akhbār ad-daula as-saljūqiyya* 6. One might speculate that the manuscript of the work on the physical and moral attributes of the Prophet known to have been in the possession of Sultan 'Abd ar-Rashīd in the middle of the previous century and then in that of a Syrian merchant in the 6th/12th century (see for this manuscript, above, Ch. 1, p.40), could have come into circulation as a result of Ghūrid or perhaps Oghuz plunderings.

21 Jūzjānī, I, 242, 341–5, tr. I, 110–11, 347–55; Ibn al-Athīr, ed. Tornberg, XI, 107–9, ed. Beirut, XI, 165–6; Niẓāmī 'Arūḍī *Chahār maqāla* 46, revised tr. 30–1; Fakhr-i Mudabbir *Ādāb al-ḥarb*, ms. India Office, f. 122b, ed. Khwānsārī, 437, tr. Shafi, 227; Gulam Mustafa Khan, op. cit., 206–11; Bosworth in *Cambridge history of Iran* V, 160; idem *EI²* art. 'Gh̲ūrids'.

22 Ibn al-Athīr, ed. Tornberg, XI, 109, ed. Beirut, XI, 166; cf. Wiet, in A. Maricq and G. Wiet *Le minaret de Djam, la decouverte de la capitale des sultans ghorides (XIIe–XIIIe siècles)* (Paris 1959) 34–5.

23 See Bosworth, ibid.

24 *Ādāb al-ḥarb*, ms. India Office, ff. 122b–123b, ed. Khwānsārī, 437–42, tr. Shafi, 227–9, cf. Gulam Mustafa Khan, op. cit., 208–9.

25 Jūzjānī, I, 345, tr. I, 355. It may be that the long-awaited volume from

the Délégation archéologique française en Afghanistan on the site and architecture of Lashkar-i Bāzār—the volume *II. Les trouvailles* appeared in 1963—will answer these questions concerning the last years of the palaces.

26 See J. Sourdel-Thomine 'Stèles arabes de Bust (Afghanistan)' *Arabica* III (1956) 285–306.

27 An anecdote of Daulat Shāh's refers to Bahrām Shāh's escape in conditions of severe winter cold, i.e. in the second half of 545/winter 1150–1, see his *Tadhkirat ash-shu'arā'*, 85–6, and Gulam Mustafa Khan 'A history of Bahrām Shāh of Ghaznīn' 210–11.

28 *Dīwān* 279–80; Gulam Mustafa Khan, op. cit., 213–14.

29 See his *Ta'rīkh-i guzīda* 401.

30 Ibn al-Athīr, ed. Tornberg, XI, 124, ed. Beirut, XI, 188.

31 Jūzjānī, I, 242, tr. I, 111.

32 See Gulam Mustafa Khan, op. cit., 76–9.

33 ibid., 214–17. In support of this later date we have the note of Raverty's *Ṭabaqāt-i Nāṣirī*, tr. I, 114 n., giving information known to him about a coin struck by Khusrau Shāh at Lahore in 552 'the first year of his reign', according to the reverse legend. Unfortunately, he does not name the coin catalogue involved or any other source for this statement; but since Raverty was, despite his strong prejudices, usually knowledgeable, one may tentatively accept his information as uncorroborated support for the evidence of the literary sources, discussed by Gulam Mustafa Khan, loc. cit.

34 Jūzjānī, I 242, n. 5, tr. I, 111.

35 *EI*[2] art. 'Ghaznawids'.

36 Jūzjānī, tr. I, 112–14 n. 5.

37 cf. Mīrkhwānd, ed. and tr. Wilken, text, 133–5, tr. 272–3.

38 Jūzjānī, I, 242–3, tr. I, 111; cf. Gulam Mustafa Khan, op. cit., 225.

39 Sayyid Ḥasan *Dīwān* 12 (cf. also Shams-i Qais *al-Mu'jam fī ash'ār al-'Ajam*, ed. Muḥammad b. 'Abd al-Wahhāb Qazwīnī and Mudarris Riḍawī (Tehran 1314/1935) 325–6), 139; Jūzjānī, I, 242, tr. I, 111. It is unclear whether the poems dedicated to Khusrau Shāh by Sayyid Ḥasan (*Dīwān* 12–16, 42–3, 72–3, 137–40, 188–91) were written during the reign of his father Bahrām Shāh—as poems of his written for others of that sultan's sons certainly were—or after Khusrau Shāh had succeeded to the throne; Sayyid Ḥasan himself probably died at some date between 555/1160 and 557/1162, see Riḍawī, Introd. to the *Dīwān*, pp. *lām-ṭā'* to *mīm*.

40 Thomas *JRAS* IX (1848) 372; Lane Poole *Additions to the Oriental Collection*, Part I, 250–1, nos. 580d–p; C. J. Rodgers *Catalogue of the coins collected by Chas. J. Rodgers and purchased by the Government of the Panjáb. Part II. Miscellaneous Muḥammadan coins* 44; idem *Catalogue of the coins in the Government Museum, Lahore*, Supplement, 13–14.

41 Jūzjānī, I, 348, tr. I, 362; Fakhr-i Mudabbir *Ādāb al-ḥarb*, ms. India Office. ff. 132a–133a, ed. Khwānsārī, 479–82, tr. Shafi, 232–4; cf. Gulam Mustafa Khan, op. cit., 216–17, and 'Aufī *Lubāb al-albāb*, notes of Qazwīnī, 569–70.

42 Ibn al-Athīr, ed. Tornberg, XI, 169, ed. Beirut, XI, 271; Jūzjānī, I, 348, 396, tr. I, 362, 448.

43 Ibn al-Athīr, ed. Tornberg, XI, 163, ed. Beirut, XI, 262; Jūzjānī, I, 242–3, tr. I, 111–13.

44 ibid., I, 243, tr. I, 114 and note; 'Aufī *Lubāb al-albāb* 94, 472–3. The dedications of the two odes of the court poets of Khusrau Malik mentioned above also refer to the sultan as 'Abū l-Muluk' (the title given in early Islamic times to the Umayyad caliph 'Abd al-Malik), which as Qazwīnī remarked, ibid., 596, seems in retrospect very curious for a ruler who was the last of his line. With regard to the form of address *Sulṭān-i Ḥalīm*, Fakhr-i Mudabbir, *Ādāb al-ḥarb*, ms. India Office ff. 81a, 125a, 132a, ed. Khwānsārī, 271, 446, 480, tr. Shafi, 218, 229, 232, applies it to Khusrau Malik's father Khusrau Shāh; it is probably impossible now to discover to whom the original attribution was made.

45 Thomas *JRAS* IX (1848) 373; Lane Poole *Catalogue of oriental coins in the British Museum* II, 179–80, nos. 581–8; idem *Additions to the Oriental Collection*, Part I, 252, nos. 580aa–ii; Rodgers *Catalogue of the coins collected by Chas. J. Rodgers* . . . Part II, 45–6; idem *Catalogue of coins in the Government Museum, Lahore* 33, Supplement, 14.

46 Ibn al-Athīr, ed. Tornberg, XI, 202, ed. Beirut, XI, 305–6; Jūzjānī, I, 243, 357, tr. I, 111–12, 376; Mīrkhwānd *Historia Gasnevidarum*, text, 133–4, tr. 272 (follows Jūzjānī here).

47 See Bosworth in *Cambridge history of Iran* V, 151–7, for details of the Oghuz interlude in Khurasanian history.

48 Ibn al-Athīr, ed. Tornberg, XI, 110, ed. Beirut, XI, 167; Fakhr-i Mudabbir *Ādāb al-ḥarb*, ms. India Office, f. 133a, ed. Khwānsārī, 482, tr. Shafi, 234.

49 Ibn al-Athīr, loc. cit.; Jūzjānī, I, 243, 396, tr. 112, 448–9.

50 See J. W. Spain *The Pathan borderland* (The Hague 1963) 48; Bābur had clashed with the Khiḍr Khēl clan of the Shinwarīs in the early 10th/16th century, see Sir Olaf Caroe *The Pathans 550 B.C.–A.D. 1957* (London 1958) 163.

51 Ibn al-Athīr, ed. Tornberg, XI, 110, ed. Beirut, XI, 167–8; Jūzjānī, I, 357–8, 396, tr. I, 376–7, 449.

52 Jūzjānī, I, 243, tr. I, 114. His reign was, indeed, the fourth longest one in the Ghaznavid dynasty, coming after those of Ibrāhīm, Bahrām Shāh and Maḥmūd in order of length.

53 cf. J. F. Richards 'The Islamic frontier in the east: expansion into South Asia' *South Asia* (Perth, Western Australia, Oct. 1974) 92–3.

54 *Ādāb al-ḥarb*, ms. India Office, ff. 81a–b, ed. Khwānsārī, 271–2, tr. Shafi, 218.

55 See for example the *qaṣīda* of Jamāl ad-Dīn Muḥammad b. 'Alī Sirājī, cited in 'Aufī *Lubāb al-albāb* 473.

56 H. C. Ray *The dynastic history of northern India* I, 535–6.

57 cf. Aziz Ahmad *An intellectual history of Islam in India* (Edinburgh 1969) 71–2. For Mas'ūd-i Sa'd's career, see Ch. 3, pp. 65–6. Concerning Abū l-Faraj Rūnī, although certain authorities aver that Rūn was a village in the Nīshāpūr region, yet Aufī, op. cit., 419, says that he was

born and brought up in the vicinity of Lahore, 'and this district, by virtue of his never-ending excellence, has pride of place and of splendour over all other lands.'

58 ʿAufī, op. cit., 87–9.

59 ibid., 90, 93; see also M. Nizamuddin *EI*[2] art. "ʿAwfī'.

60 The fact that all these poets of the last period of the Ghaznavids are found with elaborate *laqab*s, and not all of them seem to have acquired them as the concomitants of official or court posts, indicates how, in eastern Islam, these honorific titles had by the middle of the 6th/12th century percolated downwards from the strata of the rulers, the military and the civilian officials to the middle ranks of society.

61 ʿAufī *Lubāb al-albāb* 90–7.

62 ibid., 472–4, 539–40. The better-known Seljuq poet of a century before, Abū ʿAbdallāh Muḥammad b. ʿAbd al-Malik Muʿizzī, of course derived his *nom-de-plume* from his patron Muʿizz ad-Dīn Malik Shāh.

63 ibid., 474–8, 541–4.

64 Such as the various ones listed by Iqbal Husain in the bibliography to his *The early Persian poets of India* and used by him in Bankipore MSS.

65 Jūzjānī, I, 396, tr. I, 449; Mīrkhwānd, in Defrémery 'Histoire des Sultans Ghourides' *JA*, Ser. 4, vol. III (Jan.–June 1844) text, 265, tr. 283.

66 The Muslim historians describing this expedition, e.g. Jūzjānī, I, 397, tr. I, 451–2, describe Muʿizz ad-Dīn Muḥammad's adversary as Rājā Bhīma, who in fact succeeded his elder brother Mūlarājā in the early part of 1178; but internal evidence, according to D. C. Ganguly, clearly shows that the victorious Hindu ruler was Mūlarājā, see Ganguly in *The struggle for Empire*[2] 78, 106, 117–18.

67 Ibn al-Athīr, ed. Tornberg, XI, 110, ed. Beirut, XI, 168.

68 Jūzjānī, I, 244, 397, tr. I, 115, 452–3.

69 ibid., I, 398, tr. I, 543–5 and n. 4; cf. Sir Wolseley Haig, in *Cambridge history of India*. III *Turks and Afghans* (Cambridge 1928) 39, and P. Saran and R. C. Majumdar in *The struggle for empire*[2] 118. Jūzjānī's father Maulānā Sirāj ad-Dīn became *qāḍī* of the Muslim forces in India, with his court based at Lahore, under the governorship of ʿAlī Karmākh, see *Ṭabaqāt-i Nāṣirī* I, 398, tr. I, 456.

70 This verse is by the *mukhaḍram* poet Abū Khirāsh al-Hudhalī, in which he laments the metaphorical fetters which the prescriptions of the new faith of Islam had brought in place of the old Jāhiliyya freedom, cf. *Dīwān al-Hudhaliyyīn*, ed. Aḥmad az-Zain (Cairo 1364–9/1945–50) II, also in *Aghānī* XXI, ed. R. Brünnow (Leiden 1888) 59. If Khusrau Malik really did cite this most apposite verse, it is a tribute to the high standard of learning which personally characterised the Ghaznavid sultans from the time of Muḥammad and Masʿūd b. Maḥmūd onwards.

71 Ibn al-Athīr, ed. Tornberg, XI, 110–11, ed. Beirut, XI, 168–9.

72 Jūzjānī, I, 244, 398, tr. I, 115, 456–7, cf. also Mīrkhwānd *Historia Gasnevidarum*, text, 135, tr. 272–3.

73 Partial facs. edn. by Ramaḍānī, 152 = Niẓámu d-Dín *Introduction to the* Jawámiʿu l-ḥikáyát *of Muḥammad al-ʿAwfī* 168, no. 729.

74 *Bābur-nāma*, tr. A. S. Beveridge (London 1922) 219.

APPENDIX A

1 Samʿānī, facs. edn. by D. S. Margoliouth (London 1912) f. 437b. Elsewhere, *s.v.* 'al-Basāsīrī', Samʿānī further quotes Ibn Bābā on the origin of the Turkish amīr Arslan Basāsīrī's *nisba*, as cited in the history of Abū l-Wafā' al-Akhsīkathī (facs. edn. f. 80a = ed. ʿAbd ar-Raḥmān al-Yamānī and ʿAbd al-Muʿīd Khān (Hyderabad 1382–6/1962–6) II, 218–19).

2 Yāqūt *Irshād al-arīb*, ed. Margoliouth (London 1907–26) I, 230–2. Both V. A. Hamdani (see below) and following him, the present writer in the article of his cited below, were misled into assuming an identity of the two Aḥmad b. ʿAlī al-Qāshānīs.

3 *Muʿjam al-buldān* (Beirut 1374–6/1955–7) IV, 296–7. Yāqūt quotes Ibn Bābā as ridiculing the messianic expectations of the ignorant and credulous Shīʿīs of Qāshān. The introducing by Ibn Bābā into his book of this anecdote seems to indicate that, despite his presumed Qāshānī origin, he himself was no fanatical Shīʿī.

4 'Some rare manuscripts in Istanbul' *JRAS* (1938) 562–3.

5 ʿAẓīmu 'd-Dīn Aḥmad *et alii*, *Catalogue of the Arabic and Persian manuscripts in the Oriental Public Library at Bankipore. XV. History* (Patna 1929) III, no. 1044.

6 The folio numbers indicated refer to the Istanbul Turhan Valide 234 manuscript.

Bibliography

of the principal works consulted

PRIMARY SOURCES

Anon. *Ḥudūd al-ʿālam*, English tr. V. Minorsky, '*The regions of the world*', *a Persian geography 372 A. H.—982 A.D.*, Gibb Memorial Series, N.S. XI (London 1937)

—*Mujmal at-tawārikh wa-l-qisas*, ed. Malik ash-Shuʿarā' Bahār (Tehran 1318/1939)

—*Ta'rīkh-i Sīstān*, ed. Bahār (Tehran 1314/1935)

ʿAufī, Sadīd ad-Dīn Muḥammad. *Jawāmiʿ al-ḥikāyāt wa-lawāmiʿ ar-riwāyāt*, partial facsimile edn. by Muḥammad Ramaḍānī (Tehran 1335/1956); analysis by Muḥammad Niẓámu'd-Dín, *Introduction to the Jawámiʿu 'l-Ḥikáyát . . . of Muḥammad al-ʿAwfí*, Gibb Memorial Series, N.S. VIII (London 1929)

—*Lubāb al-albāb*, ed. Saʿīd Nafīsī (Tehran 1335/1956)

—Baihaqī, Abū l-Faḍl. *Ta'rīkh-i Masʿūdī*, ed. Qāsim Ghanī and ʿAlī Akbar Fayyāḍ (Tehran 1324/1945); ed. Saʿīd Nafīsī, 3 vols. (Tehran 1319–32/1940–53); Russian tr. A. K. Arends *Istorya Masʿūda (1030–1041)*, 2nd. edn. (Moscow 1969)

Baihaqī, ʿAlī b. Zaid (called Ibn Funduq), *Ta'rīkh-i Baihaq*, ed. Aḥmad Bahmanyār (Tehran 1317/1938)

al-Bākharzī, Abū l-Ḥasan. *Dumyat al-qaṣr wa-ʿuṣrat ahl al-ʿaṣr*, partial edn. by Muḥammad Rāghib aṭ-Ṭabbākh (Aleppo 1349/1930); full edn. by ʿAbd al-Fattāḥ Muḥammad al-Ḥilū, 2 vols. (Cairo 1388/1968)

al-Bundārī, al-Fatḥ b. ʿAlī. *Zubdat an-nuṣra wa-nukhbat al-ʿuṣra*, ed. M. T. Houtsma, in Recueil de textes relatifs à l'histoire des Seljoucides, II (Leiden 1889)

Daulat Shāh Samarqandī. *Tadhkirat ash-shuʿarā'*, ed. Muḥammad ʿAbbāsī (Tehran 1337/1958)

Fakhr-i Mudabbir Mubārak Shāh. *Ādāb al-ḥarb wa-sh-shajāʿa* or *Ādāb al-mulūk wa-kifāyat al-mamlūk*, India Office Persian ms. 647 (Ethé 2767); ed. Aḥmad Suhailī Khwānsārī (Tehran 1346/1967); English tr. of the anecdotes pertaining to the Ghaznavids by Miss I. M. Shafi, 'Fresh light on the Ghaznavids' *IC* XII (1938) 189–234

Farrukhī Sīstānī. *Dīwān*, ed. ʿAlī ʿAbd ar-Rasūlī (Tehran 1311/1932)

Firishta, Muḥammad b. Hindūshāh. *Gulshan-i Ibrāhīmī* or *Ta'rīkh-i Firishta*, Manchester ms. Lindesiana, Persian 380; abridged English tr. J. Briggs, *History of the rise of Mahomedan power in India till the year A.D. 1612*, I (repr. Calcutta 1966)

Gardīzī, ʿAbd al-Hayy. *Kitāb Zain al-akhbār*, ed. Muḥammad Nāẓim (Berlin 1928); ed. ʿAbd al-Ḥayy Ḥabībī (Tehran 1347/1968)

Ḥamdallāh Mustaufī Qazwīnī. *Taʾrīkh-i guzīda*, ed. ʿAbd al-Ḥusain Navāʾī (Tehran 1339/1960)

al-Ḥusainī, Ṣadr ad-Dīn. *Akhbār ad-daula as saljūqiyya*, ed. Muḥammad Iqbāl (Lahore 1933)

Ibn al-Athīr, ʿIzz ad-Dīn. *al-Kāmil fī t-taʾrīkh*, ed. C. J. Tornberg, *Chronicon quod perfectissimum inscribitur*, 14 vols. (Leiden 1851–76); ed. 13 vols. (Beirut 1385–7/1965–7)

Ibn Bābā al-Qāshānī. *Kitāb Raʾs māl an-nadīm*, ed. Muḥammad Ṣāliḥ Badawī, unpublished Ph.D. thesis, 2 vols. (Manchester 1975)

Ibn Funduq, see Baihaqī, ʿAlī b. Zaid

Jūzjānī, Minhāj ad-Dīn. *Ṭabaqāt-i Nāṣirī*. ed. Ḥabībī, 2nd edn., 2 vols. (Kabul 1342–3/1963–4); English tr. H. G. Raverty, 2 vols. (London 1881–99)

Khwāndamīr, Ghiyāth ad-Dīn. *Dastūr al-wuzarāʾ*, ed. Saʿīd Nafīsī (Tehran 1317/1938)

Kirmānī, Nāṣir ad-Dīn Munshī. *Nasāʾ im al-asḥār min laṭāʾ im al-akhbār*, ed. Jalāl ad-Dīn Ḥusainī Urmawī Muḥaddith (Tehran 1338/1959)

Manūchihrī Dāmghānī. *Dīwān*, ed. and French tr. A. de Biberstein Kazimirsky, *Menoutchehri, poète persan du 11ième siècle de notre ère (du 5ième de l'hégire)* (Paris 1886); ed. Muḥammad Dabīr-Siyāqī (Tehran 1338/1959)

al-Marwazī, Sharaf az-Zamān. *Ṭabāʾicʿ al-ḥayawān*, partial edn. and English tr. by V. Minorsky, *Sharaf al-Zamān Ṭāhir Marvazī on China, the Turks and India* (London 1942)

Masʿūd-i Saʿd-i Salmān. *Dīwān*, ed. Rashīd Yāsimī (Tehran 1319/1940)

Mīrkhwānd, Muḥammad. *Rauḍat aṣ-ṣafāʾ fī sīrat al-anbiyāʾ wa-l-mulūk wa-l-khulafāʾ*, section on the Ghaznavids ed. and Latin tr. F. Wilken, *Historia Gasnevidarum persice et latine* (Berlin 1832); section on the Ghūrids ed. and French tr. Ch. Defrémery, 'Histoire des Sultans Ghourides. Extraite de l'Histoire universelle de Mirkhond, traduite et accompagnée de notes' *JA*, Ser. 4, vol. II (July–Dec. 1843) 176–200, vol. III (Jan.–June 1844) 258–91.

Niẓāmī ʿArūḍī Samarqandī. *Chahār maqāla*, ed. Mīrzā Muḥammad Qazwīnī, Gibb Memorial Series, XI/1 (London 1910); revised English tr. E. G. Browne, XI/2 (London 1921)

Niẓām al-Mulk. *Siyāsat-nāma*, ed. H. Darke (Tehran 1340/1962); English tr. idem *The book of government or rules for kings* (London 1960)

al-Qalqashandī, Shihāb ad-Dīn. *Ṣubḥ al-aʿshā fī ṣināʿat al-inshāʾ*, ed. Muḥammad ʿAbd ar-Rasūl Ibrāhīm, 14 vols (Cairo 1331–8/1913–20)

Rāwandī, Muḥammad b. ʿAlī. *Rāḥat aṣ-ṣudūr wa-āyat as-sarūr*, ed. Muḥammad Iqbāl, Gibb Memorial Series, N.S. II (London 1921)

Rūnī, Abū l-Faraj. *Dīwān*, ed. K. I. Chaykin (Tehran 1304–5/1925–6); ed. Maḥmūd Mahdawī Dāmghānī (Mashhad 1347/1968)

as-Samʿānī, ʿAbd al-Karīm. *Kitāb al-Ansāb*, facsimile text by D. S. Margoliouth, Gibb Memorial Series, XX (London 1913); partial edn.

by ʿAbd ar-Raḥmān b. Yaḥyā al-Yamānī and Muḥammad ʿAbd al-Muʿīd Khīd Khān, 6 vols. (Hyderabad 1382–6/1962–6)
Sanā'ī Ghaznavī, Ḥakim. *Dīwān*, ed. Mudarris Riḍawī (Tehran 1341/1962)
Sayyid Ḥasan Ghaznavī. *Dīwān*, ed. Riḍawī (Tehran 1328/1949)
Shabānkāra'ī, Muḥammad. *Majmaʿ al-ansāb fī t-tawārīkh*, Istanbul Persian ms. Yeni Cami 909
ʿUnṣurī Balkhī. *Diwān*, ed. Yaḥyā Qarīb (Tehran 1323/1944)
ʿUqailī, Saif ad-Dīn Faḍlī. *Āthār al-wuzarā'*, India Office Persian ms. 1569 (Ethé 621); ed. Urmawī (Tehran 1337/1959)
ʿUthmān Mukhtārī. *Dīwān*, ed. Jalāl ad-Dīn Humā'ī (Tehran 1341/1962)
Yāqūt al-Hamawī. *Irshād al-arīb li-maʿrifat al-adīb*, ed. Margoliouth, Gibb Memorial Series, VI/1–7, 7 vols. (London 1907–26)
—*Muʿjam al-buldan*, 5 vols. (Beirut 1374–6/1955–7)

SECONDARY SOURCES

Arberry, A. J. *Classical Persian Literature* (London 1958)
Barthold, W. *Turkestan down to the Mongol invasion*, 3rd edn. C. E. Bosworth, Gibb Memorial Series, N.S. V (London 1968)
Bombaci, A. *The Kūfic inscription in Persian verses in the court of the royal palace of Masʿud III at Ghazni*, Instituto Italiano per il Medio ed Estremo Oriente, Centro Studi e Scavi Archeologici in Asia, Reports and Memoirs, V (Rome 1966)
Bosworth, C. E. 'Ghaznevid military organisation' *Der Islam* XXXVI (1960) 37–77
—'The early Islamic history of Ghūr' *CAJ* VI (1961) 116–33
—'The imperial policy of the early Ghaznawids' *Islamic Studies, Journal of the Central Institute of Islamic Research, Karachi* I/3 (Sept. 1962) 49–82
—'The titulature of the early Ghaznavids' *Oriens* XV (1962) 210–33
—'Early sources for the history of the first four Ghaznavid sultans (977–1041)' *IQ* VII (1963) 3–22
—*The Ghaznavids, their empire in Afghanistan and eastern Iran 994–1040*, 1st edn. (Edinburgh 1963) 2nd edn. (Beirut 1973)
—'Notes on the pre-Ghaznavid history of eastern Afghanistan' *IQ* IX (1965) 12–24
—*The Islamic dynasties: a chronological and genealogical handbook*, Islamic Surveys 5 (Edinburgh 1967)
—'The early Ghaznavids' in *Cambridge history of Iran. IV. From the Arab invasion to the Saljuqs*, ed. R. N. Frye (Cambridge 1975) 162–97
—'The political and dynastic history of the Iranian world (A.D. 1000–1217)' in ibid., V, *The Saljuq and Mongol periods*, ed. J. A. Boyle (Cambridge 1968) 1–202
Browne, E. G. *A literary history of Persia*, 4 vols. (London and Cambridge 1902–24)
Clauson, Sir Gerard. *An etymological dictionary of pre-thirteenth century Turkish* (Oxford 1972)
Elliot, Sir H. M., and Dowson, J. *The history of India as told by its own historians*, 6 vols. (London 1867–77)

Flury, S. 'Le décor épigraphique des monuments de Ghazna' *Syria* VI (1925) 61–90

Ganguly, D. C. 'The historical value of Dīwān-i Salmān' *IC* XVI (1942) 423–8

Gardin, J.-C. *Lashkari Bazar, une residence royale ghaznévide. II. Les trouvailles. Céramiques et monnaies de Lashkari Bazar et de Bust*, Mémoires de la Délégation Archéologique Française en Afghanistan, XVIII (Paris 1963)

Gelpke, R. *Sulṭan Mas'ūd I. von Ġazna. Die drei ersten Jahre seiner Herrschaft (421/1030–424/1033)* (Munich 1957)

Haig, Sir Thomas W., ed. *The Cambridge history of India. III. Turks and Afghans* (Cambridge 1928)

Hennequin, G. 'Grandes monnaies sāmānides et ghaznavides de l'Hindū Kush 331–421 A.H., étude numismatique et historique' *Annales islamologiques* IX (Cairo 1970) 127–77

Hodivala, S. H. *Studies in Indo-Muslim history: a critical commentary on Elliot and Dowson's 'History of India as told by its own historians'* I (Bombay 1939)

Husain, Iqbal *The early Persian poets of India (A.H. 421–670)* (Patna 1937)

Kafesoğlu, I. *Sultan Melikşah devrinde Büyük Selçuklu imparatorluğu* (Istanbul 1953)

Khan, Gulam Mustafa. 'A history of Bahrām Shāh of Ghaznīn' IC, XIII (1949) 62–91, 199–235 (also published as a separate monograph)

Köprülü, M. F. 'Kay kabîlesi hakkında yeni notlar' *Belleten* VIII (1944) 421–52

Lane Poole, R. S. *Catalogue of oriental coins in the British Museum*, 8 vols. (London 1875–83)

—*Additions to the Oriental Collection 1876–88*, 2 vols. (London 1889–90)

—*The Mohammadan dynasties, chronological and genealogical tables with historical introductions* (London 1894)

Le Strange, G. *The lands of the Eastern Caliphate* (Cambridge 1905)

Majumdar, R. C., *et alii*, eds. *The history and culture of the Indian people. V. The struggle for empire*, 2nd edn. (Bombay 1966)

Maricq, A., and Wiet, G. *Le minaret de Djam. La découvert de la capitale des sultans ghorides (XIIe–XIIIe siècles)*, Mémoires de la Délégation Archéologique Française en Afghanistan, XVI (Paris 1959)

Marquart, J. *Ērānšahr nach der Geographie des Ps. Moses Xorenac'i* in *AGGW, N.F.* III/2 (Berlin 1901)

Mercil, Erdoğan. 'Sebüktegin'in Pend-nâmesi (Farsça metin ve türkçe tercümesi)' *Islâm Tetkikleri Enstitüsü Dergisi* VI/1–2 (Istanbul 1975) 203–33

Muḥammad Riḍā. *Riyāḍ al-alwāḥ, mushtamil bar katībahā-yi qubūr va abniya-yi Ghazna* (Kabul 1346/1967)

Nāẓim, M. *The life and times of Sulṭān Maḥmūd of Ghazna* (Cambridge 1931)

—'The Pand-Nāmah of Subuktigin' *JRAS* (1933) 605–28

Pritsak, O. 'Die Karachaniden' *Der Islam* XXXI (1953–4) 17–68 (Turkish version in *Islam Ansiklopedisi*, art. 'Karahanlılar')

[Qazwīnī], Mírzá Muḥammad. 'Mas'úd-i-Sa'd-i-Salmán' *JRAS* (1905) 693–740, (1906) 11–51

Radloff, W. *Versuch eines Wörterbuches der Türk-Dialecte*, 4 vols. (St Petersburg 1893–1911)
Ray, H. C. *The dynastic history of northern India (early mediaeval period)*, 2 vols. (Calcutta 1931–6)
Rodgers, C. J. *Catalogue of the coins in the Government Museum, Lahore* (Calcutta 1891)
—*Catalogue of the coins collected by Chas. J. Rodgers and purchased by the Government of the Panjáb. Part II. Miscellaneous Muḥammadan coins* (Calcutta 1894)
—*Catalogue of coins in the Indian Museum* (Calcutta 1896)
Rypka, J., *et alii*. *History of Iranian literature* (Dordrecht 1968)
Sourdel, D. *Inventaire des monnaies musulmanes anciennes de Musée de Caboul* (Damascus 1953)
—'Un trésor de dinars ġaznawides et salǧūqides découvert en Afghanistan' *BEtO*, XVIII (1963–4) 197–219
Sourdel-Thomine, J., 'Stèles arabes de Bust (Afghanistan)' *Arabica* III (1956) 285–306
Spuler, B. *Iran in früh-islamischer Zeit* (Wiesbaden 1952)
Stern S. M. 'A manuscript from the library of the Ghaznawid Amīr 'Abd al-Rashīd' in *Paintings from Islamic lands*, ed. R. Pinder-Wilson (Oxford 1969)
Thomas, E. 'On the coins of the Kings of Ghazní' *JRAS* IX (1848) 267–386
Zambaur, E. von. 'Contributions à la numismatique orientale' *WNZ* XXXVI (1904) 43–122, XXXVII (1905) 113–98
—*Manuel de généalogie et de chronologie pour l'histoire de l'Islam* (Hanover 1927)

Index